# Eat Fit, Be Fit

## Health and Weight
## Management Solutions

Join us on the web at

**culinary.delmar.com**

# Eat Fit, Be Fit
## Health and Weight Management Solutions

## Linda Arpino, MA, RD, CDN

**THOMSON**

**DELMAR LEARNING**™    Australia   Canada   Mexico   Singapore   Spain   United Kingdom   United States

**THOMSON**
™
**DELMAR LEARNING**

**Eat Fit, Be Fit: Health and Weight Management Solutions**
by Linda Arpino

**Vice President, Career Education Strategic Business Unit:**
Dawn Gerrain

**Acquisitions Editor:**
Matthew Hart

**Product Manager:**
Patricia M. Osborn

**Editorial Assistant:**
Patrick B. Horn

**Director of Production:**
Wendy A. Troeger

**Content Project Manager:**
Ken Karges

**Director of Marketing:**
Wendy E. Mapstone

**Channel Manager:**
Kristin McNary

**Marketing Coordinator:**
Scott Chrysler

**Cover Design:**
Joe Villanova

**Cover Image:**
Mark Thomas/Foodpix

For permission to use material from this text or product,
contact us by
Tel (800) 730-2214
Fax (800) 730-2215
www.thomsonrights.com

Library of Congress Cataloging-in-Publication Data

Arpino, Linda.
    Eat fit, be fit/health and weight management solutions / Linda Arpino.
        p. cm.
    Includes bibliographical references and index.
    ISBN-13: 978-1-4180-3843-4 (alk. paper)
    ISBN-10: 1-4180-3843-1 (alk. paper)
    1. Weight loss. 2. Reducing diets. 3. Nutrition.
        4. Reducing exercises.
I. Title.
    RM222.2.A77 2006
    613.2'5—dc22

2006022271

**NOTICE TO THE READER**

# Contents

## SOUPS • 180

### ABOUT BROTH • 180

# A Word from the Author

For more than thirty years, I have been in private practice treating patients who have health concerns or who seek preventative strategies by altering lifestyle habits. During that time, I have seen how changes in diet and exercise can powerfully affect one's overall health. A combination of healthy lifestyle choices—such as physical activity, personal time, and a nutritious diet—has helped thousands of my patients. I have seen first hand how medications can be eliminated, reversal if abnormal levels of triglycerides, cholesterol, and sugar and many other disorders positively affected by diet. Although I am not funded by research, there is research supporting these profound effects.

I was always passionate about exercise and nutrition. Growing up in an Italian family, I was always called the "string bean," but that changed as I got older. In my teens, I danced and was a gymnast, and I swore that I would try hard not to become overweight, despite the fact that my family seemed genetically destined to obesity. Everyone on my dad's Italian side seems to be overweight or obese. My mother's side, who is Finnish, genetically seemed to have less of a tendency toward obesity, but the problems with weight stilled prevailed.

After watching my dad's father struggle with complications from diabetes when I was in high school, I decided that I wanted to study nutrition. The science of nutrition was always fascinating to me no matter how powerful genetic traits were for diabetes and weight gain. I was intrigued by how diet and lifestyle choices could reduce those risk factors and keep our lives in balance, so I chose to get my bachelor's and master's degrees in clinical and community nutrition. I studied how diet, exercise, and stress play a role in managing health. My master's thesis evaluated whether medications could be reduced or eliminated in Type 2 diabetes with nutrition education and changes in diet and exercise. My hypothesis was correct. After my patients in the study were given an exercise routine and a diet rich in fiber and plant-based foods and low in sugar, fats, and refined carbohydrates, many of them were able to eliminate or reduce the medication they were taking not only for their diabetes but also to regulate cholesterol and blood pressure.

Science has come a long way since then, and we see now that thousands of nutrients in high fiber–rich plants help regulate blood sugar and appetite as well as the immune system, the aging process, and overall health.

Now in my practice, I see toddlers at age 3 who are thirty pounds overweight and children and teenagers who are thirty to seventy-five pounds above their desirable weight. This was not always so. In the 1970s and '80s, the average person came to lose fifteen to thirty pounds.

The effects of making lifestyle changes can be profound—and these are what have inspired me to write this book. I have seen patients lower cholesterol and triglycerides, go into total remission after a diagnosis of cancer, improve bone density and liver enzymes, eliminate hot flashes in menopause, and reduce their medications for regulating blood pressure, cholesterol, and diabetes. My goal is to reach as many people who need guidance as I can.

In this book I have tried to do this in simple ways, keeping terms and explanations easy to read. By discovering easy recipes with nutrient balance, variety, and flavor, you will see how changing your dietary choices does not have to be bland, boring, or restrictive. They are recipes for life that can be easily incorporated and long-lasting. I hope after reading this book that you will see the importance of taking time out to plan meals, to rest, to find quiet time to reflect, and to give thanks to what is positive. I also consider myself a "foodie" and love great taste and flavor. I do not want food that seems tasteless in many books on eating healthy. I want to have fun and enjoy my food. When combined, the elements of nutrition, exercise, fun, and positive outlook are powerful tools for health. Enjoy!

Sincerely,
Linda Arpino, M.A.
Registered Dietitian,
Certified Dietitian and Nutritionist

# Preface

*Eat Fit, Be Fit: Health and Weight Management Solutions* is a plan for health that goes beyond diets, exercise, and the usual quick-fix approach. This book looks to the core of our society's values and how they mess with our well-being. Here we consider certain foods to be "Gold" because they preserve health, while other foods are "Dirt," meaning they are useless or harmful. This book will help you put an abundance of Gold foods into your diet with simple, delicious, and easy recipes that can be prepared in minutes.

The Centers for Disease Control and Prevention reports that approximately 20.8 million people—7 percent of the U.S. adults aged 18 and over—have diabetes. An estimated 129.6 million Americans, or 64 percent, are obese or overweight. The prevalence of obesity among adults aged 18 and over in 2005 has risen to 25.4 percent. The highest is 29 percent among adults aged 40–59 years old, and highest in men. The numbers of deaths from diabetes has increased 45 percent. From 2003 to 2005, the death toll rose by 14 percent. Diabetes remains a leading cause of heart disease, stroke, blindness, and kidney disease. This killer and cancer are related to a lack of healthy lifestyle habits such as diet and exercise.

Alarmingly, more than 16 percent of American children and teenagers from 6 to 19 are also overweight, and the number increases each year. Overweight and obesity increase the risk that a person will develop serious health problems, including heart disease and Type 2 diabetes. Behind much of this is our society's obsession with values of "more," "bigger," "faster," and "easier."

The statistics show that the citizens of many countries, including the United States, are growing larger in body size, reducing the quality of their lives. Furthermore, depression seems more widespread than ever before.

This book will guide you on how to look at yourself from the inside, examine social barriers that make change difficult, and your own readiness for change. You will be given options for change. The book helps you examine your feelings about food and life, and offers ways in which to create new ways of making choices. You will be given information about the causes of debilitating conditions, the cost of ignoring unhealthy lifestyle habits, the benefits of selecting certain foods, guidelines to becoming more physically active, and how to use your personal time to reduce stress and maintain focus.

In summary, the guidelines and recipes are kept simple. Our lives are complicated enough. The simpler and healthier our meals, activities, and schedules, the more our health and feelings of inner peace will be renewed. Remember, *good nutrition is a weigh of life!* Stay focused on what is important.

# Acknowledgments

Inspiration to write this book came from my lifelong friend, Dr. Gary Federici. Thanks! I am deeply grateful for your support and suggestions.

Jessica and Rebecca Levine, my children, thanks for your patience and understanding while I wrote, tested recipes, and asked you to sample them. All your suggestions have been great.

Persistence in completion of this book was truly driven by the kind and encouraging words of so many, but the most important were those of my mother, Dorothy, and stepfather, Bill Court. My mother is a true chef, and both are great mentors.

Gratitude goes to Dr. Judith Gilbright, 2006 president of the American Dietetic Association, and Dr. Wahida Karmally, Registered Dietitian, Certified Diabetes Educator, and Director of Nutrition, Associated Research Scientist, at the Irving Center for Clinical Research of Columbia University Medical Center, for their guidance and support.

Discipline is a key ingredient to success and was taught to me by dad, John, and grandfather, Amodio. They were motivating forces to write this book because they struggled between controlling their love of food with their weight and diabetes. I hope this book helps others who have diabetes or need to control their weight.

This book is also in memory of my close friends Claudia Powers and Francine Berger, who both lost their struggles against cancer. I hope this book helps others who face the same challenges.

I am grateful to all the physicians and other professionals who have referred patients to me to understand the obstacles we confront in achieving health, and who have tested these recipes over the past twenty-five years.

My commitment to publish has been realized because of a dear mentor, Julie Gillard, author and chef. Her relentless guidance through this process has allowed me to achieve my goal.

Contributors, my heartfelt thanks for your recipes, analysis, typing, editing, and suggestions: Brian MacMenamin, chef and owner of MacMenamin's Grill and Chefworks; Amodio Arpino; Carla Arpino; John Arpino; Rosanne Bordes; Dorothy

Court; Dr. Gary Federici; Michelle Jackson; Dr. Barbara Lewis; Jessica Levine; Rebecca Levine; Dr. Wahida Karmally; Lisa O'Gorman; Phyllis Schondorf; Paulette Schneider; Ada Wochowski; Yanelli Vargas; and my patients, interns, and staff.

Most important, thanks to Matt Hart, Patricia Osborn, and the entire staff at Delmar Learning who made this book a reality.

In the event I failed to acknowledge anyone or mistakenly made errors or omissions, please forgive me as it was not intended. If errors are cited, they were not intentional. The data were collected, analyzed, and written through years of research. God gives us the grace to help others; I hope this is achieved.

Linda Arpino, MA, RD, CDN
July, 2006

# Introduction

*Eat Fit, Be Fit: Health and Weight Management Solutions* is a book that offers simple healthy solutions—especially for people who are challenged by obesity, diabetes, and high blood pressure. It is perfect for people who want to just eat better or achieve a healthier weight. There are a variety of heart healthy, delicious meals for both meat eaters and vegetarians to help you achieve a balance between diet and exercise and find inner peace.

Whatever a person's weight—normal, over-, or underweight—stress and hectic schedules can cause imbalances in how he or she sleeps, eats, and exercises. This can promote illness and unwanted medical conditions. The guidelines in this book teach how to break barriers that are caused by our society's influences: the food industry, television, the restaurant industry, and culture. Taking control over your environment by cooking and choosing foods differently is the key to success. The recipes in this book are designed to help you boost nutrients in your body to control blood sugar and appetite, increase your energy, alter the distribution of foods from animal based high protein choices to lower protein plant based choices, and improve your immune system. You will learn how to live and enjoy a healthier, active life.

The food combinations in *Eat Fit, Be Fit: Health and Weight Management Solution* will have a positive effect on brain function and hormonal balance. Food addictions are not only initiated by brain chemistry imbalances but also by emotional imbalances. The focus of these recipes and the information provided is to help you take charge of your diet, health, and weight through cooking and lifestyle change. Use the recipes as a tool to maintain your and your family's health. Menus teach meal balance to lower glycemic index. This helps insulin work better for blood sugar regulation and weight control. Portion control helps to eliminate those supersized meals that cause weight gain and cancer.

## ABOUT THE RECIPES

Nutrition symbols code each recipe as rich in calcium, fiber, phytonutrients, or antioxidants and low in cholesterol, sodium, and fat. Serving sizes and exchanges make it easy to keep portions balanced for people who are trying to lose weight or must control their diabetes. Many of these recipes alter traditional recipes to reduce fat, sodium, and sugar and are encouraged as a substitute for processed foods, which are excessive in these nutrients as well as food additives and fillers such as sugar substitutes, modified corn starch, and high fructose corn syrup. Even better, the recipes enhance flavor naturally with herbs and spices that provide added health benefits.

As a registered dietitian in private practice, I see people with all kinds of nutritional problems, including diabetes, obesity, high cholesterol, polycystic ovary syndrome, eating disorders, menopause, and cancer. What experience has taught me is people must try to find better balance in their diet in six main areas:

1. fat and sugar intake;

2. portion control;

3. increasing fiber and phytonutrients;

4. daily, adequate calcium intake from food; and

5. lower sodium.

6. shift from excess animal to small to moderate amounts of vegetable protein.

Menus are offered with the entrées to teach you how to have a balanced meal. People who try these meals say they feel less stressed, have more energy, sleep better, and have reduced appetites.

## Exchanges

The nutrition information and the recipe design support the goals set forth in the 2005 version of *Dietary Guidelines for Americans* published jointly by the U.S. Department of Health and Human Services and the U.S. Department of Agriculture. The recipes also support the goals of American Diabetes Association Meal Planning Food Groups, which can be found online at www.diabetes.org/nutrition-and-recipes/nutrition/diabetes-meal-plan.jsp. By using exchange information you can learn the correct portions before you take your next serving of something, which will help you with weight management and diabetic control.

Exchanges found in each recipe tell you what food group the recipe counts for in a measured, cooked, or edible serving size. Food groups are starch, fruit, milk (fat free or 1% fat, reduced fat 2%, whole milk with 3.5% fat), vegetables, meats and meat substitutes (very lean, lean, medium fat and high fat), and the fat group.

The chart on page xxiii provides the nutrients in each food group and what one exchange means in nutrients.

This is a healthy way to maintain healthy portions and nutrients to meet your food group needs. Using the Food Pattern guides in this book you can decide how many portions you need from each group. By keeping record you can add up how much you eat using the exchange guides in recipes. The total at the end of the day should add up to the number of servings recommended for you.

| One Exchange for Each Group Is Listed Below | | | |
|---|---|---|---|
| | Carbohydrate (Grams) | Protein (Grams) | Fat (Grams) | Calories |
| Starch | 15 | 3 | 0–1 | 80 |
| Fruit | 15 | 0 | 0 | 60 |
| Milk | | | | |
| Fat-free | 12 | 8 | 0–3 | 90 |
| Reduced fat | 12 | 8 | 5 | 120 |
| Whole | 12 | 8 | 8 | 150 |
| Vegetables | 5 | 2 | 0 | 25 |
| Meat and alternates | | | | |
| Very lean | 0- varies if beans | 7 | 0–1 | 35 |
| Lean | " | 7 | 3 | 55 |
| Medium fat | " | 7 | 5 | 75 |
| High Fat | " | 7 | 8 | 100 |
| Fat Group | 0 | 0 | 5 | 45 |

## Recipe Symbols

Nutrition codes next to the recipe titles make it easy to see nutrient benefits. After each recipe title there may appear specially marked symbols:

 **High Fiber:** Recipes with this symbol contain at least 3 grams of fiber per serving. It is recommended by most leading health organization that adults include 25 grams to 50 grams of fiber daily in their diets. Children and teenagers, requirements vary with body weight, but a typical amount would be 15 grams to 30 grams. Another way to estimate fiber for a child is to use their age plus five. For example, 8 + 5 = 13 grams or more per day.

 **Rich Phytonutrients and Antioxidants:** These recipes contain at least two types of phytonutrients or antioxidants. Thousands of different phytonutrients exist, and research is finding that each one has amazing qualities in helping us stay healthy. Antioxidants such as vitamins E and C and beta-carotene are abundant in these recipes.

 **Heart Healthy:** Recipes for entrées with this symbol contain less than 90 milligrams of cholesterol and less than 15 grams of fat. Recipes for side dishes with this symbol contain less than 60 milligrams of cholesterol and less than 5 grams of fat. It is recommended by the American Heart Association that you limit cholesterol intake to 300 milligrams or less daily.

**Low Sodium:** These entrées have less than 480 milligrams of sodium, and side dishes have less than 150 milligrams. Total daily sodium should be 2,300 milligrams or less if you are at risk for high blood pressure.

 **Calcium Rich:** These recipes contain at least 125 milligrams of calcium in balance with other minerals that promote strong bones. The dairy foods used in this cookbook enhance absorption because they are in natural balance with other important nutrients such as magnesium, phosphorus, and protein. These guidelines are the same or below the standards set by the Food and Drug Administration's food labeling guidelines.

## Abbreviations Used in This Cookbook

The following abbreviations are used in this book's recipes:

oz. = ounce

lb(s). = pound(s)

tsp. = teaspoon

Tbsp. = Tablespoon

In addition, the nutrition bar code at the bottom of each recipe includes information on the following nutritional elements: Calories, Carbohydrates (in grams), Protein (in grams), Fat (in grams), Cholesterol (in milligrams), Calcium (in milligrams), Potassium (in milligrams), Sodium (in milligrams), and Fiber (in grams). Warnings about polluted fish species are also provided.

By following the ideas and recipes in this book, you will learn to rethink the word *diet,* toss the idea of restrictions, and gain the notion of freedom to become healthy.

A younger face, a firmer figure, an easier existence, and a healthier body is what we all want. As easy as it is to go out and buy a donut, it is easy to achieve these healthier lifestyle habits with a little guidance and discipline. This book is designed to teach you how to create action plans using six basic principles:

1. Be honest with and faithful to yourself.
2. Examine yourself, not others.
3. Be fit—do physical activity each day.
4. Eat unprocessed, naturally occurring environmentally safe foods.
5. Plan each day.
6. Love yourself before you worry about others.

If you do this, you will be a better person to everyone, including and especially yourself.

> Please note the internet resources are of time-sensitive nature and URL addresses may often change or be deleted.

# Learning to Eat Fit

# Chapter 1

# BREAKING THE BARRIERS: CHANGING THE WAY WE EAT

Learning to eat healthier not only will help you improve your health and the way you age but also successfully manage your weight. Learning to eat fit means eating against our society's cultural norms.

## WHY CHANGE?

People who come to my office to make lifestyle changes often say to me, "Eating healthy is boring and has no flavor." I say, "This is the wrong way to think."

Taste rules, but health counts. Learning to cook with flavorful and tasty herbs and spices can achieve a balance and produce the satiety you are looking for in your diet without the excess fat, sugar, and salt found in many convenience foods. Eating fresh, unprocessed foods can make all the difference to long-term health and being in great shape. When we eat a lot of foods high in sugar, fat, and sodium foods—Bam! Our health becomes out of balance.

If you think your eating habits could improve, then learn to step aside and look at how you have gotten to this point. This is an important step in making changes. You probably are reading this book because you need to change some things to eat better and feel healthier.

## WHAT INFLUENCES OUR FOOD CHOICES?

Let's look at the two principal parts of our living environment: home and society.

### Home

The way we are taught to eat as we grow up has a big effect on our food choices. Studies show that the choices a pregnant mother makes will influence her baby's weight. If the mother is overweight, the baby is more likely to overeat later in life and also become overweight. Think about it: If you are an adult who looks for a candy bar every time you are stressed, maybe it is because you were taught early in life that you could feel better with that little chemical fix called *chocolate.* Yes, foods contain chemicals that stimulate hormones such as serotonin, which makes us feel calm. Chocolate contains theobromine and caffeine that can stimulate the heart rate and blood pressure. Another chemical chocolate contains is phenylethylamine (PEA), which is reported to trigger *endorphins;* these are the natural chemicals that give a "high" feeling that is similar to being in love. No wonder we like it so much!

What we learn in our homes as we grow up will provide us with adult behaviors that are deeply rooted. Think of how we learn to connect emotions with food. If your child is acting up, do you automatically offer something to eat? If your baby is crying, do you automatically give a bottle? If your teenager does well in something, do you automatically reward with an ice cream cone or celebrate over pepperoni pizza? All of these responses teach children to connect food with emotional eating. There is nothing wrong with celebrating with food, but avoid using it all the time to appeal to emotions.

On the other hand, associating food with everyday activities also can lead to poor eating habits. Many studies have shown that breakfast is more important than heavy, rich meals late in the evening. If a child only knows how to eat breakfast in front of a video without a parent, then the warm feeling of relaxing with another person and eating slowly is never learned. Once that child becomes older, it will be hard for a parent to convince that teenager that sitting down and eating together is important.

## Society

Not only do our home lives and emotions influence our health and our food choices but also our environment. Sandra Bernabei, clinical social worker and certified alcohol and substance abuse counselor, is an educator and liberation psychotherapist. She shares a comparison of the reality of the Western—and predominantly American—way of thinking of what is "best" and how this influences our eating choices. She contrasts ideal image with less than ideal image.

| Ideal Image | Less than Ideal Image |
| --- | --- |
| Skinny | Fat |
| Blonde hair | Not blonde |
| Good physical build | Flabby |
| Lots of money | Not affluent |
| Own big house | Rent |
| Own big car | Do not have a car |
| Bigger is better (except in body size) | Anything small except your butt |
| Eating out a lot | Do not eat out |
| Lots of food | "Skimpy" portions |

The list goes on and on and on.

If you do not fit any or most of these "ideal images," then you may feel less than adequate. Now let's look at other cultures' ways of thinking.

| Ideal Image | Less than Ideal Image |
|---|---|
| Not skinny | Skinny |
| Hair does not matter | None |
| Physical build is not an issue because everyone is using muscle | None |
| No one drives a big van because they just don't make sense for the environment or car or budget. Most people bicycle or use mass transit. | Driving a big van or car |

How you feel from the last set of comparisons may be quite different from how you feel about the first.

Patients frequently come to me saying that it is hard to eat in healthy ways with others. An example is a 15-year-old overweight girl. She asks, "How am I supposed to lose weight if when I walk to school in the morning and I smell chocolate chip cookies baking and have not eaten breakfast—and all I want is that cookie? Then I walk into the cafeteria at lunch and there are all these high-fat foods: cheeseburgers, fries, chips, pizza, and wedges!" Even when she chooses salad, it is not fresh, and there are no low-fat protein options such as beans or low-fat cheese. Her friends are all eating those higher fat foods but are not overweight. How do you think that makes her feel? It will take a lot of persistence to not feel different in such circumstances, and you will have to work hard to eat healthier despite your surroundings and the attitudes of others.

## LIBERATE YOURSELF

What our society *thinks* is right and the accepted norm has a powerful influence on us. In trying to change, you may feel deprived instead of empowered. Learning to let go of these beliefs is part of the liberation process. It can free us from feeling less than adequate and from holding onto destructive habits.

### "Stuffing" Feelings

Often I see patients who are "stuffing" their feelings with food. At an early age, some of us have learned (usually from our mothers) that others come before us. In most cases, mothers tend to be the ones who get up when their children awaken in the middle of the night, take them for special therapy if they have disabilities, and give up their time off so their spouses can golf or pursue other recreations. A child may not be given a voice and may always be told what to do, when to do it, and how to do it. This compensation or suppression of needs eventually explodes as anger, moodiness, sleeplessness, overeating, or other problems such as compulsive eating, cigarette smoking, overspending, or excessive alcohol drinking.

Learning to live by your own inner voice and not by the voices of those around you will help you feel more satisfied and positively influence other aspects of your life, including emotional eating. As parents, this means checking to see if your children's voices are really being heard and their needs supported in positive ways. We all make mistakes in parenting, but change starts by recognizing a problem. If this is happening in your life, then a counselor or psychotherapist may help you cope differently than you have in the past.

Next, we must look at what other messages we get from those around us.

## Toss Out Society's "Must Do" Messages

Change often means going against the norm. Here are six common challenges we face when making changes in our food choices—and possible solutions.

### 1. More Is Not Always Better when It Comes to Eating

At your favorite burger joint or fast food chain, advertising promotions frequently offer "two-for-one" or supersizing deals. They sound enticing, but do not go that route! Choose the smaller healthier options even if they seem to cost more. In the long run, it will likely cost you less in health care costs.

### 2. Keeping Up with the Jones's School Lunch Bag

A "junk" snack—a non-nutritious item such as cake, cookies, and chips—in a child's lunch bag may seem "necessary" because everyone else has them. Perhaps instead you can provide a piece of fresh fruit, a vegetable, yogurt, or a whole grain food four out of five days while offering one junk food one or fewer days a week and another at home on the weekend. This teaches your children better boundaries both in and out of the home. When they become older and go to work, they may well continue what they have learned from your example.

### 3. Office Breakfasts and Eating at the Desk

When you eat bagels or donuts in the office because that is what is there and easiest, you are headed toward a health disaster. Set a new trend! Bring a bag of goodies from home. Pack great and healthy snacks from this book. If you do go to a deli, choose fruit and yogurt, salad, or other plain vegetables. If you have any influence on what foods are bought for the general office staff, ask for fresh fruit and vegetables, whole wheat bread, rolled oats to make oatmeal, and perhaps herbal tea. Even if it contains less fiber and more sodium than the old-fashioned type, unsweetened instant oatmeal in packets is healthier than donuts and bagels.

Healthy office practices include the following:

- With coffee, use skim milk powder instead of half-and-half.
- Drink herbal teas and water.
- Forget donuts and bagels and offer whole grain breads and oatmeal (not instant).
- Cut the candy and offer fruit and raw veggies.
- Vending machine options: fruit, yogurt, raisins, nuts and seeds, baby carrots.

### 4. Boardroom Lunch and Dinners

Deadlines and smaller staffs can sometimes create a need for workers to have their meals ordered in while they work. In these situations, step up to the plate with a fierce conversation about what to order. If you are forced to eat while working, the least that could happen is that the choices are lower in fat and offer fresh fruit and vegetables. In many medical offices, more often than not pharmaceutical company salespeople bring lunch when they visit. The food is usually high in fat, salt, and sugar—foods that can cause the problems that people need medication for! Take time to think about how you can change and improve this environment.

### 5. Coffee with the Girls

Instead of a high-fat drink such as a mocha frappucino, choose hot tea or steamed fat-free milk with cinnamon.

### 6. After a "Boys" Golf or Baseball Outing

Choosing beer, scotch, or martinis followed by Buffalo wings or pizza instead of a trip to the salad bar, fish, or a turkey on rye bread with a virgin Mary drink or seltzer with lemon will pack in calories and pounds. If you must have an alcoholic beverage, then go for just one and make it a light beer. The list of remedies goes on. Remember, breaking the strong forces of such habits is downright hard, but it *can* be done.

## THE POWERFUL INFLUENCES OF BIG BUSINESS

### Media

We are bombarded with many misleading messages. Examples are television "reality shows" that are far from reality and that exploit people who are struggling with issues to entertain us. Many shows encourage unhealthy lifestyle habits with excessive eating and sedentary and inactive lifestyles as being "cool." Networks offer more commercial time than program viewing and entice us to eat. Newspapers' unbalanced reporting about tragedy and violence crowd out positive news. Magazines and television emphasize beauty in the form of thin people, and radio promotes the latest fad diet or supplements that "melt fat way." Jingles associated with bad products begin the connection and brand marketing during toddler years such as McDonalds. Day after day we are influenced. This erodes our ability to think positively about change.

## The Food Industry

Food packaging in huge quantities yields big bucks! Why not get fifty sticks of cheese for three dollars more instead of just ten or an extra burger (two-for-one deals)? Two donuts and coffee is cheaper than milk, fruit, and whole wheat bread in fast food chains; a 20-ounce soda is ten cents more than a 10-ounce soda, so why not spend a little bit more? Food labels make sugar-coated cereals seem healthy because they say "whole grain"; fruit rollups are loaded with sugar but use the term "real fruit"; frozen vegetables can be loaded with high-fat sauces; oil labels bragging that their products contain "no cholesterol" are loaded with calories; and sugar-loaded chocolate-flavored milk boasts only 1 percent fat.

Food manufacturers know that foods mean more than just helping us to stay healthy. Why do you think those sugar-coated boxes of cereal look so appealing to children? Let's call them for what they really are: the beginnings of the "weapons of body mass destruction." Gradual changes in food-processing methods—adding more and more additives, sugar, salt, and fat—has affected our metabolism, our cravings, our moods, and are now linked to an increased chance of food addiction.

## The Restaurant Industry

If you take a trip and use an airport or ride a ferry or go to a baseball game, can you get healthy small portions and healthy choices? No. It does not stop there. Most places that service families make it hard to avoid what tempts children the most: french fries, pizza loaded with whole-milk cheese, fried or sautéed foods loaded with oil at Chinese restaurants, children's party centers that serve only pizza, hot dogs, chips, and fries. The list goes on. There is too much saturated fat in all of it.

These are reasons why setting healthy boundaries is important. And this is all the more reason to use this book to help you set a better balance.

# GETTING STARTED

Great nutrition starts by what you decide to put in your body. Our bodies need six main categories of nutrients for optimal health:

> carbohydrates
>
> proteins
>
> fats
>
> vitamins
>
> minerals
>
> water

The importance of these nutrients will be addressed in the following chapters.

We now know that hundreds of phytonutrients found in plants also have powerful effects in our body when they are digested. Each different color of food contains different phytonutrients, so choosing a variety of colors in foods helps boost nutrients to enhance health. For example, *resveratrol,* a chemical found in the skin of purple grapes, may help prevent cancer. *Polyphenols* in green tea may help protect the colon from cancer caused by the generation of free radicals formed from iron. *Capsaicin,* which is found in cayenne peppers, chilis, and red peppers, acts as an anti-inflammatory agent by preventing toxic molecules from invading and damaging cells and causing inflammation. *Isoflavones*—found in beans, peas, peanuts, and tofu—may help reduce women's risk of breast and ovarian cancer.

In the chapters to follow, you will learn more about what these nutrients do in our body, and the benefits of planning, preparing, cooking, and eating a variety of foods that contain these powerful nutrients. This book will help you take charge of your diet and start creating new lifestyle habits. You may have to go through a series of stages to start.

## STAGES OF CHANGE

Whether you are trying to lose weight, lower your blood sugar levels, exercise, or just eat healthier, major lifestyle changes usually include five stages as defined by the transtheoretical model: precontemplation, contemplation, preparation, action, and maintenance.

### Precontemplation

*Precontemplation* means that you are not yet thinking about change. Sometimes the contemplative process starts when our physician points out our deteriorating health or problems that can be remedied by lifestyle changes.

### Contemplation: Getting Motivated

You have this book, so you have already moved beyond precontemplation. In *contemplation,* you are intrigued by what you have heard about foods for health and being physically fit. Reading about how food choices and exercise benefits your health, or hearing about it from a friend, registered dietitian, or doctor has stimulated your interest in starting change for yourself. At this stage, you work on getting motivated, thinking about your goals, and asking yourself what you want to get out of this change. This is also the time to address possible obstacles and find ways to overcome them.

> For some people, one stage flows easily and naturally into the next within a relatively short period of time and without major problems. But many of us get hung up at one stage or another. Keep in mind that it often takes several attempts to change one's way of life. Stay with it. You will find that the effort pays off in ways you never imagined.

## Preparation: Starting Your Journey

You are ready to take action once you have thought about your motivations and goals. During *preparation,* you take steps to prepare for new eating and related lifestyle habits. You buy new food, set aside the physical space needed to do exercises, and buy any equipment you may need. You look at your schedule to see where you might fit in time to shop, plan meals, and cook. You set specific exercise days and times to ensure it gets done.

## Action: Adopting the Plan

*Action* is the exciting stage. You are learning to cook in new ways, select new foods, and exercise regularly and consistently. You are beginning to see the results of your work. You may have more energy, sleep better, and become less anxious. Technically, the action stage continues as long as you are engaged in the change. But after six months or so of doing all these lifestyle changes to eat fit and be fit, you will have graduated to the maintenance stage.

## Maintenance: Progressing and Staying on Track

*Maintenance* is the stage at which eating fit and being fit becomes a way of life. When you reach this point, there is a good chance that you will find it hard to imagine not doing this. As you progress, you may add new foods and exercises to your routine and new activities to your life.

## Achieved Change or Relapse

Remember, relapse can occur between each stage of change. You can only change yourself. If you live with others, do not *force* change on someone who is at a different level than you. Do seek support, however, from those who will help you through your change.

# TRACKING CHANGE

Look at three main areas when making change: your emotions, your values, and your confidence.

## Check Your Emotions

How do you and your family (or your child) feel about you making changes? Do you sabotage success after every daily crisis?

## Check Your Values

What does food mean? Love, comfort, reward, punishment? Think about it: If you connect food with these feelings, it will be harder to want to give up this. Remember these things.

## Check Your Confidence

How confident are you that you can change?

## SETTING WEEKLY GOALS

For example, you might set a goal of losing one to two pounds per week by doing the following:

**Week 1** Get rid of junk; add healthier options.

**Week 2** Control portions and establish calorie levels and number of servings from each food group (see Table 2-5 in Chapter 2).

**Week 3** Start adding physical activity and limit eating to only the kitchen or cafeteria.

**Week 4** Check and correct poor meal timing. Restrict eating to every four to five hours and be sure each meal contains three food groups.

**Week 5** Recheck portions and increase activity.

**Week 6** Look at stress and create calmer, more meaningful eating experiences.

## THE CHALLENGE

Make sure you consistently eat foods rich in nutrients. Most fast food lacks nutrient density and boosts empty calories—that is, calories without real nutritional value. This is a real problem. It is easy to eat convenience foods such as power bars, powdered shakes, and soda instead of foods that naturally contain the right balance of all vital nutrients. The most important natural foods to eat are whole grains, vegetables, fruit, low fat milk and yogurt, fish and lean meats, and beans. Eating convenience foods is okay once in a while, but it should not be every day or substituted for a well-balanced meal. That gets us to the next issue.

## THE MIND–BODY CONNECTION

How you feel emotionally and spiritually are important to how you feel physically.

## Stress and the Fast-Paced Life

Stress can have an effect on how we eat because powerful hormones are produced in our bodies when we are stressed. This change in body chemistry affects how we react, how we think, and how we feel. Think of a caveman thousands of years ago picking blueberries in the fields. Life is peaceful until a saber-toothed tiger arrives. Startled, the man's brain is suddenly alerted and the fight-or-flight syndrome kicks in. He takes flight and runs for his life to the safety of his cave. The tiger is gone, and the caveman recovers from the anxiety of the event.

In our society, we wake up in the morning, then for many of us the fight-or-flight syndrome starts and does not end until we go to bed. There is no recovery! For example, you wake up, rush to work with no time to make breakfast, fight traffic and road rage, rush to pick up a bagel, sit on the telephone and eat at the computer, and then rush after three hours to lunch, grab a pizza, return to the office to find you missed an important call, work the rest of the day, then miss your child's sports game because of traffic, pick up some Chinese food, and eat it in the car because you are so hungry. Once home, you sit down to television and listen to who bombed who, the murder of so and so, the downturn of the market, a reality show in which someone is fired, and then, bored out of your mind, try to get a good night's sleep.

### The Buildup of Adrenaline and Cortisol from Lack of Down Time

Lack of calm time has an accumulative effect on our organs, especially our pancreas and liver. It may even trigger the rise of a substance, C-reactive protein. This protein may be either the leading cause of or associated with many disease states such as atherosclerosis and heart disease, inflammation, and possibly cancer, according to emerging studies. If we do not give ourselves time to recover from stressful events, then our body eventually forces us to by becoming ill—sometimes by diabetes, heart attack, or even cancer. The more quiet time you get, the more relaxed you become and the more creativity seems to emerge.

### Overscheduled, Unplanned Meals Sabotage Successful Change

Many people will overeat or choose the wrong foods because their rushed, overscheduled lives lead to meals that are unplanned. When you are rushed, hormones are surging. This often triggers a false sense of hunger. What do you go for? This is when you are the most vulnerable to sweets, chips, donuts, and refined carbohydrates such as bagels. Lack of time also forces you to rely on convenience or fast foods. The vicious cycle keeps on going.

## JUNK FOOD EQUALS BODY MASS DESTRUCTION

The food industry knows how to create processed foods. Candy, soda, chips, and commercial muffins are made to comfort us and make it easy to increase our food addiction. We learn early that candy tastes good; and the more we have, the more we want. The problem is that usually after a binge on junk, we really only feel bad. As we keep food addictions going, we become heavier, more sluggish, and moody. This can make us depressed, sleepless, jumpy, and anxious. Foods that are loaded with sugar, fat, and sodium and low in fiber may temporarily make us feel good, but in the end we feel worse.

This book discourages eating those foods. Replace them with new recipes that create nutrient-dense, energy-producing, and mood-calming foods. Create your own healthy fast food, which I call a "weapon of body *fat* destruction." This is in contrast to the high-fat, high-sugar, highly refined carbohydrate, high-sodium, and low-fiber fast foods are more like "weapons of *body mass* destruction." Finally, let's look at emotional and spiritual well-being and eating.

## ABOUT ADDICTIONS

For those who are affected with addictions such as work, alcohol, or eating disorders, there are beneficial programs that include relying on others. When we open ourselves up to share our negative experiences in life, we free ourselves of the shame and guilt often associated with addictions. Sharing also gives others hope to resolve their own issues. If you suffer from an addiction, seek expert help.

## BREAKING OLD HABITS TO EAT FIT

Identify those habits that are linked to negative eating and that keep you overeating. Start by making a list of behaviors you want to change. Start with the areas below.

### Where Do You Eat?

Take a look at your usual eating places. Do they include in front of the television, in the car, at your desk at work, or in front of the computer?

### Take Ownership of Your Eating

Your mother, your spouse, and your doctor may all try to help you eat better, but ultimately you alone must do it.

Certain negative behaviors, such as those listed below, lead to overeating. Fortunately, there are solutions.

| The Problem | The Solution |
| --- | --- |
| Lack of sleep | Get plenty of rest |
| Not planning meals and snacks | Plan meals |
| Eating quickly | Eat slowly |
| Eating in front of the television or computer | Turn off all distractions when eating |

Why not television? Food commercials and anxiety-producing shows may increase your desire to eat. Studies have shown that excessive viewing of television is linked to obesity. In fact, pediatric experts recommend limiting television to no more than two hours a day for children—and adults, that means that you should set that example. Replace this sedentary activity with something fun and physical activity and a peaceful meal together.

## THE REWARD FOR CHANGE

If you make gradual changes consistently over a few months, then you may lose inches around your waist if you are trying to lose weight, your energy level may improve, you may sleep better, and your moods may improve.

## GETTING STARTED: CREATING A POSITIVE ENVIRONMENT AROUND YOU

Take an inventory of all the places you spend time eating, sleeping, working, and having fun. Ask yourself, "Do I need to change the environment I live in to support a better lifestyle?"

Follow the guide below and check what you think you must change.

Do you need to clean out your food cabinets at home? _____ at work? _____ at school?_____
Do you need to move the television out of the kitchen? _____
Do you have to get organized (because too much clutter creates lots of anxiety) at home? _____ at work? _____ at school? _____

### Identify Your Lifestyle History

It is hard to go forward if you do not know what needs to change. Answering the following lifestyle survey can help you identify areas in your life that you may want to address.

### Lifestyle Survey

Circle any that apply in each category.

1. Have you experienced any of the following in the past year?
   - excessive weight
   - high cholesterol
   - high blood pressure
   - high blood sugar
   - low blood sugar
   - digestive problems
   - binge eating
   - anorexia
   - compulsive overeating
   - fatigue
   - food allergies
   - difficulty sleeping
   - depression
   - other problems _____

2. Have you experienced any of the following?
   - irritability
   - nervousness

## Lifestyle Survey (*Continued*)

- moodiness
- restricting activities

3. If yes, circle the affected areas in your life:
   - spouse or significant other
   - job performance
   - productivity
   - ability to have quality time away from work
   - patience with others
   - sleep

4. Do you have a family history of any of the following?
   - arthritis
   - cataracts or macular degeneration
   - depression
   - diabetes
   - alcoholism
   - heart disease
   - cancer
   - high blood pressure
   - high cholesterol
   - osteoporosis
   - hypo- or hyperthyroidism

5. Do you eat based on any of the following?
   - the clock
   - energy needs
   - emotional needs
   - hunger
   - tension or stress

6. Habits are usually learned. Growing up, did any of these apply?
   - forced feeding
   - eating alone
   - limited meals with family together
   - put on "diets" or deprived of certain foods
   - rushed meals
   - fast family eating even if not rushed
   - told there are starving people and to "clean your plate"
   - meal conversation was unpleasant

(continued)

## Lifestyle Survey (*Continued*)

7. Do you have any of the following personal concerns?
   - skipping meals
   - eating quickly
   - fear of weight gain
   - portion control
   - food cravings or binging
   - emotional eating
   - vomiting after meals
   - eating in front of television
   - eating in inappropriate locations (standing, in car, at desk)

8. How many meals do you prepare yourself each day?
   - none
   - one to two
   - all of them

9. How many times a week do you eat fast foods?
   - breakfast: _____
   - lunch: _____
   - dinner: _____

10. Do you have food allergies to or exclude any of the following foods?
    - milk
    - wheat or gluten
    - soy
    - peanuts or nuts
    - all dairy
    - other: _____

Looking at your answers, identify and highlight a few things that you want to focus on and explain why. For example:

1. Your father may have been overweight or had diabetes and you want to reduce your risk of these problems.

2. Growing up you may have learned to eat fast and you want to slow things down.

3. You never eat at home and want to find better ways to make this happen so that you are more in control of what you eat.

If you are overwhelmed with many issues, a registered dietitian may be able to help you sort everything you may need.

# EASY BEGINNINGS

## Buying Sensibly

Start making positive changes by shopping for healthier foods. At first, it might take more time check out labels, but in the end you will gain confidence in knowing your choices are the right ones.

Get rid of foods like potato chips, soda, candy, and refined grains such as sugar-coated cereals, low-fiber and higher fat crackers (e.g., Goldfish), and high sodium noodle soup. No, your children do not need them either—and it is likely they will get them elsewhere!

## Reading and Becoming Educated about Food Labels

If you find products you are not sure about, the following guidelines for reading labels may be of help. Labeling can be confusing because there are loopholes in the system that food manufacturers use to exploit us. For example, an instant oatmeal cereal may be marketed as "high fiber for weight loss" but contain fibers that are not usually found in unprocessed oats. These types of foods are processed or have added sugar or a sugar substitute. Be aware of the terms *instant, quick, honey,* and *crunch.* Why? Such products have higher levels of sweeteners that may stimulate your desire for more sweets or be lower in fiber.

Under regulations from both the Food and Drug Administration (FDA) (a part of the U.S. Department of Health and Human Services) and the Food Safety and Inspection Service (part of the U.S. Department of Agriculture, or USDA), food labels offer more complete, more useful, and more accurate nutrition information than ever before. By reading food labels, you can learn a lot, including new information on food allergies (e.g., whether nuts or milk products have been used) and trans fats. If the government required all the phytonutrients to be listed on the labels of healthy plant foods, there would be no room, but that does not mean these nutrients are less important.

With today's food labels, consumers get the following:

nutrition information about almost every food in the grocery store;

distinctive, easy-to-read formats that enable consumers to more quickly find the information they need to make healthful food choices;

information on the amount per serving of saturated fat, cholesterol, dietary fiber, and other nutrients of major health concern;

nutrient reference values, expressed as "% Daily Values" that help consumers see how a food fits into an overall daily diet;

uniform definitions for terms that describe a food's nutrient content—such as *light, low-fat,* and *high-fiber*—to ensure that they mean the same for any product on which they appear;

claims about the relationship between a nutrient or food and a disease or health-related condition, such as calcium and osteoporosis, and fat and cancer. These are helpful for people who wish to select foods that may help keep them healthier longer;

standardized serving sizes that make nutritional comparisons of similar products easier; and

total percentage of fruit juice in juice drinks so that consumers know exactly how much juice is in a product.

## Nutrition Information Panel

Under the label's "Nutrition Facts" panel, manufacturers are required to provide information on certain nutrients. The mandatory (*italicized*) and voluntary components and the order in which they must appear are as follow:

total calories

calories from fat

calories from saturated fat

total fat

saturated fat

polyunsaturated fat

monounsaturated fat

trans fats

cholesterol

sodium

potassium

total carbohydrate

dietary fiber

soluble fiber

insoluble fiber

*sugars*

sugar alcohol (for example, sugar substitutes such as xylitol, mannitol, and sorbitol)

other carbohydrates (the difference between total carbohydrate and the sum of dietary fiber, sugars, and sugar alcohol if declared)

*protein*

*vitamin A*

percent of vitamin A present as beta-carotene

*vitamin C*

*calcium*

iron

other essential vitamins and minerals

If a claim is made about any of the optional components, or if a food is fortified or enriched with any of them, nutrition information for these components becomes mandatory.

These mandatory and voluntary components are the only ones allowed on the Nutrition Facts panel. The section titled "Percent Daily Values" is based on a diet of 2,000 calories. If you require fewer calories, then the daily values may be higher or lower. Remember to follow the number of recommended servings in each food group based on your calorie pattern (listed in Chapter 2).

## General Guidelines for Food Groups when Comparing Labels

At a quick glance, you can check the following: serving size, calories, carbohydrate, protein, fat, sodium, fiber, and sugar.

### Dairy Group (Milk and Yogurt)

*Serving size:* 8 ounces

| | | | |
|---|---|---|---|
| Calories | 80–120 | Carbohydrate | 12 grams |
| Protein | 8 grams | Total fat | 0–2 grams |
| Sodium | 90–120 milligrams | Natural sugar | 11 grams or less |
| Fiber | 0 grams | | |

Greek yogurt will usually have more protein and less carbohydrate but the same calories as other milk products. For dairy alternatives such as soy milk, check the percentage of calcium.

### Fruit

*Serving size:* One portion or one diabetic exchange

| | | | |
|---|---|---|---|
| Calories | 15 | Carbohydrate | 12 grams |
| Protein | 0 grams | Total fat | 0–2 grams |
| Sodium | 0–5 milligrams | Added sugar | 0 grams |
| Fiber | 1–6 grams | | |

### Bread, Pasta, Potato, Rice, Cereal, Cracker

*Serving size:* One portion or one diabetic exchange

| | | | |
|---|---|---|---|
| Calories | 80–100 | Carbohydrate | 15 grams |
| Protein | 3 grams | Total fat | 0–1 grams |
| Sodium | 60–150 milligrams | Sugar | 0–3 grams |
| Fiber | 2–12 grams | | |

### Meat, and Meat Substitute Group (Beans, Tofu, Egg, Turkey, Chicken, Beef, Lamb, Bison, Buffalo, and Other Poultry)

*Serving size:* 1 ounce or one diabetic exchange

| Calories | 70–90 | Carbohydrate | 0 grams |
|---|---|---|---|
| Protein | 4–8 grams | (except beans | 5 grams) |
| Sodium | 10–80 milligrams | Total fat | 0–7 grams |
| Fiber | 0–7 (beans) grams | Sugar | 0 grams |

## Fats

Oil or vegetable spreads without trans fats or partially hydrogenated anything. *Serving size:* 1 teaspoon (no, that is not a typo); "lite" or "whipped" or "reduced fat" may offer 1 Tablespoon for 45 calories.

| Calories | 45 | Carbohydrate | 0 grams |
|---|---|---|---|
| Protein | 0 grams | Fat | 0–5 grams |
| Sodium | 0–4 milligrams | Sugar | 0 grams |
| Fiber | 0 grams | | |

## Vegetables

*Serving size:* 1/2 cup cooked or 1 cup raw serving or one diabetic exchange

| Calories | 20–30 | Carbohydrate | 5 grams |
|---|---|---|---|
| Protein | 0–2 grams | Fat | 0–2 grams |
| Sodium | 0–9 milligrams | Sugar | 0 grams |
| Fiber | 1–8 grams | | |

## Pointers to Reading Labels and Using the Nutrition Facts Label

People look at food labels for different reasons. But whatever the reason, many consumers would like to know how to use this information more effectively and easily. The following label-building skills are intended to make it easier for you to use nutrition labels to make quick, informed food choices that contribute to a healthy diet.

## THE NUTRITION FACTS LABEL–AN OVERVIEW

The information in the main or top section (see #1-4 and #6 on the sample nutrition label, Figure 1-1), can vary with each food product; it contains product-specific information (serving size, calories, and nutrient information). The bottom part (see #5 on the sample label) contains a footnote with Daily Values (DVs) for 2,000 and 2,500 calorie diets. This footnote provides recommended dietary information for important nutrients, including fats, sodium, and fiber. The footnote is found only on larger packages and does not change from product to product.

**FIGURE 1-1 Sample label for Macaroni & Cheese**

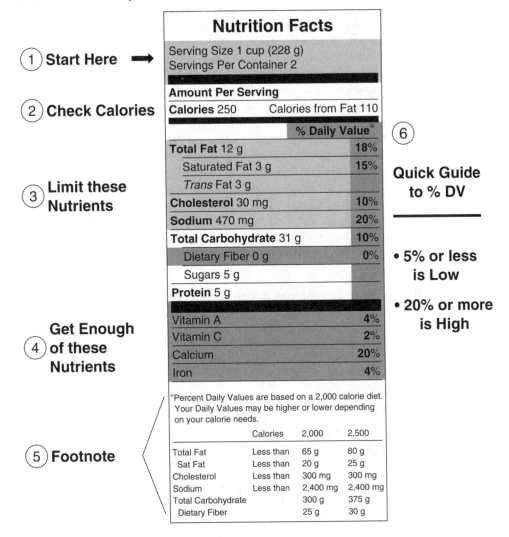

In the Nutrition Facts label certain sections are highlighted to help you focus on those areas that will be explained in detail. You will not see these highlights on the food labels on products you purchase.

①The Serving Size

(#1 on sample label):

Serving Size 1 cup (228 g)
Servings Per Container 2

The first place to start when you look at the Nutrition Facts label is the serving size and the number of servings in the package. Serving sizes are standardized to make it easier to compare similar foods; they are provided in familiar units, such as cups or pieces, followed by the metric amount, e.g., the number of grams.

The size of the serving on the food package influences the number of calories and all the nutrient amounts listed on the top part of the label. **Pay attention to the serving size, especially how many servings there are in the food package. Then ask yourself, "How many servings am I consuming?" (e.g., ¹/₂ serving, 1 serving, or more).** In the sample label, one serving of macaroni and cheese equals one cup. If you ate the whole package, you would eat **two** cups. That doubles the calories and other nutrient numbers, including the % Daily Value as shown in the sample label.

## ②Calories (and Calories from Fat)

Calories provide a measure of how much energy you get from a serving of this food.

| Amount Per Serving | |
|---|---|
| **Calories** 250 | Calories from Fat 110 |

Many Americans consume more calories than they need without meeting recommended intakes for a number of nutrients. The calorie section of the label can help you manage your weight (i.e., gain, lose, or maintain.) **Remember: The number of servings you consume determines the number of calories you actually eat (your portion amount).**

(#2 on sample label):

In the example, there are 250 calories in one serving of this macaroni and cheese. How many calories from fat are there in ONE serving? Answer: 110 calories, which means almost half the calories in a single serving come from fat. What if you ate the whole package content? Then, you would consume two servings, or 500 calories, and 220 would come from fat.

---

**General Guide to Calories**

- 40 calories is low
- 100 calories is moderate
- 400 calories or more is high

---

The **General Guide to Calories** provides a general reference for calories when you look at a Nutrition Facts label. This guide is based on a 2,000-calorie diet. If you need less calories each day this increases the percent of your daily nutrition value from the food you consume. Simply do not eat over the calories you need each day. **Eating too many calories per day is linked to overweight and obesity. So remember** Calories are for the serving size listed. The next time you drink a 20-ounce bottle of soda, check out the calories listed, the serving size, and then figure out what the calories are for the amount you drank for the entire bottle! If you do not check the serving size and only look at calories, then you may be getting double or triple those calorie amounts if you consume the whole package. This is important for chips, cookies, and many other convenience foods.

## ③④The Nutrients: How Much?

(#3 and 4 on sample label):

Look at the top of the nutrient section in the sample label. It shows you some key nutrients that impact on your health and separates them into two main groups:

(#3 on sample label):

The nutrients listed first are the ones Americans generally eat in adequate amounts, or even too much. They are identified in Figure1-1 as **Limit these Nutrients.** Eating too much fat, saturated fat, trans fat, cholesterol, or sodium may increase your risk of certain chronic

| | % Daily Value* |
|---|---|
| **Total Fat** 12 g | 18% |
| Saturated Fat 3 g | 15% |
| *Trans* Fat 3 g | |
| **Cholesterol** 30 mg | 10% |
| **Sodium** 470 mg | 20% |

diseases, like heart disease, some cancers, or high blood pressure. Sodium levels of 20 percent or more are too much. Eating too much fat may increase your risk of chronic diseases such as heart disease. Total fat per serving should be 10 percent or less in animal proteins such as meat and poultry, and it should be zero percent in fruit, vegetables, and most grains, except those with seeds or nuts. Trans fats are usually found in crackers, cookies, pastries, cakes, and margarine. Zero trans fat would be better!

**Important: Health experts recommend that you keep your intake of saturated fat, trans fat, and cholesterol as low as possible as part of a nutritionally balanced diet.**

(#4 on sample label):

Most Americans don't get enough dietary fiber, vitamin A, vitamin C, calcium, and iron in their diets. They are identified in Figure 1-1 as **Get Enough of these Nutrients**. Eating enough of these nutrients can improve your health and help reduce

| Dietary Fiber 0 g | 0% |
|---|---|
| Vitamin A | 4% |
| Vitamin C | 2% |
| Calcium | 20% |
| Iron | 4% |

the risk of some diseases and conditions. For example, getting enough calcium may reduce the risk of osteoporosis, a condition that results in brittle bones as one ages (see calcium section below). Eating a diet high in dietary fiber promotes healthy bowel function. Additionally, a diet rich in fruits, vegetables, and grain products that contain dietary fiber, particularly soluble fiber, and low in saturated fat and cholesterol may reduce the risk of heart disease.

**Remember: You can use the Nutrition Facts label not only to help** *limit* **those nutrients you want to cut back on but also to** *increase* **those nutrients you need to consume in greater amounts.**

**This information was obtained from: The Food and Drug Administration Website. http://www.cfsan.fda.gov/~dms/foodlab.html**

Here are seven more items to keep in mind when you examine a food product label.

## 1. Read the Ingredients

This list is found usually directly below the Nutrition Facts on the food label. Ingredients are listed in order of abundance of the ingredient in the product. If a product lists sugar, high fructose corn syrup, or modified corn syrup, beware that these ingredients are of concern because as these ingredients have been added to foods so has the rise of obesity and other health problems. For diabetics names of different sugars take different forms—dextrose, malt, honey, sorbitol to name a few. See the website for the American Diabetes Association that defines these in more detail. A registered dietitian can help you understand these terms more easily.

## 2. Look at Fiber

Most Americans do not get enough. Eat more fiber-containing foods such as fruit, vegetables, and whole grains with more than 2 grams per serving.

New functional foods have been tampered with. In May 2005, *Nutrition Action Healthletter* reported about examples such as Dannon's Light 'N Fit Yogurt with Fiber. The consumer might assume from the picture of fruit on the package label that the fiber comes from the fruit in the yogurt. Wrong. Maltodextrin, a nondigestible carbohydrate isolate, has been added. It is not the same as dietary fiber that is naturally found in foods.

Another deception can be found with Breyer's CarbSmart ice cream with 3 grams of fiber per serving from polydextrose, a chemical combination of dextrose (corn syrup) and sorbitol (a sugar alcohol).

Another name for functional fiber is *inulin*. Even wood pulp can be found as an ingredient to boost fiber in some breads. Because functional fiber is poorly digested, it counts as fiber. Functional fibers, although deemed safe, do not provide you with all of the nutrient-dense benefits of foods containing dietary fiber in fruits, vegetables, and whole grains. Isolated fibers are usually lower in phytonutrients. Most studies that show evidence that fiber helps lower the risk of heart disease, cancer, and diabetes are including "dietary" fiber, not "functional" fiber. The key is to get at least the following amount of fiber daily: women, 25 grams; women over age 50, 21 grams; men, 38 grams; men over age 50, 15–30 grams; and children, based on their weight, another way to figure it is a child's age plus 5.

## 3. Know that "Sugar Free" Does Not Mean "Calorie Free"

For example: Pepperidge Farm's Sugar Free Milano Chocolate Chip Cookies have only 3 fewer calories than the regular cookies. Regular and lower-sugar versions may be equal in calories, and sometimes it is only the portion or the serving size that changes. Be sure to check the portion for calories before you change.

## 4. Do Limit Sugar Substitutes

Some people think that foods sweetened with sugar substitutes are better than those without. Not really. Many sugar substitutes taste 200 to 600 times sweeter than regular sugar. This heightened sensation for sweetness, studies are showing, may cause you to want more. Furthermore, the safety of some sugar substitutes remains debatable. Those containing aspartame and acesulfame are of concern. Be sure to check what you are eating.

## 5. Not all Calcium Absorbs the Same

Check the calcium in foods you substitute for dairy products such as soy milk or orange juice. They should contain at least 30 percent of the daily value (DV) for calcium. Remember, these products differ in the content of vitamin D, protein, and phosphorous than cows milk. The balance of these nutrients is important for calcium absorption and the mineral's use in building and maintaining our bones.

### 6. Know Your Nutrient Needs

The percentages of nutrients on the food are for 2,000 calories. If you need less to lose weight then this percentage is not the same for you. Always remember total nutrient-dense calories are important to track when wanting to lose weight.

### 7. Know the Differences in Grains

According to the FDA, grains are divided into two groups: *whole grains* and *refined grains.* Whole grains contain the entire grain kernel: bran, germ, and endosperm. Examples include whole wheat flour, bulgur (cracked wheat), oatmeal, whole cornmeal, and brown rice. The problem is that the food industry can call something "whole grain" if it only contains 51 percent whole grain. More important, look for the total dietary fiber and limit the functional fibers. Refined grains have been milled, a process that removes bran and germ. This is done to give grains a finer texture and improve their shelf life, but it also removes dietary fiber, iron, and many B vitamins. Examples of refined grain products are white flour, degermed cornmeal, white bread, and white rice.

Most refined grains are *enriched.* This means certain B vitamins (thiamin, riboflavin, niacin, and folic acid) and iron are added back after processing. Fiber is not added back to enriched grains or often a functional fiber is added. Check the ingredient list on refined grain products to make sure that the word *enriched* is included in the grain name. In Table 1-1, Grains Comparison, the USDA's MyPyramid summarizes some food products that are made from mixtures of whole grains and refined grains.

Now that you have taken the next step in change, you are reading food labels and buying healthier food products. Once you create a healthy home environment, you can begin to set your life on a different path. The next step is fighting obstacles that prevent success.

## FIGHTING OBSTACLES

Change may take time if you live with others who are opposed to change. The more support you gain with family and friends, the easier change will probably be. Remember: You can only control your own choices. Those choices may beneficially influence the people around you, but ultimately each individual has to learn how to make better choices. So remember: Work on your own habits and do not police others—not even your child's eating habits—but do offer structure and guidance. For those who are willing to change with you, great.

**TABLE 1-1 Grains Comparison**

| Whole Grains | Refined Grains |
|---|---|
| Grains to use more often with greater than 2 grams of fiber | Grains to use less often if they have 2 or fewer grams of fiber (these are still better than high-sugar options) |
| Brown rice | Cornbread* |
| Buckwheat | Corn tortillas* |
| Bulgur (cracked wheat) | Couscous* |
| Oatmeal | Crackers* |
| Popcorn | Flour tortillas* |
| Unsweetened, whole grain, ready-to-eat breakfast cereals: | Grits |
| Whole wheat cereal flakes | Noodles* |
| Shredded wheat | Pasta* |
| Other high fiber cereals | Spaghetti |
| Whole grain pasta | Macaroni |
| Whole grain barley | Pitas* |
| Whole grain cornmeal | Pretzels |
| Whole rye | Some ready-to-eat breakfast cereals |
| Whole wheat bread | Corn flakes |
| Whole wheat crackers | White bread |
| Whole wheat pasta or pasta with flaxseed meal added | White sandwich buns and rolls |
| Whole wheat sandwich buns and rolls | White rice |
| Whole wheat tortillas | |
| Wild rice | |

| Less Common Whole Grains |
|---|
| Amaranth |
| Millet |
| Quinoa |
| Sorghum |
| Triticale |

*Most of these products are made from refined grains. Check the ingredient list for the words *whole grain* or *whole wheat* to decide whether they are made from a whole grain and the total fiber. Some foods are made from a mixture of whole and refined grains. The first listed ingredients are the most abundant. Refer to the grocery guide for recommended grains. If a grain is processed, it is not as beneficial as unprocessed organic grains. For more information about food labels, refer to "Food Labels: Nutrient Content Claims."

*Source:* www.mypyramid.gov

# PROMOTING POSITIVE EATING HABITS

Here are five rules for parents and families to promote positive eating habits.

## 1. Plan Ahead

Grocery shop, make a list of what is needed and keep to that list. Avoid impulse buying or purchasing large quantities. Plan meals, and work meal times into your schedule without rushing. Too often we do not make the time to eat, then we become overly hungry and grab junk.

## 2. Purchase Healthy Snacks

Limit the purchase of junk foods such as cookies, cake, pastry, and soda perhaps to one type in the house each week or just one or two on special occasions. Remember: Snacks should be foods that provide nutrients that are not consumed at mealtime, *not* empty calories that provide excess sugar, fat, and sodium without natural fiber. Avoid using breakfast bars and shakes all the time as meal replacements and as snacks. They may provide too many calories if not used in balance with other foods. Set up the picture perfect refrigerator and food pantries with fat-free milk, fat-free plain yogurt, 1 percent cottage cheese, fresh oranges and apples, carrots, dark green lettuce, and sliced chicken.

## 3. Eat Meals without Television

Limit television, computer, or video games to two or fewer hours per day.

## 4. Set Limits to What Is Available for Meals

Do not become a short-order cook if you eat with others. Often wives and husbands who work late tell me that the person at home cooking is making one meal each for a finicky child, a fussy teen, and a spouse. They pick on everything and anything. This is a sure plan for disaster with your weight and your health. Create one meal, and even if you cannot eat together all the time, try to set a few days a week for all family members to eat together.

## 5. Create a Relaxing Atmosphere at Meals and Between-Meal Snacks

Studies show that children eat better if they eat with someone—and so do adults. Put on relaxing music, perhaps light candles, add flowers, avoid answering the telephone, and avoid anxiety-producing conversation.

## Using a Food Diary

Begin your first week of change by keeping a food diary.

## Directions

1. Write down everything you have eaten right after your meal.
2. Be accurate with the amount you have eaten.

## Food Diary

| | Date | Time | Food Eaten | Amount | Location Eaten* | Mood |
|---|---|---|---|---|---|---|
| Breakfast | | | | | | |
| Snack | | | | | | |
| Lunch | | | | | | |
| Snack | | | | | | |
| Dinner | | | | | | |

*H = Home   D = Desk   C = Car   R = Restaurant   S = Standing

3. Use the codes for your location (R, restaurant; H, home; D, office desk; C, car; K, kitchen table, etc.).

4. Identify your mood: tired, relaxed, sad, happy, bored, rushed.

### Tips

1. Be accurate in your recording.

Weighing and measuring will help you see the actual number of portions you are consuming. Be sure your portions are not too large or too small. See Table 1-2.

### Keeping Track Pays Off

By keeping track of your intake, you will begin to see what habits need to change so you can eat fit and be fit.

After a full week of keeping a record, answer the following questions.

1. Do you have regular meal times?

2. Are meal times usually four to five hours apart?

3. Do meals contain at least three food groups from dairy *or* beans; meat, fish, or poultry plus fruit or vegetables or both; plus whole grains?

4. Do fluids include at least four glasses of water?

5. Are you consuming at least two servings of milk or yogurt or milk substitute?

6. How many fats servings are you eating per day?

7. Are portions larger than the number of servings you should have?

If you cannot yet answer *yes* to these questions, keep writing the food record. Be sure you are not eating smaller portions than what your body needs. Restricting too much is as harmful as eating too much.

Change will become easy once you educate yourself on how certain foods have excessive amounts of fat, salt, and sugar and do not provide enough fiber and nutrients such as calcium. Check your waist measure again and see if the number of inches are improving. This is the beginning. Even if you are really trying and nothing is happening on the scale, remember, *weight loss is a gradual*

**TABLE 1-2 A Guide to Serving Size**

Listed below are examples of selections from the major food groups, followed by real-life size equivalents, to assist you in meal preparation.

| Breads, Cereals, Rice, and Pasta | | Fruit | | Vegetables | |
|---|---|---|---|---|---|
| Item | Size | Item | Size | Item | Size |
| Average bagel | Hockey puck | 1 medium fruit | Tennis ball | 1 cup lettuce | 4 leaves |
| Medium potato | Computer mouse | 1 cup | Baseball | 1 cup chopped | Fist |
| 1 cup rice or pasta | Personal cassette player | ½ cup chopped | 15 marbles | ½ cup chopped | Standard light bulb |
| ½ cup cooked rice | Cupcake wrapper | ¼ cup raisins | 1 large egg | | |
| 1 cup dried cereal | Large handful | | | | |

| Meat | | Dairy | | Fats, Oils, and Sweets | |
|---|---|---|---|---|---|
| Item | Size | Item | Size | Item | Size |
| 3 ounces meat | Deck of cards, cassette tape, or bar of soap | 1½ ounces natural cheese | 3 dominoes, 9-volt battery, or bar of hotel soap | ½ cup ice milk, frozen yogurt | Tennis ball |
| 1 ounce meat | Match box or floppy diskette | 1 ounce cheese | 4 dice | 2 Tablespoons tub margarine, salad dressing, mayonnaise | Ping pong ball |
| 3 ounces grilled fish | Checkbook | | | 1 teaspoon tub margarine, salad dressing, mayonnaise, jelly 1 ounce larger-sized snack foods (pretzels, chips) | Top of thumb to first joint or one die (dice) 1 large handful |

For your information: 1 cup is the size of a softball or an orange.

*process.* The reward of making lifestyle changes is as important as the reward of losing weight. Continue following the guidelines in "Forty Days to Jump Start Your Health."

## ABOUT ACTIVITY

Activity helps burn calories and keeps the body toned. The less activity you have, the less you should eat. One big cheeseburger requires approximately six hours of walking just to burn off the stored calories.

Your exercise or activity should use a variety of muscles. Try to do three types: (1) daily aerobic activity, (2) daily strength conditioning or weight resistance alternating muscle groups, and (3) daily stretching as long as your doctor has given you the okay to engage in these activities.

1.  Daily aerobic activity types: walking, swimming, bicycling, elliptical machine
    Minimum activity = 300 calories/hour

    | | |
    |---|---|
    | Walking | 3 miles per hour |
    | Bicycling | 5.5 mph |
    | Dancing | Medium level of activity |
    | Aerobics | Low impact |

    Try using a step counter; ten thousand steps is suggested.

    Recommended: One hour a day for adults, two hours for children.

2.  Daily strength conditioning exercises: Pushups, barbells, free weights, and weight-resistant gym equipment. Alternate days using different muscle groups. For children, playing active sports and jumping jacks will help. These activities help maintain good bone density.

3.  Daily stretching (10–15 minutes or more): Yoga, Pilates, and isometric types of exercises will offer a well-rounded program to help you maintain muscle tone and flexibility.

### Why Do All Three Types of Exercise?

You have more than 600 different muscles in your body, and each of them needs your attention.

### Components of Physical Activity

#### Cardiorespiratory Endurance

*Cardiorespiratory endurance* is your body's ability to access stored fuel during sustained exercise. If you become tired quickly, then your endurance is low. If you can exercise for long periods of time, then you have a high endurance—a good thing!

Aerobic activities such as walking, bicycling, and swimming help cardiorespiratory endurance.

## Muscular Strength and Muscle Endurance

*Muscular strength* is a measure of your muscles' ability to exert force during an activity, and *muscle endurance* measures the level of fatigue.

To improve both muscular strength and muscle endurance, try walking, dancing, bicycling, and jogging.

## Flexibility

*Flexibility* is determined by the range of motion around a joint. When you are less flexible, activity is harder. More flexibility helps you achieve greater range of motion more easily.

Good flexibility is achieved by stretching every day. Pilates, yoga, and dance are good forms of stretching.

## Body Composition

*Body composition* is your body's ratio of muscle, bones, fat, and other vital body parts. The goal of being fit is to have more muscle and less fat.

## Getting Started with Activity

You may want guidance from professionals such as certified personal trainers, yoga and Pilates instructors, or health clubs. Another inexpensive alternative may be to use DVDs, CDs, audiotapes, or videos from the library or watch cable exercise and fitness channels to help motivate you and to follow a routine. It is great if you can be active with a partner or a friend, but do not let that be an excuse if that is not possible.

Experts advise that people with chronic diseases such as heart conditions, arthritis, diabetes, or high blood pressure talk with their physicians about what types and amounts of physical activity are appropriate. If you have symptoms of extreme shortness of breath, heart palpitations, chest pain (especially when brought on by exertion), loss of balance (especially when it can lead to a fall), dizziness, and passing out (loss of consciousness), then have your primary care physician check it out.

For more information, see Chapter 2's matrix plan for exercise.

# SUMMARY

Change can be hard, but after you start and feel better, you will be glad you made the effort. You have learned the different levels of readiness for change, you have assessed your lifestyle habits using the survey, and you have learned about reading food labels, buying healthier foods, and exercising.

Recheck food labels from time to time to be sure the products you are buying have not changed in the amounts of sugar, sodium, fat, and calories. Food manufacturers continually change their food products, so we must stay alert. Remember: Change is gradual. There may be relapses along the way. If you go back to old ways, do not beat yourself up, just keep on trying. Shop, plan meals, cook sensibly, and exercise. Those people who are the most successful are those who are persistent.

# Chapter 2

# THE BASICS: NUTRITION GUIDELINES TO EAT FIT AND BE FIT

The key to *eating fit* is giving your body the right balance of nutrients so that you feel great, avoid illness, have a fit body shape, and have more energy. The following simple guidelines will help you create this balance.

## SECTION 1

### What Is a Healthy Diet?

The 2005 U.S. Department of Agriculture's *Dietary Guidelines for Americans* describe a *healthy diet* as one that:

- emphasizes fruits, vegetables, whole grains, and fat-free or low-fat milk and milk products;
- includes beans, eggs, nuts, poultry, fish, and lean meats; and
- is low in saturated fats, trans fats, cholesterol, salt (sodium), and added sugars.

In light of environmental changes and a world full of overprocessed food, I would like to add the following:

- Include foods that are environmentally safe; free of pesticides and hormones.
- Choose from unprocessed foods that are rich in natural dietary fiber and low in sodium, fat, and sugar.
- Choose healthy lifestyle habits "24/7" (that is, twenty-four hours a day seven days a week).

I describe foods that fit this description as *Gold Choices*. To take it a step further, plant-based foods should fill most of your plate at meal time.

The USDA's dietary guidelines revised and updated the food pyramid in 2005, calling it "MyPyramid." The anatomy of the food pyramid is shown in Figure 2-1. The main difference from the old pyramid is that one size does

33

# FIGURE 2-1 Anatomy of MyPyramid

**One size doesn't fit all**
USDA's new MyPyramid symbolizes a personalized approach to healthy eating and physical activity. The symbol has been designed to be simple. It has been developed to remind consumers to make healthy food choices and to be active every day. The different parts of the symbol are described below.

**Activity**
Activity is represented by the steps and the person climbing them, as a reminder of the importance of daily physical activity.

**Moderation**
Moderation is represented by the narrowing of each food group from bottom to top. The wider base stands for foods with little or no solid fats or added sugars. These should be selected more often. The narrower top area stands for foods containing more added sugars and solid fats. The more active you are, the more of these foods can fit into your diet.

**Personalization**
Personalization is shown by the person on the steps, the slogan, and the URL. Find the kinds and amounts of food to eat each day at MyPyramid.gov.

**Proportionality**
Proportionality is shown by the different widths of the food group bands. The widths suggest how much food a person should choose from each group. The widths are just a general guide, not exact proportions. Check the Web site for how much is right for you.

**Variety**
Variety is symbolized by the 6 color bands representing the 5 food groups of the Pyramid and oils. This illustrates that foods from all groups are needed each day for good health.

**Gradual Improvement**
Gradual improvement is encouraged by the slogan. It suggests that individuals can benefit from taking small steps to improve their diet and lifestyle each day.

MyPyramid.gov
STEPS TO A HEALTHIER YOU

USDA U.S. Department of Agriculture
Center for Nutrition Policy
and Promotion
April 2005 CNPP-16

*USDA is an equal opportunity provider and employer.*

| GRAINS Make half your grains whole | VEGETABLES Vary your veggies | FRUITS Focus on fruits | MILK Get your calcium-rich foods | MEAT & BEANS Go lean with protein |
|---|---|---|---|---|
| Eat at least 3 oz. of whole-grain cereals, breads, crackers, rice, or pasta every day | Eat more dark-green veggies like broccoli, spinach, and other dark leafy greens | Eat a variety of fruit | Go low-fat or fat-free when you choose milk, yogurt, and other milk products | Choose low-fat or lean meats and poultry |
| 1 oz. is about 1 slice of bread, about 1 cup of breakfast cereal, or ½ cup of cooked rice, cereal, or pasta | Eat more orange vegetables like carrots and sweet potatoes | Choose fresh, frozen, canned, or dried fruit | If you don't or can't consume milk, choose lactose-free products or other calcium sources such as fortified foods and beverages | Bake it, broil it, or grill it |
| | Eat more dry beans and peas like pinto beans, kidney beans, and lentils | Go easy on fruit juices | | Vary your protein routine — choose more fish, beans, peas, nuts, and seeds |

not fit all. Each food group now contains lower-calorie foods at the bottom and higher-calorie foods at the top of the pyramid. Therefore, foods at the base are the ones to consume more often, especially if you are not physically active and are not trying to gain weight. Eating foods on the top of the pyramid means you have to be more active to burn them up or build muscle, otherwise they will just make you fat. For example, at the base of the pyramid you have white breast chicken with very few calories, at the top a higher-fat sausage or fried chicken wings. I recommend eating the foods at the bottom more often if you are overweight or trying to control your blood sugar because you have diabetes. These foods are less calorie dense and often more nutrient dense.

To improve your health and achieve a desirable weight, start using foods at the base of the food pyramid. As you move toward the top, consider ranking your choices from *Gold* to *Silver* to *Bronze* to *Dirt*. Gold has the highest nutrients for the fewest calories in the food group (at the bottom), and dirt has higher number of calories and lower nutrients per food group (at the top).

The USDA's dietary guidelines are recommendations based on scientific evidence for lowering the risk of chronic disease and promoting health. The recommendations in the 2005 MyPyramid are for people over 2 years of age. MyPyramid is not a therapeutic diet for any specific health condition. Individuals with chronic health conditions should consult with a health care provider such as a registered dietitian to determine what dietary pattern is appropriate for them.

The differences between MyPyramid food groups and the diabetes exchange groups of the American Diabetes Association (ADA) are few but important. In MyPyramid, the grouping of cheese is in the dairy *and* meat group, and potatoes are in the vegetable group. The diabetes exchanges will not include cheese in the dairy group. Potatoes, corn, butternut squash, and other starchy vegetables are in the grain group, not the vegetable group. The diabetic exchanges are recommended for weight loss and for persons with diabetes. The list of diabetes exchanges are found on pages 53–55 of this chapter.

## ALL ABOUT CALORIES

*Should I worry about calories if I am overweight or underweight?*
Yes.

*So what are calories anyway?*
A calorie is a unit of energy. After you eat, you must burn up the energy you have consumed in the food or it will be stored as fat.

*What is calorie density?*
The energy content of food per unit of volume or weight is usually expressed as *kilocalories* or kcal:

$$1,000 \text{ calories} = 1 \text{ kcal.}$$

The more calories in a food, the more energy dense it is. The fewer calories in a food, the less energy dense it is. This book uses many foods of lower-calorie density to benefit weight management. MyPyramid has lower-calorie dense foods at the base of the pyramid. These are "gold" choices.

*What do calories have to do with activity balance?*
The old saying is "Energy in equals energy out." Calorie balance is important. The body burns calories for energy. If you consume calories beyond your energy needs, then you will gain weight. The more calories you consume, the more activity you must have to stay in balance with your weight. Eating a bacon club or deli hero or sub sandwich means you need approximately five or more hours of physical activity to burn it off. If you are sedentary and overweight, choose a lower-calorie option.

On the other hand, too few calories will keep your body from functioning safely and lead to being underweight. Serious health problems such as infertility, depression, and anemia may occur. This may cause bone softening (osteoporosis), hair loss, low body temperature, headaches, and even heart attack.

The caloric density of foods can be seen in the following sources:

| | |
|---|---|
| Carbohydrate | 4 calories per gram |
| Protein | 4 calories per gram |
| Fat | 9 calories per gram |
| Alcohol | 7 calories per gram |

## CHOOSING CALORIES WISELY

To wisely and effectively use calories from food, follow the guide below.

### Carbohydrate Calorie Sources

*Gold Choices* are nutrient dense in grains. They can be found in the following foods:

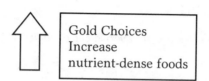

Gold Choices
Increase
nutrient-dense foods

- whole grains (with 2+ grams of fiber) and beans such as barley, oats, whole grain bread, pasta, rice, beans, and lentils;
- vegetables and herbs (all plain, unsalted, unsweetened, and without sauce and available fresh, frozen, or canned);
- dairy foods that are unsweetened, low-fat, fat-free, or sugar-free; and

- fruits that are plain, unsweetened and available fresh, canned, or frozen (use sparingly).

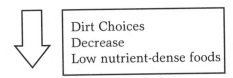

Dirt Choices
Decrease
Low nutrient-dense foods

Dirt Choices are foods with empty calories—that is, they are not nutrient dense. They include the following:

- junk foods such as chips, candy, and fruit rollups;
- sweets such as donuts, cookies, cake, and soda; and
- refined flour products such as white breads, crackers, and sweetened cereals.

### Why Cut Down on Junk Foods?

Junk foods not only lack essential nutrients but also make you want to eat more. Think of an umbrella: nutrient-dense food is like a large umbrella protecting you; junk food not dense in nutrients is like a tiny umbrella full of holes.

## Protein Calorie Sources

Gold Choices are those that are lean or fat-free and come from both meatless and meat sources such as the following:

| Meatless Sources | Meat Sources |
|---|---|
| Fat-free, 1 percent, reduced, or low-fat dairy* | Lean meat |
| Beans | Lean fish, nonpolluted |
| Tofu | Lean poultry |
| Whole grains | Eggs* |

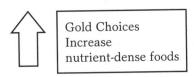

Gold Choices
Increase
nutrient-dense foods

*Not included in vegan diets because it is from an animal. For more details, see the section in this chapter on vegetarian diets.

If your cholesterol is high, then limit your intake of higher-fat dairy, animal meats, and egg yolks to three servings per week or less and most shellfish and organ meat (liver) foods to once a month or less. If you like eating eggs more often than that, use an egg substitute such as Egg Beaters or egg whites. (Note that an egg yolk can provide a lot of other essential nutrients.) Look for food labels on eggs, meat, and poultry that increase Omega-3 fats from natural feeding and grazing methods.

Dirt Choices should be used sparingly (perhaps no more than once a month) to help you control weight, excess fat, and calories. These include the following:

| | |
|---|---|
| Fried chicken | Ribs |
| Sausage | Bacon |
| Pepperoni | Skirt, rib-eye, or T-bone steak |
| Hot dogs | Gorgonzola and Brie cheeses |
| Fatty cold cuts such as pastrami, bologna, liverwurst, and salami | Pizza made from whole milk cheese |
| Fattier ground meats less than 85 percent lean (typically in restaurants or fast food stores) | |

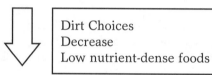

Dirt Choices
Decrease
Low nutrient-dense foods

## Fat Calorie Sources

Gold Choices are small portion-controlled amounts of the following:

| | |
|---|---|
| Nuts | Seeds |
| Canola, flax, or olive oil | Olives |

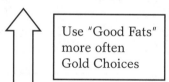

Use "Good Fats"
more often
Gold Choices

Use Dirt Choices sparingly (three or fewer times a week). They include the following:

| | |
|---|---|
| Butter | Margarine |
| Cream cheese | Mayonnaise |
| Heavy cream | Half-and-half |
| Sour cream | Ice cream |
| Whipped cream | Bacon |
| Olives | Gravy |
| Fried foods | Sauces |
| Cream soups | Junk foods (donuts, vegetable chips, potato chips) |
| | Other desserts (e.g., whole milk pudding) |

> Dirt Choices
> Decrease use of
> low-nutrient density
> "Bad Fats"

To lose weight, limit foods that are fried, stir fried, or sautéed in oil, butter, or other fat. Examples include Chinese food cooked in fat (oil) instead of being steamed or grilled and fried foods such as eggplant parmesan. (Yes, eggplant is a vegetable but this preparation packs in a lot of fat. Instead try the lower-fat version in this book.)

## Fluid Calorie Sources

Gold Choices include water ($H_2O$), 1 percent fat or fat-free milk that has not been sweetened (no chocolate milk).

Silver Choices include unsweetened tea, 100 percent fruit juice, and fat-free (under 2 grams sugar per ounce) chocolate milk. If you are trying to lose weight, then stick with water or fat-free milk.

Bronze Choices include sports drinks such as Gatorade (you do not need the calories unless you are intensely active and sweating for two or more hours), smoothies, or yogurt drinks with sugar or sweeteners added.

Use Dirt Choices sparingly. These include all soda or fruit drinks that have been artificially sweetened or regularly sweetened.

> Dirt Choices
> Decrease
> Low nutrient-dense foods

## Alcohol Calorie Sources

Remember that alcoholic drinks pack 150 to 200 calories per serving. Those calories are found in the following serving sizes by type of alcohol:

| | |
|---|---|
| Wine | 2–4 ounces |
| Beer | 12 ounces |
| *100-proof Spirits* | |
| Gin | 1 ounce |
| Cordials | 1 ounce |
| Vodka | 1 ounce |
| 80 proof | 1½ ounces |

Remember, alcohol should be consumed by adults only, and servings should be limited to two or fewer per week. And pregnant women should never consume alcohol in any form.

## Summary

Looking at your own intake of foods, determine whether you are making the healthiest choices.

Next, your personal calorie needs are based on the following:

1. your resting metabolic rate,
2. your activity level, and
3. your body frame.

Using Table 2-1, determine your calorie level based on your age.

Now that you see the amount of calories recommended for your age and activity level, you may see differences from your own intake. If you are overweight, you will need to cut down total calories and portion sizes. If you are underweight, then you will have to increase portions. This may sound simple, but it is not in our society.

## PORTION SIZES

Remember: The food industry's normal portion sizes do not mean "healthy portions." The total number of calories you consume should be adequate to maintain a healthy weight or, if you are overweight, to help you lose weight. If you are overweight, then your portions may be too large.

Table 2-2 shows the changes in just the sizes of fast food portions over the last twenty years.

Activity helps us maintain balance, but it cannot make up for today's portions. As a result, obesity is an epidemic in the United States, with more than 105 million people now obese or overweight, according to the National Institutes of Health (NIH). Many health experts believe this number to be even higher. And obesity has been strongly associated with increased risk of heart disease, cancer, diabetes, arthritis, and stroke.

## ASSESSING YOUR RISK

According to the NIH's National Heart, Lung, and Blood Institute's guidelines, assessment of overweight involves three key measures:

1. body mass index (BMI),
2. waist circumference, and
3. risk factors for diseases and conditions associated with obesity.

See Table 2-3.

The BMI is a measure of your weight relative to your height. Waist circumference measures abdominal fat. Combining these measures with information about your additional risk factors yields your risk for developing obesity-associated diseases.

### Looking at Your Body Mass Index

BMI charts provide healthy weight ranges for people of average size. Separate BMI charts are provided for children ages 2 to 20 and adults older than 20. For adults over 20 years, age and gender do not matter. There is one chart for all.

**TABLE 2-1 MyPyramid Food Intake Pattern Calorie Levels**

| Activity Level | Males | | | Females | | |
|---|---|---|---|---|---|---|
| Age | Sedentary* | Moderately Active* | Active* | Sedentary* | Moderately Active* | Active* |
| 2 | 1000 | 1000 | 1000 | 1000 | 1000 | 1000 |
| 3 | 1000 | 1400 | 1400 | 1000 | 1200 | 1400 |
| 4 | 1200 | 1400 | 1600 | 1200 | 1400 | 1400 |
| 5 | 1200 | 1400 | 1600 | 1200 | 1400 | 1600 |
| 6 | 1400 | 1600 | 1800 | 1200 | 1400 | 1600 |
| 7 | 1400 | 1600 | 1800 | 1200 | 1600 | 1800 |
| 8 | 1400 | 1600 | 2000 | 1400 | 1600 | 1800 |
| 9 | 1600 | 1800 | 2000 | 1400 | 1600 | 1800 |
| 10 | 1600 | 1800 | 2200 | 1400 | 1800 | 2000 |
| 11 | 1800 | 2000 | 2200 | 1600 | 2000 | 2000 |
| 12 | 1800 | 2200 | 2400 | 1600 | 2000 | 2200 |
| 13 | 2000 | 2200 | 2600 | 1600 | 2000 | 2200 |
| 14 | 2000 | 2400 | 2800 | 1800 | 2000 | 2400 |
| 15 | 2200 | 2600 | 3000 | 1800 | 2000 | 2400 |
| 16 | 2400 | 2800 | 3200 | 1800 | 2000 | 2400 |
| 17 | 2400 | 2800 | 3200 | 1800 | 2000 | 2400 |
| 18 | 2400 | 2800 | 3200 | 1800 | 2000 | 2400 |

(continued)

**TABLE 2-1** (*Continued*)

| Activity Level | Males | | | Activity Level | Females | | |
|---|---|---|---|---|---|---|---|
| | Sedentary* | Moderately Active* | Active* | | Sedentary* | Moderately Active* | Active* |
| 19–20 | 2600 | 2800 | 3000 | 19–20 | 2000 | 2200 | 2400 |
| 21–25 | 2400 | 2800 | 3000 | 21–25 | 2000 | 2200 | 2400 |
| 26–30 | 2400 | 2600 | 3000 | 26–30 | 1800 | 2000 | 2400 |
| 31–35 | 2400 | 2600 | 3000 | 31–35 | 1800 | 2000 | 2200 |
| 36–40 | 2400 | 2600 | 2800 | 36–40 | 1800 | 2000 | 2200 |
| 41–45 | 2200 | 2600 | 2800 | 41–45 | 1800 | 2000 | 2200 |
| 46–50 | 2200 | 2400 | 2800 | 46–50 | 1800 | 2000 | 2200 |
| 51–55 | 2200 | 2400 | 2800 | 51–55 | 1600 | 1800 | 2200 |
| 56–60 | 2200 | 2400 | 2600 | 56–60 | 1600 | 1800 | 2200 |
| 61–65 | 2000 | 2400 | 2600 | 61–65 | 1600 | 1800 | 2000 |
| 66–70 | 2000 | 2200 | 2600 | 66–70 | 1600 | 1800 | 2000 |
| 71–75 | 2000 | 2200 | 2600 | 71–75 | 1600 | 1800 | 2000 |
| 76 and up | 2000 | 2200 | 2400 | 76 and up | 1600 | 1800 | 2000 |

*Calorie levels are based on the *estimated energy requirements* (EER) and activity levels from the Institute of Medicine Dietary Reference Intakes Macronutrients Report, 2002.

Sedentary = less than 30 minutes a day of moderate physical activity in addition to daily activities.

Moderately Active = at least 30 minutes up to 60 minutes a day of moderate physical activity in addition to daily activities.

Active = 60 or more minutes a day of moderate physical activity in addition to daily activities.

*Source:* Adapted from United States Department of Agriculture, Center for Nutrition Policy and Promotion, April 2005, CNPP-XX

**TABLE 2-2 Changes in Fast Food Portion Sizes**

| French Fries | Twenty Years Ago | Now |
| --- | --- | --- |
| Calories | 210 | 610 |
| Size | 2.4 ounces | 6.9 ounces |

| Spaghetti and Meatballs | Twenty Years Ago | Now |
| --- | --- | --- |
| Calories | 500 | 1,025 |
| Size | 1 cup and 3 meatballs | 2 cups and 3 meatballs |

Even fruit has now been genetically engineered for larger sizes. A strawberry variety that was once the size of a nickel is now the size of a small apple!

Not everyone needs to lose weight or count calories! If you are at a healthy weight and making good choices, keep it up. For some people, too few calories may be associated with eating disorders or digestive disorders.

BMI is a reliable indicator of total body fat, which is related to the risk of disease and death, but it does have some limitations:

- It may overestimate body fat in athletes and other people who have a muscular built.
- It may underestimate body fat in older persons and others who have lost muscle mass.

## Obese Versus Overweight

To determine whether an adult is obese rather than merely overweight, we start by looking at Tables 2-3 and 2-4. You can also ask a registered dietitian to help you, or search the Internet using the key term BMI. Many Web sites exist to calculate your BMI. BMI is not a direct measure of body fatness, but it can be considered a good approximation of the amount of body fat you have. The NIH Web site is www.nih.gov.

**TABLE 2-3 Adult Body Mass Index Classification of Overweight and Obesity**

| | Body Mass Index |
| --- | --- |
| Underweight | Below 18.5 |
| Normal | 18.5–24.9 |
| Overweight | 25.0–29.9 |
| Obesity | 30.0–39.9 |
| Extreme obesity | 40 and above |

*Source:* www.nhlb.nih.gov/guidelines/obesity/sum_clin.

**TABLE 2-4 Adult Body Mass Index Chart**

| BMI Height (inches) | Normal | | | | | | Overweight | | | | | Obese | | | | | | |
|---|---|---|---|---|---|---|---|---|---|---|---|---|---|---|---|---|---|---|
| | 19 | 20 | 21 | 22 | 23 | 24 | 25 | 26 | 27 | 28 | 29 | 30 | 31 | 32 | 33 | 34 | 35 | 36 |
| | | | | | | | | | Body Weight (pounds) | | | | | | | | | |
| 58 | 91 | 96 | 100 | 105 | 110 | 115 | 119 | 124 | 129 | 134 | 138 | 143 | 148 | 153 | 158 | 162 | 167 | 172 |
| 59 | 94 | 99 | 104 | 109 | 114 | 119 | 124 | 128 | 133 | 138 | 143 | 148 | 153 | 158 | 163 | 168 | 173 | 178 |
| 60 | 97 | 102 | 107 | 112 | 118 | 123 | 128 | 133 | 138 | 143 | 148 | 153 | 158 | 163 | 168 | 174 | 179 | 184 |
| 61 | 100 | 106 | 111 | 116 | 122 | 127 | 132 | 137 | 143 | 148 | 153 | 158 | 164 | 169 | 174 | 180 | 185 | 190 |
| 62 | 104 | 109 | 115 | 120 | 126 | 131 | 136 | 142 | 147 | 153 | 158 | 164 | 169 | 175 | 180 | 186 | 191 | 196 |
| 63 | 107 | 113 | 118 | 124 | 130 | 135 | 141 | 146 | 152 | 158 | 163 | 169 | 175 | 180 | 186 | 191 | 197 | 203 |
| 64 | 110 | 116 | 122 | 128 | 134 | 140 | 145 | 151 | 157 | 163 | 169 | 174 | 180 | 186 | 192 | 197 | 204 | 209 |
| 65 | 114 | 120 | 126 | 132 | 138 | 144 | 150 | 156 | 162 | 168 | 174 | 180 | 186 | 192 | 198 | 204 | 210 | 216 |
| 66 | 118 | 124 | 130 | 136 | 142 | 148 | 155 | 161 | 167 | 173 | 179 | 186 | 192 | 198 | 204 | 210 | 216 | 223 |
| 67 | 121 | 127 | 134 | 140 | 146 | 153 | 159 | 166 | 172 | 178 | 185 | 191 | 198 | 204 | 211 | 217 | 223 | 230 |
| 68 | 125 | 131 | 138 | 144 | 151 | 158 | 164 | 171 | 177 | 184 | 190 | 197 | 203 | 210 | 216 | 223 | 230 | 236 |
| 69 | 128 | 135 | 142 | 149 | 155 | 162 | 169 | 176 | 182 | 189 | 196 | 203 | 209 | 216 | 223 | 230 | 236 | 243 |
| 70 | 132 | 139 | 146 | 153 | 160 | 167 | 174 | 181 | 188 | 195 | 202 | 209 | 216 | 222 | 229 | 236 | 243 | 250 |
| 71 | 136 | 143 | 150 | 157 | 165 | 172 | 179 | 186 | 193 | 200 | 208 | 215 | 222 | 229 | 236 | 243 | 250 | 257 |
| 72 | 140 | 147 | 154 | 162 | 169 | 177 | 184 | 191 | 199 | 206 | 213 | 221 | 228 | 235 | 242 | 250 | 258 | 265 |
| 73 | 144 | 151 | 159 | 166 | 174 | 182 | 189 | 197 | 204 | 212 | 219 | 227 | 235 | 242 | 250 | 257 | 265 | 272 |
| 74 | 148 | 155 | 163 | 171 | 179 | 186 | 194 | 202 | 210 | 218 | 225 | 233 | 241 | 249 | 256 | 264 | 272 | 280 |
| 75 | 152 | 160 | 168 | 176 | 184 | 192 | 200 | 208 | 216 | 224 | 232 | 240 | 248 | 256 | 264 | 272 | 279 | 287 |
| 76 | 156 | 164 | 172 | 180 | 189 | 197 | 205 | 213 | 221 | 230 | 238 | 246 | 254 | 263 | 271 | 279 | 287 | 295 |
| 58 | 177 | 181 | 186 | 191 | 196 | 201 | 205 | 210 | 215 | 220 | 224 | 229 | 234 | 239 | 244 | 248 | 253 | 258 |

| | | | | | | | | | | | | | | | | | | |
|---|---|---|---|---|---|---|---|---|---|---|---|---|---|---|---|---|---|---|
| 59 | 183 | 188 | 193 | 198 | 203 | 208 | 212 | 217 | 222 | 227 | 232 | 237 | 242 | 247 | 252 | 257 | 262 | 267 |
| 60 | 189 | 194 | 199 | 204 | 209 | 215 | 220 | 225 | 230 | 235 | 240 | 245 | 250 | 255 | 261 | 266 | 271 | 276 |
| 61 | 195 | 201 | 206 | 211 | 217 | 222 | 227 | 232 | 238 | 243 | 248 | 254 | 259 | 264 | 269 | 275 | 280 | 285 |
| 62 | 202 | 207 | 213 | 218 | 224 | 229 | 235 | 240 | 246 | 251 | 256 | 262 | 267 | 273 | 278 | 284 | 289 | 295 |
| 63 | 208 | 214 | 220 | 225 | 231 | 237 | 242 | 248 | 254 | 259 | 265 | 270 | 278 | 282 | 287 | 293 | 299 | 304 |
| 64 | 215 | 221 | 227 | 232 | 238 | 244 | 250 | 256 | 262 | 267 | 273 | 279 | 285 | 291 | 296 | 302 | 308 | 314 |
| 65 | 222 | 228 | 234 | 240 | 246 | 252 | 258 | 264 | 270 | 276 | 282 | 288 | 294 | 300 | 306 | 312 | 318 | 324 |
| 66 | 229 | 235 | 241 | 247 | 253 | 260 | 266 | 272 | 278 | 284 | 291 | 297 | 303 | 309 | 315 | 322 | 328 | 334 |
| 67 | 236 | 242 | 249 | 255 | 261 | 268 | 274 | 280 | 287 | 293 | 299 | 306 | 312 | 319 | 325 | 331 | 338 | 344 |
| 68 | 243 | 249 | 256 | 262 | 269 | 276 | 282 | 289 | 295 | 302 | 308 | 315 | 322 | 328 | 335 | 341 | 348 | 354 |
| 69 | 250 | 257 | 263 | 270 | 277 | 284 | 291 | 297 | 304 | 311 | 318 | 324 | 331 | 338 | 345 | 351 | 358 | 365 |
| 70 | 257 | 264 | 271 | 278 | 285 | 292 | 299 | 306 | 313 | 320 | 327 | 334 | 341 | 348 | 355 | 362 | 369 | 376 |
| 71 | 265 | 272 | 279 | 286 | 293 | 301 | 308 | 315 | 322 | 329 | 338 | 343 | 351 | 358 | 365 | 372 | 379 | 386 |
| 72 | 272 | 279 | 287 | 294 | 302 | 309 | 316 | 324 | 331 | 338 | 346 | 353 | 361 | 368 | 375 | 383 | 390 | 397 |
| 73 | 280 | 288 | 295 | 302 | 310 | 318 | 325 | 333 | 340 | 348 | 355 | 363 | 371 | 378 | 386 | 393 | 401 | 408 |
| 74 | 287 | 295 | 303 | 311 | 319 | 326 | 334 | 342 | 350 | 358 | 365 | 373 | 381 | 389 | 396 | 404 | 412 | 420 |
| 75 | 295 | 303 | 311 | 319 | 327 | 335 | 343 | 351 | 359 | 367 | 375 | 383 | 391 | 399 | 407 | 415 | 423 | 431 |
| 76 | 304 | 312 | 320 | 328 | 336 | 344 | 353 | 361 | 369 | 377 | 385 | 394 | 402 | 410 | 418 | 426 | 435 | 443 |

*Source:* http://www.nhlbi.nih.gov/guidelines/obesity/bmi_tbl.htm

**FIGURE 2-2 Apple or Pear?**

Parents should consult their children's physician or a registered dietitian to evaluate their weight and determine their body mass index.

## Waist Circumference

Are you an apple or a pear shape?

Studies show that people that are heavier on top—that is, they have an apple shape—have a greater risk of getting heart disease (Figure 2-2).

Waist circumference is a measure of abdominal fat. To determine your waist circumference, place a measuring tape snugly around your waist. If you have abdominal fat, it is another predictor of your risk for developing heart disease and other medical conditions. This risk increases with a waist measurement of more than 40 inches in men and more than 35 inches in women.

## Other Risk Factors

The NIH identifies additional risk factors other than overweight or obesity; these are listed in Table 2-5.

## Bottom Line

For people who are considered obese (BMI 30 or more) or those who are overweight (BMI of 25 to 29.9) and have two or more risk factors, the guidelines

**TABLE 2-5 Risk Factors**

| |
|---|
| High blood pressure (hypertension) |
| High LDL-cholesterol ("bad" cholesterol) |
| Low HDL-cholesterol ("good" cholesterol) |
| High triglycerides |
| High blood glucose (sugar) |
| Family history of premature heart disease |
| Physical inactivity |
| Cigarette smoking |

*Source:* Department of Health and Human Services, National Heart, Lung, and Blood Institute, Obesity Institute. *Aim for a Healthy Weight.* See www.nhlbi.nih.gov/health/public/heart/obesity.

recommend weight loss. Overweight people who do not have a large waist measurement and have less than two risk factors may need to prevent further weight gain rather than lose weight. Having lean muscle at a desirable weight is best. If you are not toned, exercise is even more important.

Consult your physician if you are at increased risk and if you must lose weight. Your physician or registered dietitian will evaluate your BMI, waist measurement, and other risk factors. For overweight people, even a small weight loss (just 10 percent of your current weight) is beneficial. If you cannot lose weight on your own, seek out the advice of a registered dietitian.

# SECTION 2

## Introduction to Weight Loss

### The Issue of Weight

If you look at the BMI chart in Section 1, you will see that weight is not the same range for everyone at the same height.

Differences in weight vary because of three factors:

1. body frame.
2. muscle frame, and
3. age.

## When Is Being Overweight a Concern?

A BMI of more than 24 may put you at greater risk for illness and medical conditions.

## Why Do People Gain Weight?

People gain weight for three primary reasons:

1. When they eat more than their body needs.
2. When they do not get enough exercise.
3. Because of genetic, psychological, and emotional factors.

## About That Word *Obesity*

*Obesity* is an excess accumulation of fat, which accumulates when energy intake is greater than energy output. If energy intake is equal to energy output, then your weight usually will remain stable (no weight loss and no weight gain). Obesity is complex, however, and not quite as simple as balancing energy in with energy out. Simply cooking and eating in healthy ways and exercising is only one piece to the puzzle called *obesity.*

Powerful fat hormones are at work once weight becomes excessive. Some of these are *leptin; tumor necrosis factor;* prothrombotic agents such as *plasminogen activator inhibitor,* which is involved in blood pressure regulation; and *peptide hormone,* which may be involved in keeping fat on your body. This may make your insulin resist working right, so it is harder to get to your desirable weight. Estrogen is another powerful hormone produced from fat cells in postmenopausal women. The body craves to make more fat cells to keep the levels of this hormone high. Exercise is the key in keeping hormonal balance in conjunction with a healthy diet. Research in the area of genetics is helping to solve the complex effects of so-called fat hormones.

## What Else Affects a Person's Ability to Lose Weight?

The following seven factors are predominant in determining how easily someone loses weight.

1. *Heredity or family history.* Our genes and family medical history can tell us a lot about ourselves.

2. *The number of times you might have dieted before.* Chronically losing and gaining can mess up your metabolism. In my experience, the more your weight goes above the desirable BMI, the harder it appears to be to lose weight.

3. *Preconceived ideas.* Parents do not just think, "Oh, it's just baby fat!" Studies are reporting that weight influences begin in the fetus, so if you are overweight and pregnant, this affects your baby. I see kids at 2 years old who are forty or fifty pounds overweight who are no different than their parents.

4. *Body composition.* The more muscle on our bodies, the more calories we can eat.

5. *Age.* As we get older, our metabolisms slow down ever so slightly each decade.

6. *Metabolism.* How fast we burn up food for energy is a genetic factor. Some people just need fewer calories than others.

7. *Psychological factors.* Feelings, emotional balance, and inner peace all influence our desire for food.

## Why Should You Lose Weight?

Losing weight may help decrease your risk of developing hypertension, noninsulin dependent diabetes mellitus (NIDDM), certain types of cancer, stroke, and heart disease. Achieving a health weight *will* help you feel better.

*How many pound per week should I lose?*
A healthy plan is calculated to help you achieve one to three pounds weight loss per week. Each week you must eat approximately 3,500 fewer calories than you normally eat to lose one pound of fat. The Eat Fit, Be Fit program for weight loss follows similar recommendations of many national programs, such as the National Cholesterol Education Program for Weight Loss, which are as follows:

| Nutrient | Recommendations |
|---|---|
| Calories | 500–1,000 cal/day reduction* |
| Total fat | 30 percent or less |
| Saturated fats | 8–10 percent or less of total calories |
| Monounsaturated fats | Up to 15 percent of total calories |
| Polyunsaturated fats | Up to 10 percent of total calories |
| Cholesterol | Less than 300 mg/day |
| Protein | Approximately 15 percent of total calories |
| Sodium chloride (salt)or sodium (naturally occurring) | 6 grams or 6,000 milligrams per day 2,400 milligrams per day |
| Calcium | 1,000–1,500 milligrams per day |
| Fiber | 20–50 grams** per day |

*To lose weight

**This is higher than the national cholesterol program, which recommends 20–35 grams per day. Our early ancestors consumed more than 60 grams. As long as you do not have symptoms of loose stools or cramps, higher amounts may aid in cholesterol and blood sugar regulation.

## Formula for Calculating Weekly Weight Loss

Your weight loss is based on the number of calories you cut out of your diet each day over the entire week. You can calculate this loss as follows:

1. Write below the total calories each day you can choose to cut out:

    _____ × 7 = _____ calories per week

2. Does it add up to 3,500 calories? If yes, you will lose approximately one pound of fat.

## Steps to Weight Loss

Next follow these steps to begin your weight loss plan:

1. Set a short-term goal for each week for how much weight you want to lose: _____ pounds per week.

2. Record the calories per day you want to consume.

    This is based on your age and activity level; use the

    MyPyramid Intake Pattern Calorie Levels: _____

    Determine if this is close to what you are currently consuming and reduce the portions by one-quarter or 500 calories less to lose approximately one pound per week. You should see the results within a week. Try not to weigh yourself more once a week.

    Another option is to use the food pyramid guide from the USDA Web site: www.myfoodpyramid.gov. You can put in your age, height, weight, and activity level to find the right calorie level.

## Determining Your Daily Servings from the Food Groups

Once you know the calories you need each day, determine the number of servings you need from each food group using Table 2-6, MyPyramid Food Intake Patterns.

## Keep a Food Journal

Use the form in the Food Diary in Chapter 1. You can also keep track of your daily exercise. Check your portions. Add up the total number of servings from each food group each day. Are you meeting your goals using the guidelines in Table 2-1?

Check what your desirable weight should be for your height and write it here_____. Write your current weight_____.

### About Weighing Yourself

If you are trying to lose weight, choose a morning once each week to check your weight. Weighing yourself every day will make you crazy, especially if you have a tendency to retain fluids. If you maintain consistency, eventually the scale will report a loss, but do not be discouraged in the beginning if it is slow.

## Determining Your Calorie Needs

Based on your age and activity level, you can decide how many calories are right for you. Remember, one size does not fit all. Refer to page 41, Table 2-1, MyPyramid Food Intake Pattern Calorie Levels.

# SECTION 3

## Do Not Be Fooled by Portion Distortion

Remember,

> 1 fist = 1 cup of starch
> 1 9-volt battery = 1 ounce

Choose the blueberry corn muffins in this book, a medium-size homemade muffin, instead of a commercial cornbread muffin that is twice the size and twice the calories.

Or choose the cookbook pizza size versus a regular pizza slice eaten out or the vegetable omelet in this book on an English muffin with tomato instead of an Egg McMuffin.

Watch your portions using the guides below. The guidelines and recipes in this book are designed to help people choose healthy portions and use techniques that lower fat, sodium, and sugar to boost health. Higher fiber foods usually contain fewer calories for a larger volume. Choose foods that are rich in nutrients to boost the immune system and add flavor. Fat and sugar are replaced or reduced; spices, herbs, and other flavorings are added.

## TABLE 2-6 MyPyramid Food Intake Patterns

These are the suggested amounts of food to consume from the basic food groups, subgroups, and oils to meet recommended nutrient intakes at twelve different calorie levels. Nutrient and energy contributions from each group are calculated according to the nutrient-dense forms of foods in each group (e.g., lean meats and fat-free milk). The table also shows the discretionary calorie allowance that can be accommodated within each calorie level in addition to the suggested amounts of nutrient-dense forms of foods in each group.

| Calorie Level[1] | Daily Amount of Food From Each Group | | | | | | | | | | | |
|---|---|---|---|---|---|---|---|---|---|---|---|---|
| | 1,000 | 1,200 | 1,400 | 1,600 | 1,800 | 2,000 | 2,200 | 2,400 | 2,600 | 2,800 | 3,000 | 3,200 |
| Fruits[2] | 1 cup | 1 cup | 1.5 cups | 1.5 cups | 1.5 cups | 2 cups | 2 cups | 2 cups | 2 cups | 2.5 cups | 2.5 cups | 2.5 cups |
| Vegetables[3] | 1 cup | 1.5 cups | 1.5 cups | 2 cups | 2.5 cups | 2.5 cups | 3 cups | 3 cups | 3.5 cups | 3.5 cups | 4 cups | 4 cups |
| Grains[4] | 3 oz. eq | 4 oz-eq | 5 oz-eq | 5 oz-eq | 6 oz-eq | 6 oz-eq | 7 oz-eq | 8 oz-eq | 9 oz-eq | 10 oz-eq | 10 oz-eq | 10 oz-eq |
| Meat and Beans[5] | 2 oz-eq | 3 oz-eq | 4 oz-eq | 5 oz-eq | 5 oz-eq | 5.5 oz-eq | 6 oz-eq | 6.5 oz-eq | 6.5 oz-eq | 7 oz-eq | 7 oz-eq | 7 oz-eq |
| Milk[6] | 2 cups | 2 cups | 2 cups | 3 cups | 3 cups | 3 cups | 3 cups | 3 cups | 3 cups | 3 cups | 3 cups | 3 cups |
| Oils[7] | 3 tsp | 4 tsp | 4 tsp | 5 tsp | 5 tsp | 6 tsp | 6 tsp | 7 tsp | 8 tsp | 8 tsp | 10 tsp | 11 tsp |
| Discretionary calorie allowance[8] | 165 | 171 | 171 | 132 | 195 | 267 | 290 | 362 | 410 | 426 | 512 | 648 |

[1]Calorie levels are set across a wide range to accommodate the needs of different individuals.

[2]Fruit group includes all fresh, frozen, canned, and dried fruits and fruit juices. In general, 1 cup of fruit, 100 percent fruit juice, or 1/2 cup of dried fruit can be considered as 1 cup from the fruit group.

[3]Vegetable group includes all fresh, frozen, canned, and dried vegetables and vegetable juices. In general, 1 cup of raw or cooked vegetables or vegetable juice or 2 cups of raw leafy greens can be considered as 1 cup from the vegetable group.

[4]Grains group includes all foods made from wheat, rice, oats, cornmeal, barley, such as bread, pasta, oatmeal, breakfast cereals, tortillas, and grits. In general, one slice of bread, 1 cup of ready-to-eat cereal, or 1/2 cup of cooked rice, pasta, or cooked cereal can be considered as a 1-ounce equivalent from the grains group. At least half of all grains consumed should be whole grains.

[5]Meat and beans group in general, 1 ounce of lean meat, poultry, or fish; one egg; 1 Tablespoon peanut butter; 1/4 cup cooked dry beans; or 1/2 ounce of nuts or seeds can be considered as a 1-ounce equivalent from the meat and beans group.

(continued)

## TABLE 2-6 (Continued)

[6] Milk group includes all fluid milk products and foods made from milk that retain their calcium content, such as yogurt and cheese. Foods made from milk that have little to no calcium—such as cream cheese, cream, and butter—are not part of the group. Most milk group choices should be fat-free or low-fat. In general, 1 cup of milk or yogurt, 1½ ounces of natural cheese, or 2 ounces of processed cheese can be considered as 1 cup from the milk group.

[7] Oils include fats from many different plants and fish that are liquid at room temperature, such as canola, corn, olive, soybean, and sunflower oil. Some foods are naturally high in oils such as nuts, olives, some fish, and avocados. Foods that are mainly oil include mayonnaise, certain salad dressings, and soft margarine.

[8] Discretionary calorie allowance is the remaining amount of calories in a food intake pattern after accounting for the calories needed for all food groups—using forms of foods that are fat-free or low-fat and with no added sugars.

*Source:* www.mypyramid.gov

### Vegetable Subgroup Amounts Are Per Week

| Calorie Level | 1,000 | 1,200 | 1,400 | 1,600 | 1,800 | 2,000 | 2,200 | 2,400 | 2,600 | 2,800 | 3,000 | 3,200 |
|---|---|---|---|---|---|---|---|---|---|---|---|---|
| Dark green veg. | 1 c/wk | 1.5 c/wk | 1.5 c/wk | 2 c/wk | 3 c/wk | 3 c/wk | 3 c/wk | 3 c/wk | 3 c/wk | 3 c/wk | 3 c/wk | 3 c/wk |
| Orange veg. | .5 c/wk | 1 c/wk | 1 c/wk | 1.5 c/wk | 2 c/wk | 2 c/wk | 2 c/wk | 2 c/wk | 2 c/wk | 2.5 c/wk | 2.5 c/wk | 2.5 c/wk |
| Legumes | .5 c/wk | 1 c/wk | 1 c/wk | 2.5 c/wk | 3 c/wk | 3 c/wk | 3 c/wk | 3 c/wk | 3.5 c/wk | 3.5 c/wk | 3.5 c/wk | 3.5 c/wk |
| Starchy veg. | 1.5 c/wk | 2.5 c/wk | 2.5 c/wk | 2.5 c/wk | 3 c/wk | 3 c/wk | 6 c/wk | 6 c/wk | 7 c/wk | 7 c/wk | 9 c/wk | 9 c/wk |
| Other veg. | 3.5 c/wk | 4.5 c/wk | 4.5 c/wk | 5.5 c/wk | 6.5 c/wk | 6.5 c/wk | 7 c/wk | 7 c/wk | 8.5 c/wk | 8.5 c/wk | 10 c/wk | 10 c/wk |

*Source:* www.mypyramid.gov

## What Is a Healthy Portion?

As noted earlier, this book adopts portions and food groupings set by the ADA's Exchange Lists for Meal Planning, not the grouping of food in the USDA food pyramid. The main difference is that we include starchy vegetables in the grain group, not the vegetable group, because of the amounts of carbohydrate they contain. Pasta, rice, and juice servings are each $^1/_3$ cup instead of $^1/_2$ cup in the USDA's MyPyramid. Cheese is in the meat, not dairy group, because of its fat content.

The seven groups of foods are:

1. grain
2. fruit
3. dairy
4. vegetable
5. meat & beans
6. fats
7. other carbohydrates (sweets)

Use this guide to watch portion sizes:

### Grain, Starch, and Bread Group

One 1-ounce slice of bread
$^1/_4$ ounce bagel
$^1/_2$ English muffin or 1 whole reduced calorie, high-fiber type
$^3/_4$ cup flaked whole grain, high-fiber cereal
$^1/_2$ cup cooked whole grain, high-fiber cereal (not instant lower fiber type)
$^1/_2$ cup peas, corn, cooked beans, yams, potato
1 cup winter squash
$^1/_3$ cup high-fiber (more than 2 grams) pasta, noodles, rice
2 cups popcorn, fat-free

### Fruit

1 cup melon or berries, fresh or frozen (or $^1/_2$ cup canned in natural syrup)
1 fresh fruit (apple, orange, pear, or large plum) the size of a tennis ball
2 kiwis or small plums
2 Tablespoons dried fruit
$^1/_2$ small banana

### Dairy Group

8 ounces fat-free milk and yogurt

### Vegetables

1 cup raw
$^1/_2$ cup cooked

## Meat and Meat Substitute

Eat a portion of your total day's meat and meat substitutes throughout your meals, not just at one meal. Three ounces is approximately the size of a deck of playing cards. Children's portions may be smaller, depending on their age. Use the food pyramid guide to establish the number of ounces you need.

### Very Lean

$^1/_2$ cup beans or lentils (cooked)

1 ounce equivalent: lean meat, fish, poultry (0–1 gram fat per ounce) white meat (breast of chicken or turkey), London broil beef, 93 percent lean ground turkey or beef

$^1/_4$ cup cottage cheese, 1 percent fat or fat-free (may be higher in sodium)

1 ounce fat-free cheese

### Lean 1-ounce equivalent of meat, fish, or poultry (3 grams of fat per ounce) 90 percent lean

Beef: sirloin or flank steak, roast (rib, chuck, or rump), or ground

Lamb: chop, leg, or roast

Fish: tuna, sardines (not in oil), or herring (smoked or pickled)

Poultry: skinless dark meat of chicken, duck, or turkey

Rabbit or goose

Bison

1-ounce equivalent cheese

$^1/_4$ cup 3.5-percent fat cottage cheese

1-ounce equivalent of hard cheese (less than 3 grams per ounce of fat) such as reduced fat Swiss or cheddar

$^1/_2$ cup tofu, low-fat type (less than 3 grams per serving)

### Medium Fat (limit to one to three times per week)

1 egg

$^1/_2$ cup tofu

$^1/_2$ cup or 2 ounces tempeh

1 ounce cheese: feta or mozzarella from whole milk

$^1/_3$ cup ricotta made from whole milk

1 cup soymilk, calcium fortified suggested

Beef: 85 percent lean ground beef, prime grades, trimmed, short ribs, and corned beef

Fish: salmon or blue fish

2 ounces reduced fat cheese

### Fats

1 teaspoon oil, light margarine, or butter

1 Tablespoon light mayonnaise, light margarine, or light cream cheese

10–15 nuts

$^1/_8$ avocado

5 medium olives

To find a registered dietitian call:

| | |
|---|---|
| American Dietetic Association | 1 800-366-1655 |
| American Diabetes Association | 1 800-342-2383 |
| American Diabetes Educators | 1 800-832-6874 |

*Source:* www.diabetes.org

2 teaspoons regular peanut butter, smooth or crunchy
1 Tablespoon peanut butter, reduced fat

**Sweets**

$^1/_2$ cup ice cream
1 small cupcake or muffin
2 small cookies

## Number of Servings from Each Group

The number of servings per day you need to eat from each group depends on your age, weight, height, and activity level. The USDA's MyPyramid food chart provided by the U.S. Department of Agriculture lists the suggested amounts of each type of food. If you have special needs, consult a registered dietitian (see box above).

## Estimated Daily Calorie Needs

To determine which food intake pattern to use for an individual, Table 2-7 gives estimates of individual calorie needs. The calorie range for each age and sex group is based on physical activity level, from sedentary to active.

Two definitions are important here:

*Sedentary* means a lifestyle that includes only the light physical activity associated with typical day-to-day life.

*Active* means a lifestyle that includes physical activity that is equivalent to walking more than 3 miles per day at 3 to 4 miles per hour in addition to the light physical activity associated with typical day-to-day life.

# SECTION 4

## Fats, Fatty Acids, Triglycerides, and Cholesterol

### Common Questions about Fats and Fatty Acids

*If I use more olive oil instead of butter, I am okay, right?*
It is not that simple. Fats are really different types of fatty acids. Some are highly beneficial because they contain essential fatty acids; vitamins A, D, and E; and other antioxidants (substances that help our body create healthy balance). They are stored in our bodies to act as reserves for times when we do not have food to eat and need energy.

**TABLE 2-7 Estimated Individual Calorie Needs**

| | Calorie Range | | |
|---|---|---|---|
| Children | Sedentary | → | Active |
| 2–3 years | 1,000 | → | 1,400 |
| **Females** | | | |
| 4–8 years | 1,200 | → | 1,800 |
| 9–13 | 1,600 | → | 2,200 |
| 14–18 | 1,800 | → | 2,400 |
| 19–30 | 2,000 | → | 2,400 |
| 31–50 | 1,800 | → | 2,200 |
| 51+ | 1,600 | → | 2,200 |
| **Males** | | | |
| 4–8 years | 1,400 | → | 2,000 |
| 9–13 | 1,800 | → | 2,600 |
| 14–18 | 2,200 | → | 3,200 |
| 19–30 | 2,400 | → | 3,000 |
| 31–50 | 2,200 | → | 3,000 |
| 51+ | 2,000 | → | 2,800 |

*Source:* U.S. Department of Agriculture, Center for Nutrition Policy and Promotion, April 2005.

*How much fat do I need?*
The range of total dietary recommended fat is 20 percent to 35 percent of our total calories. In my practice, I may recommend 25 percent to 30 percent fat if you want to lose weight; 35 percent of total calories may be needed to gain weight. Everyone is different.

*What do fatty acids do in our bodies?*
Some fats are essential for human growth and development. These fats are called *essential fatty acids* (EFAs) because our bodies do not make them. Most fat we can make in our body. We cannot make Omega-3 and Omega-6 fats, so we must consume these in our food each day. Fatty acids are extremely important for reproduction, regular menstrual cycles in women, eyes, bones, memory, mood stability, skin, and heart health. Table 2-8 shows the various types of Omega-3 fatty acids and their food sources.

*Which fatty acids are important?*
Omega-3 fatty acids are consumed in the form of alpha-linolenic acid (ALA), eicosapentaenoic acid (EPA), and docosahexaenoic acid (DHA). All Omega-3 fatty acids eventually produce DHA, a substance known to help our cells and protect against heart disease and aging.

**TABLE 2-8 Types of Omega-3 Fatty Acids and Natural Food Sources**

| Type of Fatty Acid | Food Sources |
| --- | --- |
| Eicosapentaenoic acid (EPA) | Oily coldwater fish: Tuna, salmon, and mackerel |
| Docosahexanoic acid (DHA) | Venison and buffalo |
| | Fresh seaweed |
| | Plant foods rarely contain EPA or DHA. |
| Alpha-linolenic acid (ALA) | Flaxseed, hemp seed, and flaxseed |
| | Flaxseed oil, walnuts, dark green leafy vegetables, and mango |

*What are the health benefits of Omega-3 fatty acids?*
Omega-3 fatty acids help reduce the risk of heart disease, make the blood less likely to form clots that may cause heart attack or stroke, and protect against irregular heart beats, according to the American Heart Association's 2000 statement on Omega-3 fatty acids. Other benefits may include reduced risk of insulin resistance, diabetes mellitus, rheumatoid arthritis, inflammation, psoriasis, and depression.

*Which foods contain Omega-3 fatty acids?*
Rich food sources of Omega-3 fatty acids are flaxseed and fattier fish such as salmon, herring, and mackerel. However, the fish may not always be from waters free from pollution. If you consume fish regularly, be sure it is from safe sources. The Food and Drug Administration (FDA) and certain states such as New York warn women of childbearing age, pregnant women, and women who are breast feeding may be at special risk and should limit their weekly intake of fish to no more than 12 ounces of fish containing lower levels of mercury. The Environmental Protection Agency (EPA) recommends no more than 6 ounces per week of fish from most freshwaters.

Depending on where you live, the waters may or may not have pollution. Cancer and neurological problems (for example, autism) have been linked to toxicity from methyl mercury, cadmium (in polluted oysters), and other toxic substances. You can have your blood tested for mercury by your physician if you are concerned. In my practice, I have seen levels at excessively dangerous levels in some of my patients.

Avoid eating king mackerel, tilefish, swordfish, and shark. Although both contain mercury, light canned tuna is lower in mercury than albacore tuna. Freshwater sport fish may have high levels of mercury or other toxins such as dioxin. In addition, certain toxic substances such as *polychlorinated biphenyls* (PCBs) have been reported in farm-raised salmon. Pacific salmon seem to be safer than farm-raised salmon. Always keep abreast of potential pollutants in fish by checking with your physician, especially if you are pregnant or nursing. Refer to your local health department as well as the FDA's and EPA's Web sites for further warnings.

Because of this concern over potential pollutants in fish, flaxseed and other plant sources may be better for obtaining Omega-3 fats.

*Why Omega-3 fatty acids and not Omega-6 fatty acids?*
Omega-6 fatty acids aggravate inflammation and our immune systems. Omega-3 fatty acids have little or no inflammatory activity and act to modulate platelet aggregation (which keeps blood flowing easy) and helps our immune systems.

Eating processed foods and vegetable oils causes an overabundance of Omega-6 fatty acids, commonly called Omega-6 linoleic acid. Studies have shown that increases in Omega-6 fatty acids are linked to increased inflammation, which may lead to chronic diseases such as Alzheimer's, heart disease, and cancer. Getting too much may be a concern.

*How much of these fats do I need?*
The diet can have as little as 1 percent to 2 percent of calories from Omega-6 linoleic acid, approximately 3 grams to 6 grams or 1 teaspoon vegetable oil, to meet daily needs. The average American diet contains 7 percent. Omega-3 fatty acids need to be consumed daily to gain the benefits. For example, 2 to 3 Tablespoons of flaxseed each day will help you get what you need. The recommended ratio of Omega-6 fats to Omega-3 fatty acids ranges from 4:1 to 10:1 from authorities such as the World Health Organization and the Food and Agriculture Organization.

*How can I get Omega-3 fatty acids in my diet?*
In the past, when our ancestors ate meat from wild animals that grazed on grass, their meat was rich in Omega-3. Now animals are fed cheaper grains such as corn, which lowers the Omega-3 content of their meat. It may cost more, but if you like meat, free-range, grass-fed livestock is a better option.

A less expensive means is to consume rich plant sources of Omega-3, with less saturated fat, from flaxseed, walnuts, or borage oil. You must grind the flaxseed before you eat it to get the most benefit. Ground flaxseed meal is available for purchase, but it must be stored in the refrigerator after the package is opened so it does not go rancid. Check the expiration date.

The recipes in this book use foods such as flaxseed, canola oil, mangoes, green leafy vegetables, halibut, Chinook salmon, and other environmentally safe coldwater fish, as well as nuts and seeds that are abundant in these nutrients. Many studies demonstrate it is the food, not the supplement, that works best, but if you do not consume natural sources regularly, then choose a fish oil supplement from safe sources. One Web site, www.consumerlabs.com, provides information on reputable sources of supplements.

## Summary of Fats and Fatty Acids

Flaxseed is one of the richest plant sources. Other sources are walnuts, hemp seed, and soy beans. Canola, walnut, soy, and flax oils can be used in making salad. Fish or free-range, grass-fed livestock are the main animal sources of Omega-3 fatty acids. Table 2-9 shows the types of fish with various levels of Omega-3 fatty acids.

## About Flax

## What Is Flaxseed?

Flaxseed is a seed from a plant that is no larger than a sesame seed. It is one of the richest plant sources of Omega 3-fatty acids, alpha-linolenic acid. Our ratio of Omega-3 to Omega-6 fatty acids should be 4:1; the current American diet as reported by the NIH is 20:1. Fifty-seven percent of the polyunsaturated fat in flaxseed is Omega-3.

## What Are the Nutritional Benefits?

Flaxseed is recommended not only for its Omega-3 fatty acids but also its fiber in the form of lignans. *Lignans* are phytoestrogens, plant substances that act as weak estrogen-like compounds when eaten. Flaxseed seems to be one of the best sources for lignan. This is converted to mammalian lignan and then further digested by bacteria in our colon. The ground flaxseed seems to have a lipid (fat)–lowering effect in the body and reduces the risk of heart disease. Although it does not have the lignan and fiber, flax oil has proven to make arteries more elastic, to decrease clot formation, and to protect against arrhythmias. It is the *ground flaxseed* that seems to have the most benefit. Check out the differences in nutrient below:

| Nutrient | 1 Tbsp. Flax Oil | 1 Tbsp. Ground Flaxseed |
|---|---|---|
| Calories | 124 | 36 |
| Protein | 0 | 1.6 grams |
| Fat | 14 grams | 3.3 grams |
| Alpha-linolenic acid | 8,000 milligrams | 1,900 milligrams |
| Dietary fiber | 0 grams | 2.2 grams |

## Where Do I Get Flaxseed?

Flaxseed is sold in most health food stores or organic health food supermarkets. Be sure to buy the ground flaxseed, not whole flaxseed, because the whole seed is not digested and you will get no benefit. Once you open the package, store it in the refrigerator. Be sure to use it after a few weeks because it may not maintain its nutrient benefit for long.

## How Do I Use Flaxseed in My Diet?

Use the recipes in this book that contain flaxseed and consume up to 3 Tablespoons per day to aid in health benefits. It can be used in cereals, smoothies, salads, baking, and breads.

**TABLE 2-9 Omega-3 Content of Selected Fish**

| Type of Fish | Omega-3 Content (grams) in 4-Ounce Serving | Pollutants |
|---|---|---|
| Chinook salmon | 3.6 | |
| Sockeye salmon | 2.3 | |
| Albacore tuna | 2.6 | Toxic levels of mercury |
| Mackerel | 1.8–2.6 | Toxic levels of mercury |
| Herring | 1.2–2.7 | |
| Rainbow trout | 1.0 | Some toxic mercury |
| Whiting | 0.9 | |
| Cod | 0.3 | |

## Common Questions about Fats in Our Diets

*How is fat absorbed in my body?*
Approximately 95 percent of dietary fat is absorbed in the form of triglyceride fats. Triglycerides are also made in our bodies from sugar in our diets. A high triglyceride level in your blood may mean you should reduce your total calories if you are overweight as well as reduce your intake of total fat, sweets and sugar, alcohol, and refined carbohydrates such as white bread and pasta.

A triglyceride is a glycerol molecule attached to three fatty acids. Fatty acids are chains of hydrogen and carbon atoms, and the number of carbon–carbon double bonds in the chain determines the saturation. Some beneficial fats have as many as six double bonds. Saturated fats have no double bonds, monounsaturated fats have one double bond, and polyunsaturated fats have many double bonds. Fatty acids are made from the food we eat (fat in fish, oil, seeds, and nuts), and some can be made in the body.

In summary, fatty acids (fat) can be categorized into three fat groups: saturated fat, polyunsaturated fats, and monounsaturated fats.

*What are the recommended amounts of total fat and saturated fat in grams?*
The recommended amounts depend on the number of calories you eat each day. To find that number, refer to Table 2-1, MyPyramid Intake Pattern Calorie Levels. Once you know the right amount of calories you need, use Table 2-10, Comparison of Calories and Total Fat Needed, to see what is right for you.

*Do fat requirements vary with age?*
Yes. It is recommended that persons over age 18 consume 20 percent to 30 percent of their daily calories as fat. For children ages 2 to 3, 30 percent is recommended; for ages 4 to 18, 25 percent is recommended. Fat is important in the diet for reproduction and for the absorption of important antioxidants such as vitamin E and beta-carotene. Children as old as 2 years of age need whole milk, not fat-free or low-fat, to get adequate nutrients.

**TABLE 2-10 Comparison of Calories and Total Fat Needed**

| Calorie Level | Total Fat 30% or Less (grams) | Saturated Fat Less than 10% (grams) | Saturated Fat Less than 7% (grams) |
|---|---|---|---|
| 1,200 | 40 or less | Less than 13 | Less than 9 |
| 1,500 | 50 or less | Less than 17 | Less than 12 |
| 1,800 | 60 or less | Less than 20 | Less than 14 |
| 2,000 | 67 or less | Less than 22 | Less than 16 |
| 2,200 | 73 or less | Less than 24 | Less than 17 |
| 2,500 | 83 or less | Less than 28 | Less than 19 |
| 3,000 | 100 or less | Less than 33 | Less than 23 |

*Source:* Reproduced with permission of the American Heart Association, www.americanheart.org ©2005.

*Can I eat too little fat?*
Yes. A diet that is extremely low in fat may reduce the intake of these essential nutrients and cause infertility, irregular menstrual cycles in women, mood instability, and unhealthy weight loss.

*What are saturated fatty acids?*
Saturated fat is the main dietary cause of high blood cholesterol, according to the American Heart Association. Saturated fatty acids have all the hydrogen that the carbon atoms can hold. Saturated fats are usually solid at room temperature, and they are more stable—that is, they do not combine readily with oxygen. Saturated fats and trans fats are the main dietary factors in raising blood cholesterol.

*Where are saturated fats in food?*
High saturated fat foods are not used in the recipes included in this book because they are associated with raising total and LDL ("bad") cholesterol and weight excessively.

    The main sources of saturated fat in the typical American diet are foods from animals such as meats, whole milk, cheese, milk, butter, lard, and ice cream. Fatty meats such as hot dogs, bacon, sausage, chicken skin, and cold cuts such as bologna, liverwurst, and salami are loaded with saturated fat. Plant sources are coconut oil, palm oil, and palm kernel oil (often called *tropical* oils), and cocoa butter. These fats have been frequently used in commercial muffins, cakes, and cookies.

    Too much is a Dirt Choice!

*What are trans fats?*
Trans fats are unsaturated, but they can raise total and low density lipoproteins (LDL, or bad cholesterol) and lower high density lipoproteins (HDL, or good cholesterol). Trans fats result from adding hydrogen to vegetable oils used in commercial baked goods, and for cooking in most restaurants and fast food chains.

    Dirt Choices? Yes, I consider these less beneficial than monosaturated and polyunsaturated fats.

*Where are trans fats in foods?*
Trans fats are found in partially hydrogenated oils in some baked goods. French fries, donuts, and other commercial fried foods are major sources of trans fat in the diet. Trans fats are solid, but softer in texture than saturated fat. TF is found in some margarine and fat spreads. Once again, I classify these as "Dirt Choice" if consumed in place of nutrient dense foods.

*What are hydrogenated fats?*
*Hydrogenate* means to add hydrogen or, in the case of fatty acids, to saturate. Food processing changes liquid oil, naturally high in unsaturated fatty acids, to a more solid and more saturated form. The greater the degree of hydrogenation, the more saturated the fat becomes. Many commercial products contain hydrogenated or partially hydrogenated vegetable oils to give products a longer shelf life.

Reproduced with permission www.americanehart.org ©2005, American Heart Association.

Examples are such foods as french fries, cakes, donuts, and cookies. Recent studies suggest that these fats may raise blood cholesterol. Check food labels to see what fat is listed as an ingredient.

## Summary of Fats in Our Diets

Eating fit means getting rid of or limiting foods with trans fat or hydrogenated vegetable oils and saturated fats. The recipes in this book help you do that. Excess intake of hydrogenated and saturated fats are Dirt Choices.

## Common Questions about Poly- and Monounsaturated Fats

*What and where are polyunsaturated and monounsaturated fatty acids?*
Polyunsaturated and monounsaturated fatty acids are fats from vegetable sources.

Polyunsaturated fats can be found in safflowers, sesame and sunflower seeds, corn and soybeans, and many nuts and seeds as well as their oils.

Monounsaturated fats are in canola, olive, and peanut oils, as well as in nuts, seeds, and avocados.

Both polyunsaturated and monounsaturated fats may help lower your blood cholesterol level when you use them in place of saturated fats in your diet. These are Gold Choices as long as they are consumed in balance and make up less than 20 percent to 30 percent of your total calories. A little goes a long way.

## Cholesterol

Fat can increase the cholesterol in your body. Cholesterol is a waxy, soft, fat-like substance that is produced in the body. The body requires it to make hormones such as estrogen and testosterone, body tissue, and cell membranes. Approximately 70 percent of the cholesterol in our bodies is made in our livers. Our genes dictate how much is produced. We can control about 30 percent of the cholesterol by what we eat.

Fruit, vegetables, grains, seeds, and nuts contain no cholesterol. Some of these foods can even help lower it. However, although a food product label such

**TABLE 2-11 Foods that Raise Cholesterol Most**

| Fats that Raise Cholesterol | Sources | Examples |
|---|---|---|
| Dietary cholesterol | Foods from animals | Meats, egg yolks, dairy products, organ meats (liver, etc.), fish, and poultry |
| Saturated fats | Foods from animals | Whole milk, cream, ice cream, whole milk cheeses, butter, lard, and meats |
| | Certain plant oils | Palm, palm kernel and coconut oils, and cocoa butter |
| Trans fats | Partially hydrogenated vegetable oils | Cookies, crackers, cakes, french fries, fried onion rings, and donuts |

*Source:* Reproduced with permission of the American Heart Association, www.americanheart.org ©2005.

as on a peanut butter jar may boldly say "No Cholesterol," that does not mean the food will not raise your cholesterol levels. Too many fat calories, which can cause weight gain, can boost cholesterol, too.

## The Good and the Bad Guys

In the body, we have so-called bad cholesterol (the LDLs noted above) and so-called good cholesterol (the HDLs). LDLs are almost entirely cholesterol and can build up in our arteries by attaching to their walls and clogging them, eventually causing a heart attack. HDL has minimal levels of cholesterol and helps move the LDL from the arteries to the liver to be removed from the body or reprocessed, as noted in Table 2-11, Foods that Raise Cholesterol Most.

Recent research has shown that monounsaturated fats may also help reduce blood cholesterol as long as the diet is low in saturated fat.

To help lower your overall blood cholesterol level, replace saturated fats in your diet with monounsaturated and polyunsaturated fats. The mono and polyunsaturated fats tend to help your body get rid of newly formed cholesterol. Foods that help lower cholesterol are listed in Table 2-12. Table 2-13 shows normal blood cholesterol levels for good health.

## The Bottom Line

Here is the bottom line when it comes to the use of fats and oils in our diet.

- Consume small amounts of the following more often: polyunsaturated or monounsaturated oils, vegetable oils, and margarine made without trans fats.
- Consume the following less often: Saturated and trans fats; butter, lard, and hydrogenated shortenings; cream, and chicken and meat fats.

**TABLE 2-12 Foods that Lower Cholesterol**

| Fats that May Lower Cholesterol | Sources | Examples |
|---|---|---|
| Polyunsaturated fats | Certain plant oils | Safflower, sesame, soy, corn and sunflower seed oils and nuts and seeds |
| Monounsaturated fats | Certain plant oils | Olive, canola, walnut, flax, and peanut oils as well as avocados, flaxseed, and some nuts |

*Source:* Reproduced with permission of the American Heart Association, www.americanheart.org ©2005.

**TABLE 2-13 Normal Blood Cholesterol Levels for Health**

| Substance | Levels and Health |
|---|---|
| Total cholesterol | Less than 200 milligrams/dl |
| LDL | Less than 130 milligrams/dl if you are not at risk for heart disease |
| HDL | Levels of 60 milligrams/dl or more are considered beneficial. |
| Triglycerides | Levels of 150–190 milligrams/dl are considered high, and lower levels are suggested. |

*Source:* Reproduced with permission of the American Heart Association, www.americanheart.org ©2005.

## Summary on Cholesterol

Strive to keep yourself active and watch your total fat intake to keep your cholesterol in check. Fiber is an important component that helps to get rid of LDLs in our bodies, which is a good reason to add fiber to our diets. When you get your lipid profile checked, Table 2-12 will help you know where you should be.

## The Use of Fats in This Book's Recipes

Cooking techniques used in this book's recipes include the use of these healthful fats:

- monounsaturated fats rich in vitamin E
- Omega-3 fatty acids

To lower cholesterol, eggs are used in moderation in these recipes. Other foods high in cholesterol, such as pork products, organ meats, and shellfish, are not used in this book.

## Nutrition Nugget

According to several studies, nutritional and vitamin supplements may not have the same beneficial results as food. It is the collective nutrients in the fruits and vegetables that are linked to inhibiting disease because of their phytonutrients, antioxidants, and fiber. Eating a brownie and then popping a pill will not do the trick.

Remember, fats contain more than twice the calories of either protein or carbohydrate for the same portion!

# CARBOHYDRATES

The majority of carbohydrates used in our recipes are from foods rich in phytonutrients (nutrients from plants), fiber, calcium, or all three. You may ask, why are carbohydrate foods that are rich in phytonutrients good for me? Foods rich in phytonutrients may help your body resist colds, fight inflammation and pain, enhance memory, lower cholesterol, reduce risks of cancer, arthritis, and more.

Our recipes include carbohydrates mainly from fruit, vegetables, whole grains, and low-fat or nonfat dairy products. Studies show that low-fat or nonfat dairy products consumed three times a day aid in weight loss and improved bone density.

## What Do Carbohydrates Do in My Body?

Carbohydrates—often called just *carbs*—are the key source of energy that fuel muscles, the brain, and the central nervous system; in pregnancy, it fuels the placenta and the fetus.

Many foods that contain carbohydrate are junk foods and Dirt Choices: chips, candy, cookies, soda, and snacks such as Goldfish, Fruit Loops, and fruit rollups. Do not be fooled by the word *fruit*. Once absorbed, fruit sugars convert into glucose (blood sugar), which is delivered in the blood to every cell in the body.

The body uses glucose for energy. If too much is consumed, it converts to fat. Our body needs insulin to absorb glucose into our cells. In Type 1 diabetes, the body does not make any insulin, so it must be injected. In Type 2 diabetes, the body may not be producing enough insulin. If a person is overweight, a reduction in calories is recommended. A good diet, exercise, and possible medication can help this.

## The Two Main Categories There are two main categories of carbohydrates: (1) simple or refined and (2) complex.

### Simple or Refined Carbohydrates: Dirt Choices

Simple carbohydrates are fruit sugar (fructose), table sugar (sucrose), and corn or grape sugar (dextrose or glucose). When a diet is high in sugar or refined carbohydrates from sources such as sodas, cookies, cake, candy, white bread, donuts, and bagels, the body must release a lot of insulin to digest the food. Chronic surges of insulin in the blood every day may cause the pancreas to wear out, with diabetes a possible result. There has been a 30 percent rise in diabetes in the past decade. This seems to be linked to the increased intake of refined carbohydrates that people eat as well as an increased lack of activity.

Many refined carbohydrate foods contain high fructose corn syrup made from cornstarch. It is an ingredient in many bakery products and cereals. It may be detrimental because it can cause the blood sugar to rise rapidly. Chronic surges in blood sugar and high demands for insulin are linked with the development of Type 2 diabetes and have also been associated with an increased risk of cancer. The less insulin you need to digest food, the better. In summary, refined carbohydrates should be limited. One benefit of exercise is that you need less insulin to digest food.

## Complex Carbohydrates: Gold Choices

Complex carbohydrates contain dietary fiber and are digested more slowly, allowing the body to better metabolize blood sugar. Foods containing complex carbohydrate include whole grains in cereal, pasta, and bread, as well as barley, brown rice, fruit, vegetables, beans, and lentils. It is recommended that the average adult consume at least 25–50 grams of fiber a day.

# GLYCEMIC INDEX

Glycemic index is simply a reference food to compare how quickly carbohydrate foods are absorbed into the body. Usually, white bread is the reference and is noted as 100 (see Table 2-14). Although glycemic index is not the greatest reference for what to eat and not eat, I bring it up because it has been in many diet books, so it will help you to understand what it means. High glycemic foods when eaten alone may raise blood sugar quicker than low glycemic foods, but this is not always the case. Some individuals respond differently than others. So before you eliminate high glycemic foods, know that it is the balance of food that you have to worry about.

## High Glycemic Index Foods Eaten Alone

When eaten by themselves, carbohydrate foods with higher glycemic index numbers may cause a fast rise in blood sugar and then a surge of insulin production in the body. This has a negative effect in your body. Because of a rapid rise in blood sugar, there is a rapid response and need for insulin, followed by absorption of sugar into the cells. Then blood sugar drops, making you hungrier and wanting to eat more. For a diabetic, this can cause even more havoc.

### Should I Avoid Eating High Glycemic Foods?

No, but you need to limit the use of high glycemic load foods. When planning meals, combine low with high glycemic load foods. This will help reduce the surge of insulin that would occur if the high glycemic foods were eaten alone.

**TABLE 2-14 High and Low Glycemic Index Foods**

| High Index Foods[a] | | Lower Index Foods[b] | |
|---|---|---|---|
| Baked potato | 135 | Pumpernickel bread | 78 |
| Instant rice | 124 | Old-fashioned oatmeal | 70 |
| Cornflakes | 119 | All Bran | 60 |
| Instant potatoes | 116 | Pasta, high-fiber type | 35–65 |
| Rice Krispies | 117 | Sweet potato | 54 |
| Jelly beans | 114 | Lentils and kidney beans | 40–69 |
| French fries | 107 | Milk | 49 |
| | | Cherries | 32 |
| | | Barley | 31 |
| | | Peanuts | 19 |
| | | Soy beans | 20 |
| Reference: White bread = 100 | | | |

[a]Eat less if eaten alone without other high-fiber foods.
[b]The better choice

The bottom line is that you should eat more complex carbohydrates and fewer simple carbohydrates. You do not have to get crazy over low and high glycemic foods, but it is good to know how they can affect your body. Many simple carbohydrates such as jelly beans, candy bars, and sweetened beverages such as sodas and fruit drinks have higher glycemic loads that spike blood sugar. Other foods that quickly raise blood sugar are potatoes, couscous, and refined high-sugar, low-fiber cereals.

Here is a comparison of high and low glycemic load meals:

| Higher Glycemic Load Meal | Lower Glycemic Load Meal |
|---|---|
| Sweetened cereal with milk | Unsweetened oatmeal with milk |
| Glass of juice | An egg and an orange |

There is more fiber in the lower glycemic load meal. Fiber improves *insulin sensitivity*, a measure of how well insulin works in getting blood sugar into cells.

## Low Glycemic Index Foods and Health

According to the American Diabetes Association, low glycemic index foods are of importance for long-term diabetic control. They may help reduce extreme blood sugar highs and lows. Lower glycemic load foods such as bran or whole oat cereal, beans and lentils, and brown rice are digested more slowly and may not elevate the blood sugar as rapidly. This will make you feel more satisfied for a longer period of time, so you will be less likely to overeat.

In Australia, Canada, France, New Zealand, and the United Kingdom, education on the use of foods with low glycemic index has been widely adopted. Food labels in some countries now use codes to identify low glycemic foods.

## Lowered Risk of Heart Disease

Worldwide health experts have demonstrated in their research that diets with an overall high glycemic index do increase the risk of coronary heart disease.

## Reduced Insulin Resistance

Low glycemic foods may help reduce *insulin resistance,* the inability of insulin to bring glucose (blood sugar) into cells. Persons especially with hyperinsulinemia, polycystic ovary syndrome, and obesity may benefit from eating meals with a lower glycemic load and higher fiber content. Research is still emerging in this area.

## Reduced Surges of Hunger

Low glycemic meals and snacks will make you feel satisfied longer, allow you to have better concentration, keep your moods on an even keel, and increase energy.

## Controlling High Insulin Levels Associated with Cancer

In May 2000, the American Society of Clinical Oncology released the results of a study reporting that women with breast cancer who had high insulin levels have a greater chance of the disease recurring and of dying from it. According to Pamela J. Goodwin, M.D., lead researcher of the study, "Insulin is well-known for its control of blood sugars. What's new in our study is that it also appears to have an important effect on the growth of breast cancers." Goodwin is associate professor of medicine at the University of Toronto School of Medicine and scientist at the Samuel Lunenfeld Institute at Mt. Sinai Hospital in Toronto, Canada. Eating low glycemic index meals, achieving a normal weight, and exercising helps to lower insulin levels if they are too high in the blood.

# Keeping the Glycemic Load in Meals Lower

Keeping the glycemic load in meals low is simply done by combining a mix of foods groups:

> Protein + High-fiber foods + Complex Carbohydrates
>
> Beans             Whole grains      Fruit and vegetables
> Fish
> Lean Poultry
> Nonfat or low-fat dairy

# Benefits of Lower Glycemic Load Meals

Low glycemic foods and meals are good for everyone. Research shows that diets low in sugar and fat and meals with low glycemic load lead to better weight and diabetes management and reduced risk of cancer. For children, this combination is even more important in helping to reduce the risk of excess weight gain and other health problems.

The bottom line is that the recipes in this book aim to reduce the glycemic load by mixing low with high glycemic index foods. This allows the body to digest and absorb nutrients slowly without excess demand on insulin. For this reason, the recipes and menus in this book are designed to reduce your intake of refined, processed food and teach you to use foods with greater nutrient density.

# SUGAR AND SWEETENERS

Americans consume excessive amounts of sugar. One goal of this book is to help you eliminate excess sugar or sugar substitutes in common recipes and add other flavors that not only taste great but also improve nutrient density.

*What is wrong with consuming a lot of sugar?*
There are two important reasons for reducing sugar:

1. Sugar causes fermentation in the mouth and produces acids that erode teeth enamel and cause dental caries.

2. Sugar decreases the production of healthy bacteria in the intestine. Recent studies show that this allows a possible cancer-causing bacterium to grow.

## Cravings for Sweets

If you crave sweet foods, try to decrease your need for them. Choose sugars that occur naturally within food such as those found in fruit (called *intrinsic* sugars). Reduce *extrinsic* sugars, which are added to foods through processing and preparation (such as high fructose corn syrup). Change your desire for sugar and watch your excess calories decrease. Convenience foods such as sweet-tasting cakes, muffins, cereals, and even soda, as well as common foods such as ketchup, tomato sauce, and bread, all have sugar or sugar substitutes added. Fruit juice contains natural sugar.

Artificial sweeteners are calorie-free but 200 to 800 times as sweet as regular sugar, which may enhance your desire for sweets. Use Table 2-15 as a guide when choosing sweeteners.

## Summary

The food industry wants you to eat as much sugar as possible. It is addictive, and the industry wants to keep you buying it to boost sales profits. Health is not always the industry's first priority—profits are. So, the next time you choose a convenience food loaded with sugar and calories think—weapons of body mass destruction. Buyers beware!

---

Drinking a lot of juice—sugar water with a few vitamins or minerals—is not as beneficial as eating a piece of fruit with fiber.

Although sports drinks such as Gatorade are slightly lower in sugar, limit your intake of these drinks to a glass or less a day if you are overweight or if you are filling up on these rather than fiber-rich, nutrient-dense foods. In sports, if you are intensely sweating for more than two hours, you may need to drink more of this type of beverage.

**TABLE 2-15 Sweeteners in Cooking**

| Sweeteners in Cooking | Use | Caution |
| --- | --- | --- |
| Sugar | Natural sweetening agent in beverages, desserts, cereals, tomato sauce, and candy. Raw unbleached sugar is the most natural. Contains 15 calories per gram. | Excess causes dental caries; extreme rapid rise in blood sugar, which may affect mood or diabetes. All forms interfere with white cells to destroy bacteria and increase risk of infection. |
| Stevia | Good option for diabetics and weight loss. Naturally occurring sweetener derived from a plant in Paraguay. It is not approved by FDA as a sweetening agent but as a dietary supplement because of political influences. Its use in baking may alter the sweet taste. It may also aid in reducing infections because of its antiviral properties. Contains no calories. | No studies have concluded danger in consumption by humans. Early studies tested for an association with infertility but tests offered no documented evidence. |
| Splenda | Sucralose, 600 times sweeter than sugar, is manufactured from sugar. Can be used in beverages, baking, and cooking without losing its sweet taste. No calories. If used sparingly (1 package per day), it may be a good diabetic and weight-loss option. | This substance was tested for twenty years prior to approval in the United States. Because of extra sweet taste, may increase your desire for sweet foods. From the Department of Health and Human Services, Food and Drug Administration evidence sucralose can cause cancer. "Sucralose was weakly mutagenic in a mouse lymphoma mutation assay." However, regulators felt these and other concerns were refutable and considered safe. |
| Nutrasweet and Equal | Aspartame is some 200 times sweeter than sugar. It is made by joining two amino acids—aspartic acid and methyl ester of phenylalanine. It can be used in cold foods but is not recommended for use in heating because it loses its sweetness. Zero calories. | Persons with phenylketonuria must avoid ingesting this product. Some research has suggested that this substance can overstimulate brain cells to the point of damage, therefore we do not recommend its use. Other studies have demonstrated health problems in rats. |

| | | |
|---|---|---|
| Saccharin | Calorie-free substance that is 300 times as sweet as sugar. It is stable for use in beverages, baking, and cooking. | Decades ago it was banned because of possible bladder cancer, based on animal studies. Follow-up studies show no association in humans or animals. |
| Xylitol | Naturally occurring sweetener found in fruits. Reduces cavities and plaque. Found in gum. Glycemic index of 7. May fight infections. | No known side effects. |
| Whey Low | Sweetness same as sugar but with 70 percent lower glycemic index. Can be used in cooking. Good diabetic and weight-loss option. Contains 4 calories per gram. Made from corn syrup and milk sugar but seems okay for lactose-intolerant people. Found online at http://wheylow.com. | Studies do not demonstrate fructose in this product to cause gastrointestinal problems for those with lactose intolerance. For those who have allergy sensitivities to corn caution is advised. |
| Honey | Made from bees. Adequate to use but see caution. | Pregnant woman and young children under 2 should avoid honey because of natural bacteria that could be harmful. |
| High Fructose Corn Syrup | Produced from acid-treated corn; naturally occurring glucose in the corn converts to fructose. Food manufacturers use it in everything from bread to beer to tomato sauce to soda. | High fructose diets have also been implicated in the development of adult onset diabetes. Fructose, especially "when combined with other sugars, reduces stores of chromium, a mineral essential for maintaining balanced insulin levels," according to Richard Anderson, Ph.D., lead scientist at the Human Nutrition Research Center in Beltsville, Maryland. Other data suggests it is contributing to the rise in obesity and insulin resistance, therefore limit. |

# PHYTONUTRIENTS

Phytonutrients, or phytochemicals, are nutrients in plant foods. Thousands of them exist. They concentrate in the skins of many vegetables and fruits and are responsible for their color, hue, scent, and flavor. To a lesser extent, they are also found in grains and seeds.

Phytonutrients are involved in the following highly complex roles in our bodies. They:

- help vision and reduce the risk of macular degeneration,
- boost the autoimmune system and reduce inflammation,
- fight infection and cancer,
- improve memory and cognitive thinking, and
- remove and deactivate harmful substances in the body.

Research has demonstrated that plant-based foods contain thousands of phytonutrients. As you get older, the more varied foods you eat, the better your health. When eaten, these phytonutrients have specific functions in the body. For example, *allylic sulfide (allicin)* is found in bulb plants such as garlic, onions, and chives. They intercept toxins in our body and help detoxify them. *Beta-carotene* is well known to protect the immune system and is found in carrots, squash, apricots, and peaches. *Capsicum* (an antioxidant found in paprika) and *capsaicin* (found in hot or red peppers and chilis) prevents harmful substances from invading and damaging cells. They also have anti-inflammatory properties.

*Carotenoids,* from dark green– and orange-colored plants, help block cancer-causing molecules from entering the cell and also help repair DNA.

*Flavonoids* are found in fruits, vegetables, red wine, and tea and help to prevent carcinogenic hormones from attaching to cells. *Genistein*—which is found in tofu, soy milk, and soybeans—inhibits the formation of blood vessels that assist tumors to grow. *Isoflavones,* found in peas, beans, peanuts, and tofu, have been noteworthy for reducing menopausal symptoms and decreasing the risk of breast cancer by interfering with harmful estrogen action. Other phytonutrients that deactivate carcinogens (substances that cause cancer) are *catechins, chlorogenic acid,* and *indoles* found in pepper, garlic, and other spices found in our recipes. See Table 2-16, Benefits of Phytonutrients for Health.

Thousands of phytonutrients may hold the key to health if you choose to eat a variety of food and incorporate lifestyle habits to achieve balance in your body, spirit, and mind. Taking a supplement may cover a few nutritional needs, but the balance and variety of existing naturally occurring nutrients seems to have a much stronger and more profound effect.

Using our recipes you will learn how to cook foods rich in phytonutrients and obtain their benefits. The more colorful foods on your plate, the more variety

**TABLE 2-16 Benefits of Phytonutrients on Health**

| Phytochemical or Antioxidant | Potential Benefits | Food Sources |
| --- | --- | --- |
| Alpha-linolenic acid (essential Omega-3 fatty acid) | Lowers blood cholesterol, reduces risk of heart disease, reduces risk of osteoporosis, and may aid in brain function and intelligence | Flaxseed, flax oil, fish oils, cold-pressed canola or soybean oil, walnuts or walnut oil, wheat germ |
| Anthocyanosides | Reduce risk of heart disease | Found in red, blue, and purple plants, such as grapes, raspberries, black-berries, raisins, red apples, dried plums, blueberries, eggplant, and cherries |
| Carotenoids: phytofluene, beta-cryptoxanthin, delta carotene, and lycopene | Encourage normal cell growth, reduce risk of cancer, and protect against prostate cancer (lycopene only) | Yellow-orange fruits and vegetables, red fruits, green leafy vegetables such as spinach and romaine lettuce, tomatoes, sweet red peppers, yellow peppers, sweet potatoes, winter squash, and carrots |
| Coumarin | Reduces risk of cancer | Carrots, caraway, celery, and parsley |
| Organosulfur compounds such as allylic sulfide, disulfides, and trisulfide | Reduce risk of cancer, reduce risk of heart diseases, and has antimicrobial properties | Onions, garlic, shallots, chives, and leeks |
| Dithiolthiones | Reduce risk of cancer | Cruciferous vegetables: broccoli, cau-liflower, brussel sprouts, and cabbage |
| Ellagic acid | Reduce risks of cancers of the esophagus, lung, breast, bladder, and skin | Grapes, nuts, strawberries, raspberries, cranberries, pomegranates, grapes, and walnuts |

(continued)

**TABLE 2-16** (*Continued*)

| Phytochemical or Antioxidant | Potential Benefits | Food Sources |
| --- | --- | --- |
| Flavonoids | Reduce risk of heart disease and risk of cancer | Most fruits and vegetables |
| Glucarates | Reduce risk of cancer | Citrus fruits, grains, tomatoes, and bell peppers |
| Indoles and isothiocyanates | Reduce risk of cancer | Cruciferous vegetables such as broccoli and cauliflower |
| Isoflavones | Lower blood cholesterol, reduce risk of cancer, reduce risk of heart disease, and reduce risk of osteoporosis | Soy foods and products (soybeans, Stofu, soy milk, soy protein powder) |
| Lignans | Lower cholesterol and reduce risk of cancer | Soybeans, flaxseeds, sesame |
| Polyphenols | Emerging links to lower blood pressure, improved blood flow, and possible insulin sensitivity | Dark chocolate (the active ingredient is usually not found in dark chocolates made in the United States) |
| Phenolic acids | Reduce risk of cancer | Cherry, berries, grapes, nuts, and whole grains |
| Phthalides and polyacetylenes | Reduce risk of cancer | Caraway, celery, cumin, dill, fennel, and parsley |
| Phytates and phytosterols | Reduce risk of colon cancer | Grains, legumes, and nuts |
| Phytoestrogens | Reduce symptoms of menopause | Soy products, legumes, and flaxseed |
| Phytofats and Omega-3 fatty acids | Reduce risk of heart disease and reduce risk of cancer | Fish oils (mackerel, salmon, and sardines) and flaxseed oil |

| | | |
|---|---|---|
| Saponins | Reduce risk of cancer | Potatoes, asparagus, spinach, and legumes |
| Terpenes and limonene | Aids in fighting cancer | Mushrooms and peels of citrus fruits |
| Betaine | Reduces the risk of heart disease, protects liver function, and serves as a cleansing agent | Beets and beet juice |

| Plant-Based Foods | Potential Benefits and Use | Possible Side Effects and Interactions |
|---|---|---|
| Basil | Can be used to treat nose and throat infections and aids in digestion | None known |
| Cayenne pepper | Relieves muscular tension and rheumatism | Avoid when taking anticoagulants |
| Chamomile | Can be used to treat indigestion and inflammation of skin, mouth, and pharynx | None known |
| Chili pepper | Aids in digestion | Can aggravate stomach ulcers |
| Garlic | Fights infection and can be used to treat inflammation of the mouth and pharynx; also used as a blood thinner | Contraindicated if on prescription blood thinners or anticoagulants; large intake can lead to stomach distress |
| Ginger | Reduces nausea caused by chemotherapy; acts as natural blood thinner and digestive aid | Contraindicated with use of prescription blood thinners or anticoagulants |
| Green tea | Used for stomach disorders, vomiting, and diarrhea when taken as a beverage | Contraindicated with the use of prescription blood thinners |

(continued)

**TABLE 2-16** *(Continued)*

| Phytochemical or Antioxidant | Potential Benefits | Possible Side Effects and Interactions |
|---|---|---|
| Licorice | Reduce risk of liver disease; used to treat sore throat and gastric and peptic ulcers | Contraindicated with the use of potassium-wasting diuretics; increases blood pressure |
| Peppermint | Relieves pain and indigestion; enhances ulcer healing and prevents reoccurrence | None known |
| Rosemary | Anti-inflammatory action; reduces gastrointestinal upset, gas, and indigestion; reduces risks of heart disease | Gastrointestinal disturbances with large doses |
| Soybean | Lowers cholesterol; may reduce menopausal symptoms and risk of certain types of cancer and protects liver function | Stomach pain, loose stools, and diarrhea; in certain breast cancer cases, large intake may increase cancer growth |
| Thyme | Anti-bacterial and antispasmodic; aids in digestive upsets with gas, nausea, vomiting, and abdominal bloating | None known |
| Turmeric | Aids in liver function; has anti-inflammatory and anti-ulcerogenic properties; may reduce risk of bowel, cervical, and liver cancers; reduces inflammation of osteoarthritis and rheumatoid arthritis; reduces cholesterol and triglyceride levels | Avoid large doses with anticoagulants and non steroidal anti-inflammatory, possible additive effect for bleeding may cause stomach ulcers |

*Source:* www.nps.ars.usda.gov

## Nutrition Nugget

Genetic engineering has produced tomatoes with up to three times more *lycopene*—the cancer-preventing red pigment—than normal and a shelf life that is several weeks longer. Autar K. Mattoo and colleagues at the ARS Vegetable Laboratory in Beltsville, Maryland, inserted a gene that retards plant aging, or senescence, along with a promoter that is triggered by ripening. The engineered tomatoes accumulate more lycopene and other antioxidants during the longer ripening stage. This novel approach should work in other fruits and vegetables.

of the phytonutrients you will consume to boost your immune system. Think red, blue, orange, yellow, white, and purple.

# ANTIOXIDANTS

Antioxidants are nutrients that protect cells. Oxygen is essential for life but the by-products it leaves in our body, called *free radicals,* can damage our cells. The results of free radical damage include heart disease, cataracts, and a weakened immune system. Common protectors against free radicals are vitamin C, vitamin E, and beta-carotene. They act as scavengers by removing free radicals from our body. Recent studies show, however, that in certain people too many antioxidants in supplements may not be good or and may even be harmful. Recent studies report that a gene we inherit may dictate whether a supplement will be helpful or harmful. It seems safer to obtain these nutrients from foods. The recipes in this book are high in antioxidants and taste delicious.

## The Scoop on Chocolate, Green Tea, and Vitamin E

For chocolate lovers, there may be hope. A tiny Italian study of fifteen people demonstrated that 3¹/₂ ounces of dark chocolate lowered blood pressure and boosted insulin sensitivity. But wait, the calories eaten from the chocolate totaled 480! According to Alice Lichenstein of the USDA Human Nutrition and Research Center at Tufts University, what we thought initially was beneficial is proving not always so. There is still uncertainty if it is the polyphenols, the theobromine, or something else in chocolate that gives a beneficial effect. So, before you rush out to eat dark chocolate, know that the calories from the fat and sugar in chocolate are just not worth it. Much research is going into this area, so keep on the lookout.

As for green tea, the FDA says, "there is no credible evidence supporting a relationship between green tea consumption and colon, lung, stomach, and six other cancers."

And in the case of vitamin E, the *Journal of the American Medical Association* reported in 2005 that 40,000 healthy women over a ten-year period showed no difference in stroke, heart disease, or cancer rates after consuming vitamin E in 600 international units with either aspirin or a placebo.

The moral of the story is that research is forever evolving. What we think is extremely beneficial in supplements one day may not turn out to be helpful and may even be harmful. You never hear of studies where someone has overdosed on a fruit or vegetable. Although antioxidants are important for the body, so are dietary fibers and phytonutrients. The more we learn, the more views change. My conclusion: If you eat a variety of plant-based foods, you will gain the benefits of all of these nutrients.

## PROTEIN

Protein is essential in the body and diet. The sources of protein in this book are from both animal and plant-based foods. High protein diets that incorporate more than 7 ounces a day of meat will boost their intake of saturated fats that are linked to cancer and heart disease. Excess protein adds stress on the kidneys as they try to remove the by-products of metabolism. The recommended number of servings of meat or meat alternates ranges from two to seven servings per day, depending on your total caloric needs. When animal protein is used excessively, it may replace beneficial calories from plant-based foods, robbing us of essential nutrients. Complete protein is contained in animal meats and dairy products. It contains all eight essential amino acids. An essential amino acid cannot be synthesized by the body and therefore must be supplied as part of the diet.

Humans need eight essential amino acids: tryptophan, lysine, methionine, phenylalanine, threonine, valine, leucine, and isoleucine. Two others, histidine and arginine, are essential only in children. A good mnemonic device for remembering these is "Private Tim Hall," abbreviated as: PVT TIM HALL:

| phenylalanine | valine | tryptophan | |
|---|---|---|---|
| threonine | isoleucine | methionine | |
| histidine | arginine | lysine | leucine |

Incomplete proteins—those missing one or more essential amino acids—are found in grains, nuts, seeds, and vegetables and other plant-based products. By combining these foods, a complete protein can be made. Protein from vegetables and grains boosts fiber, phytonutrients, and vitamins. Vegetarian recipes are labeled according to their type: for example, lacto-ovo or vegan. Just eating a protein bar does not make up for what our body needs, and it can be harmful when it replaces fruit, vegetable, and dairy products as a snack or meal. Below is more information on vegetarian diets.

## VEGETARIAN DIETS

The most common reasons people become vegetarians are:

1. a desire not to eat animals,
2. concern about the environment and health, and
3. religious beliefs.

This book classifies vegetarians into two categories: (1) lacto-ovo and (2) vegan.

A lacto-ovo diet includes dairy animal sources such as milk, cheese, and eggs. It restricts all meat, fish, and poultry or animal-based products such as beef and chicken broth.

A vegan diet eliminates all animal products such as meat, fish, poultry, eggs, milk, cheese, yogurt, and other dairy products. It contains only foods from grains, vegetables, fruit, legumes, nuts, and seeds. This diet is deficient in vitamin $B_{12}$, and individuals will need to take vitamin $B_{12}$ supplements. A person may also become deficient in calcium and protein if a sufficient variety of grains is not included.

## Benefits of a Vegetarian Diet

The added fiber in vegetarian diets has many benefits, including:

- regulating blood sugar better,
- adding important phytonutrients for the immune system,
- reducing stress on the kidneys,
- regulating blood pressure,
- removing toxins that could cause cancer,
- reducing insulin resistance,
- reducing hypoglycemia, and
- lowering cholesterol.

To start eating a lower-fat and more nutritious diet, try a minimum of two lacto-ovo vegetarian meals per day even if you do enjoy animal protein. Low-fat dairy is known to aid in weight management and improved bone density. Learning to cook a wider variety of meals that contain grains such as wheat berries or beans, instead of only rice and pasta, will boost fiber and other nutrients. Nonanimal protein sources from grains and vegetables lack the eight essential amino acids to make protein. By combining different food groups or grains, a complete protein is achieved.

For example,

Beans + rice *or* pasta + beans *or* corn + beans *or* tofu + rice *or* cheese + tortilla

## Common Questions

*What if I am a diabetic? Won't this boost carbohydrate foods and raise my blood sugar?* A meal containing beans and rice instead of chicken and rice not only decreases fat but also boosts fiber, which aids in keeping blood sugar from rapidly rising. Fat is important to reduce in your diabetic diet. Excess fat from meat and poultry and animal fats, such as butter and cream cheese, proves to be harmful to a person with diabetes or at risk for diabetes. Fiber is increased substantially with the whole grain food group, such as oats, beans, and lentils.

Suggestion: Try the recommended portions in this cookbook and the menus. Test your blood sugar two hours after your meal or before your next meal and see how your body reacts. You may be pleasantly surprised. By eliminating saturated fat from animal products, you reduce your risk of developing complications of heart disease, which occurs more often in persons with diabetes.

## DAIRY PRODUCTS

Recent research has confirmed that dairy foods are not only rich in calcium for bones but also are beneficial for weight management and reducing the risk of colon, breast, prostate, and stomach cancer. The use of *probiotics* (beneficial active bacteria cultures) found in yogurt and cultured buttermilk may improve immune function and affect intestinal symptoms such as diarrhea, colitis, constipation, and inflammatory bowel. Another beneficial substance is *conjugated linoleic acid,* which is found in milk products and active in reducing the risk of the cancers mentioned earlier. Clearly, most individuals need at least two to three rich calcium sources per day of dairy products or calcium equivalents. Include one fat-free yogurt or buttermilk per day to get active cultures. Active cultures are reduced in the intestine if you consume too much sugar. Sugar allows bacteria that can cause cancer to grow.

> Serving size:  8 ounces fat-free or low-fat milk or yogurt
> 1 to 2 ounces low-fat or reduced fat hard cheese
> $^1/_2$ cup 1 percent fat cottage or ricotta cheese

Dairy products contain a balance of proteins, vitamin D, calcium, and phosphorous in the right form and amount for absorption and utilization. Supplements or pills may not always have the right balance or form that is well absorbed. Some sources of calcium supplements may not be healthy, especially those from oyster shells, which may be contaminated with toxins from polluted oysters.

### Caution

The substances in dairy have a wide array of therapeutic value, but if you are sensitive to milk or dairy products, then other foods fortified with calcium or that naturally contain calcium are recommended. Casein, the protein in milk, may be difficult for some people to digest. Asthmatic symptoms and mucus can be a symptom of sensitivity. Another symptom is cramping, diarrhea, and abdominal discomfort.

With lactose intolerance, the body does not make enough of the enzyme lactase to break down lactose, the principal sugar in milk. Some yogurts and cheeses may be tolerated because they may contain less lactose. Lactase pills, such as Lactaid tablets, or Lactaid milk can also be used if you are lactose intolerant, temporarily or indefinitely. Often after not drinking milk, it may cause stomach cramping when introduced back into the diet. The body needs a little time to start producing the enzyme to start breaking down the lactose again. After a gradual increase in your milk intake, more may be tolerated. This will not help if you have other sensitivities to milk, in which case soy milk or other foods fortified with calcium should be substituted.

Other alternative sources of calcium are fish with bones such as wild canned salmon and sardines with bones, collard greens, broccoli, orange juice with added calcium, and to a lesser degree enriched cereals and breads.

This book recommends milk and dairy products from animals that are free of antibiotics and growth hormones that are given to increase milk production (choosing organic milk is a way to assure this). Avoid dairy products that contain excessive amounts of sugar in yogurts, whipped yogurt, and flavored drinks or smoothies.

## FLUIDS

Drink water regularly to help your skin stay soft and to replenish your metabolic needs. Most of the human body is made up of fluid.

Water is the best, a Gold Choice. Soda is the worst, a Dirt Choice. Water should come from safe sources and without the excessive amounts of chlorine or other contaminants found in some tap water. The Environmental Protection Agency lists safety violations by state, so check if you have a concern. The FDA usually lists warnings as well, although the information may be outdated or minimized because of politics. The more varied the sources of fluid in your diet, the better your chances are of reducing the risk of contaminants.

In our recipes, I incorporate a variety of beverages to boost nutrients such as antioxidants, calcium, beta-carotene, vitamin C, and magnesium. A variety of teas have powerful substances to aid in health. Refer to the recipes in the beverage section to learn more about teas. Fat-free milk is encouraged for its known benefit in weight loss and bone density. Three 8-ounce servings of milk a day is reported to be beneficial for weight management.

*How much fluid should I drink daily?*
The daily requirements for both children and adults is 1 liter or quart per 1,000 calories of food consumed.

In general, an average of six to eight 8-ounce glasses of fluid a day, including two to three servings of milk, is recommended. Excessive drinking to maintain a feeling of unnatural fullness is discouraged. Drinking soft drinks with lots of sugar or sugar substitute is not recommended. For infants, approximately 1.5 liters is needed, based on a ratio of 2 ounces of fluid per pound or 2 milliliters per kilogram of body weight. Ask a registered dietitian if you are not certain.

### Water Facts

- Water is a major component of our body weight, constituting 75 to 62 percent of infants' and children's weight, 55 to 60 percent of teenagers' and adult males' weight, and 45 to 50 percent of females' weight.
- Water improves hormonal function.
- Water should be replenished daily; it is part of all cells and is needed to transport nutrients to all cells and remove waste and toxins out of the body.
- The higher the environmental temperature over 75 degrees Fahrenheit, the more fluid you need.

*How much do I need for fluid replacement for physical activity?*
Hydration is important before, during, and after exercise as the following table shows:

| Timing | Amount of Water* |
|---|---|
| 2 hours before exercise | 2–3 cups |
| 10–15 minutes before | 2 cups |
| During exercise | 2–8 ounces every 30 minutes |
| After exercise | Replace 2 cups per pound lost |

*Sports drinks such as Gatorade are only recommended if exercise exceeds two hours.

Do not use drinks for fluid replacement if they contain 10 percent or more of the carbohydrates found in most sodas and juice. This can lead to cramping and bloating.

*What are the side effects of fluid imbalance?*
Fluid imbalances, excess retention, or dehydration or contaminants may cause cramps, headaches, and excess fatigue.

*What about fluids with caffeine?*
Limit coffee, tea, and caffeinated soda to one or fewer eight-ounce serving per day. Drinks with excess caffeine or sugar such as coffee (especially flavored coffees), Red Bull, and sodas with caffeine (Mountain Dew, Coke, etc.) are things to cut. The chemical dependency of caffeine has a negative effect on the human body, especially children and teens. The average homemade cup of coffee has 70 milligrams of caffeine, and a "tall" (small) cup of Starbucks is estimated to have more than 150 milligrams. If you are a coffee lover, then try to limit it to once a day, preferably to less than 100 milligrams.

*Should I be concerned about water pollution?*
Here are a couple of cautions:

- Water-treatment plants may use chlorine in the attempt to decontaminate our water. Unsafe levels of chlorine and other contaminants have been associated with cancer and other health problems. Regulatory agencies may not always be able to monitor how much or how safely it is used.
- Plastics contain toxins that, when consumed, have been associated with cancer. The softer plastic or styrofoam containers for food and fluids, especially when heated, may penetrate the contained food or beverage. If we are exposed to this continually, the question rises, will this exposure cause cancer over time? Do you want to find out this as smokers have after the matter occurs?

## Summary and Tips for Drinking

- Drink before thirst begins.
- Drink enough so that your urine will be pale yellow.

- Avoid excess fluid loss and dehydration.
- Do not be excessive beyond your need to fill up.
- Consume water from safe sources; a variety of sources helps.

## About Alcohol

Remember, alcohol is for adults only. A healthy lifestyle sets boundaries to limit alcohol consumption. Here is a rule of thumb: If you must drink, have one drink every other day or less.

In addition to the problems inherent in a mood-altering substance such as this one, alcohol also adds empty calories to your body (see Table 2-17).

*Aren't red wines good for phytonutrients to protect my heart?*
True, they are, but if you are trying to lose weight, there are better ways. Fresh fruit and vegetables have fewer calories, more fiber, and other nutrients.

*Why does red and not white wine have these phytonutrients?*
Certain red wines are not filtered and may provide phytonutrients to protect the heart while white is filtered, removing the important phytonutrients. The downside: Many red wines contain sulfites, which may be the cause of headaches hours later. Calories add up fast and will cause weight gain if consumed regularly.

### Limiting the Intake of Alcohol

There are several reasons why you should limit how much alcohol you consume:

1. Most hard liquor and beer provide empty calories with no nutritional benefit.
2. Alcohol reduces the appetite for foods that contain powerful nutrients and phytonutrients that reduce the risk of developing such killers as obesity, heart disease, cancer, and diabetes.
3. Too much alcohol causes mood swings, distorted thinking, depression, weight gain, fatigue, dehydration, liver and circulatory problems, and birth defects in pregnant women, among many other complications.
4. For athletes, performance is impaired and dehydration is accelerated.

### Tips for Quitting

Stopping the habitual and chronic use of alcohol can be difficult, so here are some suggestions to keep you focused on a change in your life that limits alcohol use:

- If you use alcohol as a way to relax, try to substitute an evening walk after work.
- Create support systems of friends and family members who do not indulge in alcohol.

**TABLE 2-17 Calories in Alcohol, Mixers, and Mixed Drinks**

| Alcoholic Beverages | | |
|---|---|---|
| Rum, whiskey, vodka, gin, brandy, scotch (80 proof) | 1½ | 115 |
| Wine | 4 | 130 |
| Beer | 12 | 160 |
| Light beer | 12 | 100 |
| Wine cooler | 10 | 120 |
| **Various Mixers** | | |
| Soft drink | 6 | 80 |
| Sugar-free soft drink (better option) | 6 | 0–1 |
| Tonic water | 6 | 60 |
| Diet tonic water | 6 | 30 |
| Seltzer or club soda (better option) | 6 | 0 |
| Orange juice | 6 | 85 |
| Low-sodium vegetable or tomato juice (better option) | 6 | 35 |
| **Various Mixed Drinks** | | |
| White Russian | | |
| with light cream | 5–6 | 450 |
| with half and half | 5–6 | 350 |
| with whole milk | 5–6 | 250 |
| Piña Colada | 8 | 375 |
| (1½ ounces light rum, 2 ounces cream of coconut, 4 ounces pineapple juice) | | |
| Rum and Cola | | |
| (1½ ounces light rum) | | |
| With 5½ ounces cola | 8 | 190 |
| With diet cola | 8 | 115 |

- Substitute reading before bed or a calming shower to relax instead of using alcohol.
- If you socialize in environments that have a lot of alcohol consumption, then consider arriving late to the cocktail hour.
- For weight loss, limit your intake to no more than one alcoholic beverage per week.
- Join Alcoholics Anonymous if you cannot do it alone.

### Limiting Drinks at Parties and Social Occasions

Remember, positive changes in your life often face the biggest challenges in social situations. Here are a few tips that may help you in such cases:

- Do not go starving! If you skip meals all day to "save up" and eat more while out, then you are setting yourself up for binging on drinks and appetizers. Choose lower-calorie options and drink lots of water or seltzer between each alcoholic beverage. If you are not hungry, the temptation will be less.
- Decide in advance to limit your drinks to one or two.
- Avoid mixed drinks that are rich in cream, ice cream, or sugar.

### Summary

Water is the best fluid we can consume because our bodies are largely made up of water. Other vegetable juices such as carrot or tomato juice are low in calories and provide rich nutrients. Using fat-free dairy beverages is another good alternative. Lastly, keep abreast of your changing environment and how it may affect the water you drink.

## BEING SODIUM SAVVY

For adults, 2,400 milligrams or less of sodium, or 6 grams of sodium chloride (table salt), per day is recommended. Too much sodium can cause excess fluid retention and may affect blood pressure. High blood pressure significantly increases the risk of heart and stroke death in overweight and obese people, according to a report in *Hypertension: Journal of the American Heart Association,* September 2005. If you eat convenience foods, then look at labels for sodium per serving. As recommended by the American Heart Association, a serving should contain fewer than 480 milligrams.

I was examining Oscar Meyer's "Lunchables" to see how much harmful fat and sodium is packed in this product. One label reads "Mega Pack." They got that right! It is packed with toxic amounts of sodium—more than 1,000 milligrams. I cringe at the thought of a child eating that, let alone an adult. It is usually the child who wants these prepackaged lunches for their sugary drinks and candy along with the sodium and fat.

When you cook your own food, you can control the sodium. The recipes in this book are designed to minimize sodium, and this will benefit you especially if you want to lose weight. Check out the nutrient analysis under each recipe to know how much you are getting. Each recipe has a symbol, including one for low sodium, to represent the nutritional merits of the recipe and why you want to eat it.

## HIGH BLOOD PRESSURE

Blood pressure is a measure of two cardiac states: (1) the force in the arteries when the heart beats (known as *systolic pressure*) and (2) the force in the same arteries when the heart is at rest (known as *diastolic pressure*). Blood pressure is measured in

**TABLE 2-18 American Heart Association Blood Pressure Categories**

| Blood Pressure Category | Systolic (mm Hg) | | Diastolic (mm Hg) |
|---|---|---|---|
| Normal | Less than 120 | and | less than 80 |
| Prehypertension | 120–139 | or | 80–89 |
| High | | | |
| Stage 1 | 140–159 | or | 90–99 |
| Stage 2 | 160 or higher | or | 100 or higher |

*Your doctor should evaluate unusually low readings.

*Source:* www.Americanheart.org.

millimeters of mercury (abbreviated mm Hg). High blood pressure (or hypertension) is defined in an adult as a blood pressure greater than or equal to 140 mm Hg systolic pressure or greater than or equal to 90 mm Hg diastolic pressure.

High blood pressure directly increases the risk of coronary heart disease (which leads to heart attack) and stroke, especially when it is present with other risk factors.

High blood pressure can occur in children or adults, but it is more common among people age 35 and older. It is particularly prevalent in African-Americans, middle-aged and elderly people, obese people, heavy drinkers, and women who are taking birth control pills. Hypertension may run in families, but many people with strong family histories of high blood pressure may never get it. People with diabetes mellitus, gout, or kidney disease are more likely to have high blood pressure, too.

The American Heart Association's recommended blood pressure levels are shown in Table 2-18.

One key element to good circulation is a balance of minerals, especially sodium. Read food labels and know the amount of sodium food products contain, especially highly processed and convenience foods. Consuming natural foods such as fruit, vegetables, and whole grains, all of which are naturally low in sodium, will help you keep balance in your diet. Regular checkups with your physician to monitor your blood pressure will help know whether you are okay.

## PHYSICAL ACTIVITY

Are you physically active or are you a couch potato?

To feel your best and to aid you in reducing your risk of chronic health conditions, a minimum of thirty minutes a day of exercise is critical. For children, sixty to ninety minutes per day of rigorous exercise is suggested by most authorities. To aid in weight loss, forty-five to ninety minutes daily of exercise is suggested for most people.

Physical activity is important. Weight-resistance exercise may enhance bone density, and aerobic activity and may also reduce the risk of developing medical conditions such as diabetes and hypertension. Studies have associated yoga with better blood sugar control in persons who have diabetes. From yoga to brisk walks and free weights, a rounded routine is best. One hour of physical exercise may burn 100 to 200 calories. Sports and dancing are fun and offer more ways to maintain good muscle tone. To keep weight off, exercise more than sixty minutes each day.

If you can work it into your schedule, use the three-to-one rule: Be active for three hours after each meal you eat. Activity not only includes fun sports, but also brisk walking, house cleaning, and physical work such as gardening. You could do wall pushups in your office, use free weights while you read your e-mails, use stretch bands at your desk, or do squats before you firmly place your butt on the couch.

People who have physical limitations have special needs. Always consult with your physician and an exercise physiologist or a physical therapist to find the best solution if you can be physically active and if you have medical conditions— especially if you are out of shape and need to recondition. Table 2-18 can help you decide what is right for you. Remember, make exercise changes gradually.

The greater the intensity of your activity, the more calories you will burn and the more muscle you will achieve. You can engage in many different types of activities, but two of the most enjoyable are *recreational sports* and *competitive recreational sports.*

Recreational sports include bicycling, running, rowing, golf, tennis, swimming, and rollerblading.

Competitive recreational sports include tennis, basketball, racquetball, hockey, soccer, gymnastics, swimming, squash, and boxing.

Using Table 2-19, you can make positive choices about what you want to accomplish. Remember, though, to always consult with your physician and a certified personal trainer, especially if you have medical conditions, to be sure a chosen exercise is right for you.

The benefits of exercise increase the quality of life and will make you smile, which is the best cure if you are feeling down.

## SUMMARY

According to the USDA's 2005 *Dietary Guidelines* advisory committee, its nine recommendations are based on significant scientific findings:

1. Consume a variety of foods within and among the basic food groups while staying within your energy needs.

2. Control your calorie intake to manage your body weight.

3. Be physically active every day.

4. Increase your daily intake of fruits and vegetables, whole grains, and fat-free or low-fat milk and milk products.

5. Choose fats wisely for good health.

6. Choose carbohydrates wisely for good health.

## TABLE 2-19 Matrix for Exercise

| | |
|---|---|
| **Flexibility** | To start: Do 2 to 3 stretching exercises a few minutes before and after other exercises. Hold stretches for 15 to 30 seconds. Try to stretch all major muscle groups. Start with 5 minutes. Minimum goal: 15 minutes daily.<br><br>Benefits: Reduces tension, may lower blood sugar and risk of injury, and improves posture.<br><br>Other types of stretching: dance, yoga, Pilates, and gymnastics. |
| **Strength Conditioning** | To start: Do 3 exercises, 8 repetitions each, and 1 to 2 sets 2 times a week. Gradually increase to 4 to 6 exercises, 10 repetitions each, and 2 sets 3 times a week; then 7 to 8 exercises, 12 repetitions each, and 3 sets 4 times a week.<br><br>Benefits: Improves posture, increases strength, promotes healthy bones and muscle tone, improves athletic performance, and enhances weight loss.<br><br>Types: yoga, Pilates, free weights, weight-resistance machines. |
| **Structured Aerobic Activity** | To start: Do 15 to 20 minutes, 3 times a week. Then increase to 30 minutes 4 times a week, then increase to 40 to 60 minutes or more 5 to 7 times a week. Ultimately, 45 to 60 minutes, 7 times per week at 60% to 90% of maximum heart rate: continuous, sustained, and rhythmical.<br><br>Types: walking, rowing, cycling, swimming, karate, cross-country ski machines, treadmills, jogging, and elliptical trainers.<br><br>Benefits: Builds cardiovascular endurance, reduces body fat, increases energy, reduces risk of heart disease and other health risk factors, and promotes weight loss. |
| **Active Lifestyle** | 30 to 90 minutes of accumulated activity on most or all days.<br><br>Activities: Walk instead of driving; housecleaning, raking leaves, shoveling, and taking stairs. |

7. Choose and prepare foods with little salt.

8. If you drink alcoholic beverages, do so in moderation.

9. Keep your food safe to eat.

   To make the list an even ten:

10. Choose environmentally safe and unprocessed food.

You now have learned nutrition basics. Congratulations! You have learned a lot about carbohydrates, glycemic index, fats, protein, fluids, phytonutrients, fiber, weight management, and sodium and the relationship of each to your overall health. Understanding why you should eat certain foods is so important to eating fit and being fit. This is the first step to change and to creating lifelong healthy habits. The next important area to understand is about vitamins and minerals in the next chapter.

# Chapter 3

# VITAMINS AND MINERALS

Vitamins and minerals are necessary for normal body function and cannot be made by the body. They are not metabolized into energy and therefore provide no calories. Both vitamins and minerals are essential for organs to do their jobs: metabolize food, carry out daily activities, assist in normal growth and development, and sustain life. Eating a wide variety of foods is the best way to meet all of your vitamin and mineral needs.

Thirteen vitamins are critical to human physiology: nine water-soluble and four fat-soluble. *Water-soluble* means that the vitamin dissolves in water (in foods or in your body). In foods, these vitamins are more likely to be destroyed or lost during cooking and storage. Once in the body, they can travel in the blood; excess amounts can be excreted in the urine. Because they are not stored in the body, you need a fresh supply every day. *Fat-soluble* vitamins dissolve in the fat in foods. These vitamins can be stored in your fat cells; if they are present in excess, they have a higher risk of toxicity than do water-soluble vitamins. Toxic amounts are unlikely from foods, as opposed to supplements.

Minerals are also separated into two categories: macrominerals and trace minerals. *Macrominerals* are needed in large quantities. For example, calcium is abundant in the body, making up the structures of bones and teeth, and present to a lesser extent in blood and muscles. *Trace minerals* are also vital, but they are only needed in small quantities.

Table 3-1 describes each fat-soluble vitamin and mineral, its functions in the body, the foods in which it can be found, what happens when you do not get enough (called a *deficiency*), what happens when you get too much (*toxicity*), and any other pertinent information. Tables 3-2, 3-3, and 3-4 provide the same information for water-soluble vitamins, macrominerals, and trace minerals, respectively. Box 3-1 shows rich sources of zinc.

**TABLE 3-1 Fat-Soluble Vitamins Needed for Human Physiology**

| Fat-Soluble Vitamins | Function in Body | Food Sources | Deficiency and Toxicity | Notes |
|---|---|---|---|---|
| **Vitamin A** | Many important roles in eyesight, cell division, bone growth, prevention of infections and diseases, and skin maintenance. | Milk, liver, fortified or enriched cereals, orange fruits and vegetables: carrots, sweet potatoes, pumpkin, peaches | Too little: Hardening of skin and hair, abnormalities in bone development, night blindness<br><br>Too much: Yellow skin, liver damage | Can be eaten as a precursor (beta-carotene, for example) and converted to vitamin A in the body. |
| **Vitamin D** | Formation of bones and teeth; aids absorption of calcium from the intestines; maintains normal levels of calcium and phosphorous in the blood. | Egg yolks, fish, fortified milk | Too little: Soft bones—called *rickets* in children and *osteomalacia* in adults<br><br>Too much: Calcification of soft body tissues | The body can make vitamin D after exposure to sunlight. The ultraviolet rays trigger vitamin D synthesis in the skin. |
| **Vitamin E** | Antioxidant that helps protect cells from damage; important for health of red blood cells | Nuts, seeds, vegetable oils, leafy green vegetables, avocados, wheat germ, whole grains | Too little: Adverse effects on the stability of membranes and cells<br><br>Too much: Stomach upset | Relatively nontoxic |
| **Vitamin K** | Essential for blood clotting; important in bone formation | Dark leafy green vegetables, egg yolks, liver, legumes, herbal tea, green tea | Too little: Profuse bleeding and bruising<br><br>Too much: Hemolytic anemia (breakdown of red blood cells) | Vitamin K is also produced in the intestines by bacteria. |

**TABLE 3-2 Water-Soluble Vitamins Needed for Human Physiology**

| Water-Soluble Vitamins | Function in Body | Food Sources | Deficiency and Toxicity | Notes |
|---|---|---|---|---|
| **Vitamin B$_1$ (Thiamin)** | Converts carbohydrates into energy; necessary for heart, muscles, and nervous system | Pork, whole wheat, beef, liver, fortified pasta, soy, peas | Too little: Beriberi—loss of energy, nerve damage, muscular weakness | |
| **Vitamin B$_2$ (Riboflavin)** | Converts food to energy. | Meats, fish, whole grains, milk, vegetables, legumes, fortified or enriched grains | Too little: Dry, scaly skin; cracked lips; vision problems; nerve damage | |
| **Vitamin B$_3$ (Niacin)** | Converts food to energy; important for nerve function | Meat, poultry, eggs, milk, cheese, fortified or enriched cereals | Too little: Weakness, pellagra, dermatitis (scaly skin), diarrhea, dementia <br><br> Too much: Flushing and itching of skin, liver damage | |
| **Vitamin B$_5$ (Pantothenic Acid)** | Important for metabolism of fats, carbohydrates, proteins | Corn, lentils, peas, egg yolk, cheese, whole grains, nuts, avocados, sweet potatoes | Too little: Dermatitis, numbness, muscle cramps | |
| **Vitamin B$_6$** | Builds amino acids; involved in protein metabolism, red blood cell metabolism, and production of hemoglobin (to carry oxygen in blood); important for nerve system and immune system; maintains blood glucose (sugar) | Meat, poultry, fish, egg yolk, beans, peanuts and walnuts, fortified or enriched cereals, potatoes, bananas, seeds, spinach | Too little: Impaired production of hemoglobin and neurotransmitters, weakness <br><br> Too much: Nerve dysfunction | |

| | | | |
|---|---|---|---|
| Folate (Folic Acid) | DNA metabolism, production of red blood cells, cell division, and tissue growth | Liver, dark green leafy vegetables, beans, peas, enriched grains, citrus fruits, poultry | Too little: Birth defects, megoblastic anemia (red blood cells so big they cannot divide)<br><br>Too much: Can mask vitamin $B_{12}$ deficiency | |
| Vitamin $B_{12}$ | Maintains healthy nerve cells and red blood cells; helps make DNA | Fish, red meat, poultry, eggs, milk, fortified or enriched cereals | Too little: Pernicious anemia (such as megoblastic anemia, folate deficiency), confusion, dizziness | Found naturally only in animal products |
| Biotin | Role in metabolism of fat, protein, and carbohydrates | Almonds, liver, soybeans, fish | Too little: Nausea, loss of appetite | Produced by intestinal bacteria |
| Vitamin C | Antioxidant, collagen formation, healing of wounds, role in immune system; increases absorption of iron; essential for healthy bones, teeth, and blood vessels | Citrus fruits, berries, kiwi, peppers, tomatoes, broccoli, spinach, potatoes | Too little: Scurvy—bleeding gums, loose teeth, anemia, poor wound healing, weakness<br><br>Too much: Diarrhea, nausea, kidney stones, rebound scurvy | |

**TABLE 3-3 Macrominerals Needed for Human Physiology**

| Macrominerals | Function in Body | Food Sources | Deficiency and Toxicity | Notes |
|---|---|---|---|---|
| Calcium | Development of bones and teeth, muscle contraction, blood vessel contraction and dilation, secretion of hormones and enzymes, sending messages through the nerve system | Milk, yogurt, hard cheeses, broccoli, dark green leafy vegetables, soy, fortified foods such as orange juice | Too little: Decreased bone density leading to osteoporosis<br><br>Too much: Deposition of calcium in soft tissues and organs | |
| Chloride | Component of stomach acid; important for regulating the body's acid–base balance | Table salt, salt substitutes; found in many animal and plant foods | Too little: Disturbances in acid–base balance, potassium loss, low body fluid<br><br>Too much: Elevated blood pressure | |
| Magnesium | Component of enzymes (substances that promote biochemical reactions in the body); essential for normal functioning of nerves and muscles; important for strong bones | Nuts, legumes, whole grains, soybeans, seafoods, leafy green vegetables, potatoes, avocados, bananas, chocolate | Too little: Muscle spasms, irregular heartbeat, leg cramps, weakness<br><br>Too much: Drowsiness, weakness, diarrhea | |
| Phosphorus | Structural component of all cells and cell membranes; critical for energy production and DNA and protein synthesis | Dairy foods, meats, fish, eggs, soft drinks | Too little: Bone pain, weakness<br><br>Too much: Disrupts calcium absorption, metabolism, and utilization | |

| | | | |
|---|---|---|---|
| **Potassium** | Helps maintain water balance and cellular integrity; involved in muscle and nervous systems | Potatoes, citrus fruits, tomatoes, dried fruits, bananas, all other fruits and vegetables, whole grains, legumes | Too little: Impaired growth, bone fragility, muscle weakness, lowered heart rate<br><br>Too much: Muscle weakness, abnormal heart rates |
| **Sodium** | Regulates body fluid volume, muscle contraction, and nerve transmission; transports other molecules across cellular membranes | Table salt, fast food, soya sauce, teriyaki sauce, processed and convenience food (canned soups, rice with seasonings, frozen meals), olives, pickles, sausage, coldcuts, meat tenderizers | Too little: Low blood pressure, muscle twitching, water toxicity<br><br>Too much: Elevated blood pressure, swelling |

**TABLE 3-4 Trace Minerals Needed for Human Physiology**

| Trace Minerals | Function in Body | Food Sources | Deficiency and Toxicity | Notes |
|---|---|---|---|---|
| Chromium | Needed for normal carbohydrate metabolism | Whole grains, meats, cheeses, eggs | Too little: Severe disturbances in carbohydrate metabolism<br><br>Too much: Inhibits insulin activity; carcinogenic activity | Foods contain chromic chloride. Supplements contain chromium picolinate, which is absorbed better. |
| Copper | Component of many enzyme systems; needed for collagen formation and synthesis of hemoglobin | Shellfish, fish, whole grains, beans, nuts, eggs | Too little: Decline in red blood cell production leading to anemia, impaired bone and hair formation, nervous system impairment<br><br>Too much: Nausea, vomiting, muscle aches, and stomach pains; destruction of red blood cells | |
| Fluoride | Essential to teeth and bones | Seafood, liver, tea, eggs, florinated water | Too little: Cavities<br><br>Too much: Destruction of teeth, vomiting | Most of the U.S. water supply is supplemented with fluoride. |
| Iodine | Essential for thyroid and production of thyroid hormone, which regulates metabolism | Seafood, iodized salt | Too little: Slowed growth and sexual development in children, mental retardation, deafness, goiter<br><br>Too much: Rash, headaches, breathing difficulty | |

| | Function | Sources | Too little / Too much | Notes |
|---|---|---|---|---|
| **Iron** | Necessary for oxygen transport by red blood cells, collagen synthesis, immune function | Heme: Red meats, other animal foods  Nonheme: Beans, dark leafy vegetables, nuts, fortified grains | Too little: Anemia (low red blood count, small red blood cells), weakness, paleness  Too much: Vomiting, cramps, constipation, severe overdoses can be deadly | Two forms of iron: heme and nonheme  Heme is absorbed better.  Acidity helps absorption of iron (tomato or citrus) |
| **Selenium** | Antioxidant; important for many enzymes | Seafood, whole grains, mushrooms, liver, meat, vegetables, depending on the soil in which they were grown | Too little: Heart problems, increased risk of cancer, impaired immune function  Too much: Tooth decay, nerve problems, hair and nail loss, heart problems | |
| **Zinc** | Essential for many enzyme reactions, healthy immune system, wound healing, DNA synthesis, normal growth and development | Seafood, meats, poultry, eggs, whole grains, beans, nuts | Too little: Diarrhea, hair loss, impaired protein synthesis and energy production  Too much: Vomiting, stomach pain, kidney failure, poor coordination, dizziness | Absorbed better from animal foods than plant foods |

## BOX 3-1 Some Rich Sources of Zinc (Zn)

| | |
|---|---|
| Barley, pearl, raw | Beans, baked |
| Beans, black, cooked | Beans, white |
| Beef, lean sirloin, cooked | Beef liver, cooked |
| Beef, round eye, cooked | Cereals, ready to eat, whole grain |
| Chick peas | Corn meal, yellow, whole |
| Cow peas (black-eyed peas), cooked | Lamb, leg, cooked |
| Lentils, cooked | Peas, split, cooked |
| Rice, white, long-grain | Ricotta cheese, part skim |
| Roast beef sub sandwich | Seeds, mature, cooked |
| Soybeans, mature, cooked | Tostada with guacamole |
| Turkey, dark meat | Wheat flavor, whole grain |
| Wild rice, cooked | Yogurt, plain fat-free |

# SECTION 2

# Recipes

# ABOUT COOKING

The cooking methods described below are recommended over sautéing foods in butter, margarine, or oil. Flavors are enhanced instead with herbs, spices, and other vegetables such as onions, peppers, and mushrooms.

## Quickest and Low Calorie

### Convection Cooking

Convection ovens offer six modes: convection bake, roast, broil, pastry, drying, and thaw serve. Because the fan moves heated air continuously throughout the oven, the cooking time is usually a few minutes less than normal cooking time. In baking, the oven automatically reduces temperature by 25°F after the conventional oven temperature is entered. The forced air penetrates food more quickly with convection, speeding up the cooking process. The even heat allows for larger quantities to be cooked at the same time. Energy savings are an added benefit.

### Conventional Baking

Although slightly longer than convection cooking, conventional baking also offers a lower fat alternative to other cooking methods. Oven cooking is easy.

### Grilling or Broiling

Grilling and broiling are easy to do, and new indoor grills allow similar effects to outdoor grills. It is recommended not to blacken foods, however, because this process increases carcinogens that could cause cancer. In Japan, the people with the highest incidences of stomach cancer are thought to have consumed large amounts of charcoaled fish over their lifetimes.

### Microwaving

Most microwaves have several settings that allow quick cooking without added fat; this causes less drying than conventional cooking. Studies demonstrate that greater nutrients are retained in food cooked by this method especially vegetables. Overcooking can dry the food, however, so be careful. One advantage is that day-old bread and muffins can be heated briefly to restore freshness. Defrosting frozen items becomes easy and can be done in minutes on days you are pressed for time.

### Poaching

Using water, wine, or broth with herbs can be a low-calorie way to cook many foods such as fish, chicken, and vegetables. Simply place food in a shallow pan over medium high heat on the stove top, cover, and poach until done.

## Steaming

Place a small amount of water in a pot on the stove top and, using a steaming rack or directly placing vegetables in the pot with water, cover the pot and bring to a boil, steaming the foods until they are tender. A good way to add great flavor without high fat butter or oil is to add herbs with the vegetables.

## Stir-Frying

Stir-frying does not require the oil used in many Asian restaurants. Over high heat, add meat, fish, vegetables, tofu, or poultry to a nonstick pan or wok. Only a tiny amount of oil or a nonstick spray is required, if any. Simply toss the food a few times; it cooks in just minutes. Broth or water may be used instead of oil in small amounts to prevent sticking.

# Chapter 4

# APPETIZERS

## BAKED TORTILLA AND CHEESE MELT

*This is a delicious way for children and adults to get calcium. Just follow this rule of thumb: Do not deprive yourself, but set healthy portion boundaries.*

**Vegetarian: Lacto-ovo**

6 oz. Baked tortilla chips, organic, unsalted (1 bag)

8 oz. Salsa, commercial, mild

8 oz. Cheddar cheese, reduced fat, shredded

Total time: Microwave, 2 minutes; conventional: 7 minutes
Serves: 6
Serving size: 3-1/3 oz. or 1/6
Exchange: 1-1/2 starch, 1 medium fat meat

### Oven Method

1. Preheat oven to 450°F.
2. Cover a cookie sheet with chips one layer deep. Spread salsa on chips and top with cheese.
3. Bake in oven for 6 minutes or until cheese is melted. Serve immediately.

### Microwave Method

1. Place chips on microwavable plate one layer deep. Spread salsa on chips and top with cheese.
2. Place in microwave and heat for 50 seconds or until cheese is melted. Serve immediately.

Rule of thumb: DON'T DEPRIVE YOURSELF, BUT SET HEALTHY PORTION BOUNDARIES!

**Nutrition Information:**

CAL 182  CHO 25G  PRO 12G  FAT 4G  CHOL 8MG  CALCIUM 283MG  POTASSIUM 151MG  SODIUM 525MG  FIBER 3G

# BEAN AND TOMATO BROCHETTE

*These brochettes are rich in antioxidants and fiber. My teenagers love this recipe, which also makes a great afternoon snack or appetizer.*

**Vegetarian: Vegan**

Total time: 10 minutes
Serves: 8
Serving size: 2
Exchange: 3 starch, 1 medium fat meat

2 medium Tomatoes, vine-ripened, diced
1 small Onion, red, chopped
1 Tbsp. Olive oil
15-1/2 oz. can Small white beans (navy), drained
2 Tbsp. Basil, fresh, chopped (or 1 Tbsp. dried)
4 drops Tabasco sauce (optional)
1 French bread loaf, 16 inches, cut in 1-inch slices

1. Mix all ingredients. Chill (optional).
2. Top each sliced baguette with bean mixture. Serve immediately.

## Serving Suggestion

This easy bean mixture can be made a day ahead. Freeze French bread to keep it fresh or buy fresh bread the day it is to be served.

Another option is to place a whole baguette on a cutting board with a knife next to the bean mixture and allow your guests or hungry teenagers to serve themselves. Tomatoes taste best in August and September when they are picked fresh from the vine and basil is fresh from the farm.

**Nutrition Information:**

CAL 255  CHO 45G  PRO 11G  FAT 4G  CHOL 0MG  CALCIUM 48MG  POTASSIUM 456MG  SODIUM 337MG  FIBER 6G

# DELICIOUS STUFFED MUSHROOMS

*These mushrooms are lower in fat, unlike most stuffed foods.*

16 large Stuffing mushrooms

1 medium Onion, chopped

2 tsp. Olive oil

1/2 cup Bread crumbs

1/4 cup White wine*

1/4 cup Chicken bouillon, reconstituted, low-sodium type

2 Tbsp. Parmesan cheese

Total time: 35 minutes
Serves: 8
Serving size: 2 mushrooms
Exchange: 1 vegetable, 1/2 fat

1. Clean mushrooms by brushing off any dirt. Remove stems and place tops in shallow casserole pan.
2. Chop mushroom stems and onion. Place in saucepan with oil and sauté until onions are translucent.
3. Add white wine and bouillon. Simmer 5 minutes.
4. Remove from heat and pour in a mixing bowl. Add bread crumbs and Parmesan cheese and mix to a smooth consistency.
5. Stuff each mushroom with enough mixture to fill its cavity.
6. Bake at 350°F for 20 minutes or until tender.

## Serving Suggestion

Make ahead and zap in the microwave about 1 minute as a great after-school snack or appetizer.

**Nutrition Information:**

CAL 67  CHO 8G  PRO 3G  FAT 2G  CHOL 1MG  CALCIUM 43MG  POTASSIUM 221MG  SODIUM 122MG  FIBER 1G

*If you choose not to use wine, double the amount of bouillon in the recipe.

# EGGPLANT CAPONATA

*This recipe contains powerful phytonutrients for memory, skin, and more.*

**Vegetarian: Vegan**

1 large Eggplant

1 medium Onion, chopped

1 Tbsp. Olive oil

4 oz. Artichoke hearts, marinated (1 jar;
  save 1 Tbsp. of liquid), drained and chopped

1-1/2 cup Tomato sauce (Classico brand: Florentine)

1/2 cup Stewed tomatoes, chopped

10 large Stuffed green olives, chopped

1/2 tsp. Garlic, minced, fresh

10 large Black olives, pitted, chopped

2 tsp. Capers, rinsed and drained

1 Tbsp. Artichoke liquid from jar (see above)

1 Tbsp. Vinegar, red wine

To taste Salt and pepper

1/4 tsp. Oregano

> Total time: 25 minutes
> Serves: 8
> Serving size: 1/2 cup
> Exchange: 1 starch, 1 fat, 1 vegetable

1. Preheat oven to 350°F.
2. Wash eggplant and place in baking dish whole. Pierce skin with fork once. Bake approximately 15 minutes or until eggplant is soft and mushy.
3. While eggplant is cooking, sauté onions in oil in a small frying pan then remove from heat.
4. Remove eggplant from oven and cut into small pieces, leaving the skin on.
5. Place eggplant pieces in a mixing bowl. Add onions, olive oil, tomato sauce, stewed tomatoes, green olives, garlic, black olives, capers, liquid from artichoke jar, red wine vinegar, salt and pepper, and oregano to eggplant and mix until blended. Serve hot or cold.

## Serving Suggestion

This goes well with thinly sliced baguettes or pita wedges for dipping. If there are leftovers, add to a marinara sauce and serve over pasta for a quick meal.

**Nutrition Information:**

CAL 119  CHO 19G  PRO 2G  FAT 5G  CHOL 0MG  CALCIUM 38MG  POTASSIUM 458MG  SODIUM 542MG  FIBER 4G

# EGGPLANT ROLLENTINI

*Paulette Schneider, Registered Dietitian, Irving Center for Clinical Research at Columbia University, Bionutrition Unit*

1 package Extra firm tofu (not silken), drained

1 large Eggplant

1/2 medium Onion, diced

1 package Frozen spinach, defrosted and drained

2 Whites from eggs

12 oz. Tomato sauce

0.5 tsp. Basil and oregano mix

1 Tbsp. Parmesan or Romano cheese, grated

As needed Basil sprigs, fresh

**Vegetarian: Lacto-ovo**

Total time: 50 minutes
Serves: 10
Serving size:
Exchange: 1 vegetable,
1 medium fat dairy

1. Preheat oven to 400°F.
2. Manually squeeze the excess liquid from the spinach until it holds together in a ball.
3. Spray cookie sheets with nonstick pan coat.
4. Cut eggplant lengthwise into 1/8-inch slices (a large eggplant should yield approximately 20 slices). Eggplant may be peeled if desired before slicing. Lay slices of eggplant on cookie sheet and bake in oven for approximately 10 minutes until slices are pliable. Let cool for a few minutes.
5. Reduce oven heat to 350°F.
6. While eggplant is baking, place the tofu in a food processor and blend until creamy consistency is achieved; it should resemble ricotta cheese. Place tofu into mixing bowl and add spinach, onions, egg whites, 1 ounce of the mozzarella, and the hard cheese (Parmesan or Romano) and mix until blended.
7. Spray casserole or baking dish with nonstick pan coat and place one-half to two-thirds of the tomato sauce into the bottom of the baking dish and set aside until needed.

*(continues)*

# EGGPLANT ROLLENTINI (Continued)

8. Layer eggplant in a single layer on cutting board or other flat work surface. Place 1-1/2 Tablespoons of filling on the larger end of the eggplant slice and roll the bottom toward the top until the ends overlap (it should resemble a cannoli). Place each roll into the bed of tomato sauce in the baking dish and repeat until eggplant or filling is gone. Sprinkle with basil and oregano and top with mozzarella.
9. Cover baking dish with foil and bake for 20 to 25 minutes or until cheese melts and sauce is bubbling. Remove foil and bake another 5 to 10 minutes or until cheese browns.
10. Serve with fresh basil sprigs as garnish.

## Serving Suggestion

Serve on a bed of angel hair pasta with a green salad and crusty bread.

**Nutrition Information:**

CAL 119   CHO 11G   PRO 10G   FAT 5G   CHOL 5MG   CALCIUM 156MG   POTASSIUM 352MG   SODIUM 93MG   FIBER 3G

# GOAT CHEESE AND TOMATO ON BAGUETTE

*This recipe is great as a meal (whole serving or as a snack half serving).*

*Becky Levine*

8 oz. Goat cheese

1 16-inch loaf French bread, cut into 1/2-inch slices

1 sprig Rosemary, fresh, minced

1 Tbsp. Parsley, fresh, minced

3 medium Tomatoes, vine-ripened, diced

1/4 cup Black olives, large, pitted, chopped

1 Tbsp. Vinegar, red wine

1 tsp. Olive oil

1/16 tsp. Garlic powder

To taste Pepper, black

**Vegetarian: Lacto-ovo**

Total time: 8 minutes
Serves: 8
Serving size: 2 slices
Exchange: 2 starch, 1 high fat meat, 1 fat

1. Spread goat cheese thinly on baguette slices.
2. Top with herbs.
3. Combine remaining ingredients and place 2 to 3 Tablespoons of tomato mixture on each baguette slice.

**Nutrition Information:**

CAL 277  CHO 32G  PRO 12G  FAT 12G  CHOL 22MG  CALCIUM 135MG  POTASSIUM 214MG  SODIUM 518MG  FIBER 2G

# GRILLED PINEAPPLE AND TOFU KABOBS

*This recipe is rich in isoflavones to help make a healthy heart.*

13 oz. Tofu, extra firm, reduced fat
 (a single container in most places)
32 chunks Pineapple, fresh, cut into
 1-inch cubes

**Vegetarian: Vegan**

Total time: 25 minutes (plus 15
minutes marinating time)
Serves: 4 to 8
Serving size: 1 skewer
Exchange: 1 medium fat meat, 1/4 fruit

## Marinade

2 tsp. Soy sauce
2 tsp. Ginger, fresh, peeled and minced
1 tsp. Garlic, fresh, minced
1 Tbsp. Sesame seed oil

1. Prepare marinade and set aside.
2. Cut tofu into 1-inch cubes, place in bowl, and coat with marinade. Set aside.
3. Cut fresh pineapple into chunks.
4. Place tofu and pineapple on skewers, alternating, and totaling four pieces each. Pour marinade over skewers and keep covered in refrigerator from 15 minutes to 5 hours. When ready to cook, remove from refrigerator and place on grill. Turn skewers as each side browns, approximately 5 minutes each.

## Serving Suggestion

Serve on a platter over a bed of lettuce greens. Garnish with dried sesame seeds.

**Nutrition Information:**

CAL 70  CHO 5G  PRO 5G  FAT 4G  CHOL 0MG  CALCIUM 81MG  POTASSIUM 133MG  SODIUM 82MG  FIBER 1G

# GRANDMA DOT'S SWEET AND SOUR MEATBALLS

*Dorothy Court*

1 lb. Ground beef, 90 percent lean

1/4 cup Flaxseed, ground

6 oz. Chili sauce, bottled (low-sodium type optional)

1/2 cup Water

1/4 cup Molasses, dark

1 Onion, chopped

1 clove Garlic, minced

To taste Pepper, black

Total time: 20 minutes
Serves: 6
Serving size: 2
Exchange: 2 medium
fat meat, 1 fruit

1. Combine flaxseed meal and ground beef, then roll into 1-1/2-inch meatballs. Place on cookie sheet and bake at 350°F until lightly browned; turn approximately 10 to 15 minutes.

2. While meatballs brown, mix chili sauce, water, molasses, onion, garlic, and pepper in saucepan and cook over a medium heat until the onion is soft.

3. Remove the meatballs from the oven and add to the sauce. Simmer for 5 more minutes. Serve hot.

**Nutrition Information:**

CAL 205  CHO 18G  PRO 15G  FAT 7G  CHOL 47MG  CALCIUM 53MG  POTASSIUM 503MG  SODIUM 419MG*  FIBER 3G

*Use low sodium chili sauce if you want to lower your sodium intake.

# HUMMUS WITH OLIVES AND PITA

*This recipe creates a hummus that is lower in fat than most store brands. It offers a great medley of fiber, antioxidants, and calcium.*

12 oz. Chickpeas (one 15-1/2-oz. can drained)

1/4 cup plain Yogurt, fat-free, Greek*

**Vegetarian: Lacto-ovo**

1 Tbsp. Tahini (sesame seed paste)

1 medium Lemon, freshly squeezed juice

1 Tbsp. Garlic, minced

1 tsp. Olive oil

12 large Black olives, diced

4 Pita pockets, 6-inch diameter, whole wheat

Total time: 8 minutes
Serves: 8
Serving size: 1/2 pita
Exchange: 2 starch, 1 lean meat

1. Place all ingredients except pita in a blender or food processor and purée.
2. Spread 3 ounces of purée on one inside of the pita pocket.
3. Cut into quarters and serve, two pieces per serving.

## Serving Suggestion

These can be served whole as breakfast or lunch sandwiches with sliced tomato and romaine lettuce or cut into wedges to serve as an appetizer.

**Nutrition Information:**

CAL 206  CHO 35G  PRO 9G  FAT 5G  CHOL 0MG  CALCIUM 63MG  POTASSIUM 250 MG  SODIUM 314MG  FIBER 7G

*If you cannot find Greek yogurt, substitute plain fat-free yogurt.

# LOW-FAT MINI PIZZA BAGELS

*These are quick and offer a good source of calcium—and a children's favorite.*

**Vegetarian: Lacto-ovo**

4 Mini bagels, each cut in half

4 oz. Marinara (Italian-style tomato sauce)

2 medium Tomatoes, sliced 1/4-inch thick

8 oz. Mozzarella cheese, part skim, shredded

Total time: 10 minutes
Serves: 4
Serving size: 2 bagel halves
Exchange: 2 fat-free milk, 1 fat

1. Preheat oven to 500°F.
2. Place bagel halves on a cookie sheet, inside face up. On each half place 1 to 2 tablespoons marinara and then 1 tomato slice; top with 1 ounce of cheese.
3. Bake for 6 minutes or until cheese melts.

## Serving Suggestion

These can be made ahead and then frozen. Serve 1 hour before a sports event to boost energy. Bagels are dense, so use the mini size to maintain calorie balance. Use whole grains if possible.

**Nutrition Information:**

CAL 272  CHO 24G  PRO 19G  FAT 5G  CHOL 31MG  CALCIUM 443MG  POTASSIUM 306MG  SODIUM 584MG  FIBER 2G

# PORTABELLO NACHOS

*Mushrooms are known for their many health benefits. This recipe will put some "Wow!" into your next party.*

*Chef Brian MacMenamin*

4 Flour tortillas* (6-inch), cut into quarters
Olive oil
1/2 lb. (approx. 2) Portabello mushrooms,
  sliced
1/4 cup Chicken broth, low-salt
1 Tbsp. Lemon juice, freshly squeezed
1 Tbsp. Soy sauce, low-sodium
1 tsp. Olive oil
2 Tbsp. Basil, fresh, chopped (or 2 tsp. dried)
1 Tbsp. Thyme, fresh, chopped (or 1 tsp. dried)
1 cup Hummus
1/3 cup Tomato sauce
1/3 cup Feta cheese, crumbled
1 Lime, zested (optional)

Total time: 15 minutes
Serves: 8
Serving size: 1
Exchange: 1 vegetable, 1 starch

1. Preheat oven to 350°F.
2. Place tortilla quarters on a baking sheet and drizzle with olive oil. Bake for 8 minutes or until crisp.
3. In a medium sauté pan, add oil and mushrooms; sauté mushrooms until crisp and then add broth, lemon juice, soy sauce, and oil, then sprinkle with basil and thyme. Add broth and continue to cook until liquid evaporates.
4. Spread 1 Tablespoon hummus over each tortilla quarter and top with mushrooms. Top each serving with 1 teaspoon tomato sauce and 1 teaspoon feta cheese.
5. Place tortilla quarters on baking sheet. Bake for 5 minutes or until tortillas are thoroughly heated.
6. Garnish nachos with lime zest if desired. Serve immediately.

**Nutrition Information:**

CAL 139  CHO 16G  PRO 6G  FAT 6G  CHOL 6MG  CALCIUM 80MG  POTASSIUM 248MG  SODIUM 310MG  FIBER 3G

*High-fiber whole wheat tortillas optional.

# SNACK ATTACK COMBO

6 Ak-Mak flat bread crackers

6 Tbsp. Hummus, premade, original flavor

30 Grapes, sliced in half

**Vegetarian: Vegan**

Total: 2 minutes
Serves: 2
Serving size: 1/2

Spread hummus on crackers, top with grapes, and munch away.

**Nutrition Information:**

CAL 307  CHO 58G  PRO 9G  FAT 5G  CHOL 0MG  CALCIUM 60MG  POTASSIUM 318MG  SODIUM 436MG  FIBER 6G

# VIETNAMESE-STYLE SPRING ROLLS

*Chef Brian MacMenamin*

| |
|---|
| Total time: 30 minutes |
| Serves: 8 |
| Serving size: 1 spring roll |
| Exchange: 1 vegetable, 1 starch |

### Dipping Sauce

1/4 cup Fish sauce (nuoc mam or Thai
  nam pla)
2 Tbsp. Green onion, thinly sliced
1-1/2 Tbsp. Lime juice, freshly squeezed
Pinch Red pepper flakes

### Spring Roll Filling

1/4 cup Cilantro, fresh, minced
1/2 cup Green onions, cut into thin strips
1/2 cup Cucumber, peeled, seeded, and cut into thin strips
1 Red pepper, julienned
1 Red onion, julienned
1 small Zucchini, julienned
1 tsp. Sesame oil
4 cups Hot water
8 Vietnamese spring-roll sheets, 6-inch diameter

1. Mix fish sauce, green onion, lime juice, and red pepper flakes in small bowl. Set dipping sauce aside.
2. Combine cilantro, green onions, cucumber, red pepper, red onion, and zucchini and toss with 1 Tablespoon of reserved dipping sauce and sesame oil.
3. Pour hot water into large bowl. Using tongs, dip 1 spring-roll sheet in water for 5 seconds and then remove from water and place on wet towel. Let stand for 30 seconds (sheet should be pliable, but if it is still stiff, sprinkle with more water).
4. Place 1 Tablespoon of spring roll filling onto moistened sheet.
5. Fold sides of sheet over ends of filling. Starting at filled side, roll sheet until completely folded and held in place by moist sheet. Repeat with remaining sheets.
6. Serve with dipping sauce.

*(continues)*

# VIETNAMESE-STYLE SPRING ROLLS (Continued)

### Serving Suggestion

The only item in this recipe that is high in sodium is the fish sauce, so if you reduce it to 1 Tablespoon, you will have a low-sodium spring roll.

**Nutrition Information:**

CAL 114  CHO 22G  PRO 4G  FAT 1G  CHOL 17MG  CALCIUM 25MG  POTASSIUM 180MG  SODIUM 722MG  FIBER 2G

# Chapter 5

# BEVERAGES

## ABOUT TEA

Whether black, herbal, or green, teas have therapeutic phytochemicals that boost our immune system and fight against cancer by the action of flavonoids, which have antioxidant properties. Research is unfolding that corroborates that the incidence of oral, rectal, stomach, skin, and colon cancers is reduced in tea drinkers. As noted in Chapter 2, antioxidants work in the body to neutralize free radicals that can damage the body over time. This damage can cause disease and promote cancer. *Catechins* are a class of flavonoids that are found in tea, fruit, and vegetables. Catechins are strongly linked to decreased colon and rectal cancers.

Research is studying the effects of teas' flavonoids in reducing lipid oxidation, which decreases the chances of cardiovascular disease such as heart attacks and stroke. Some studies have linked tea consumption with decreased cholesterol and triglyceride levels. New studies are unfolding a possible benefit for improved bone density and oral health by reducing dental caries. Some teas contain licorice root and other herbs that help fight allergies and provide other benefits such as to mood and memory. The leaves of the plants used are usually the most active sources of phytochemicals, so beware if flavorings are added. For example, raspberry tea is often used to reduce the symptoms of premenstrual syndrome, but some raspberry teas only contain artificial flavoring. A caution to pregnant women, however: Raspberry tea may induce uterine contraction.

If you drink black teas that contain caffeine, note that the tannins in tea block the action of caffeine so it will not have the same side effects as coffee. Tannins found in both decaffeinated and caffeinated teas may reduce the absorption and utilization of iron, so if you are deficient in iron, limit your daily intake to one or fewer cups.

Most research links black and green teas with health benefits, but studies also show that many herbal teas offer other health benefits. The concentration of active ingredients in some teas made in the United States such as green tea may have weaker results than those from Asia.

# CHILLED CAFÉ SOY LATTÉ

*This beverage contains isoflavones that will help reduce menopause symptoms (e.g., hot flashes), improve heart health, lower the risk of cancer, and more.*

1 cup Ice, crushed or cubed

1/2 cup Coffee, organic, decaffeinated*

1-1/2 cup Soy milk, vanilla or chocolate, 1 percent fat

2 Cinnamon sticks (optional)

**Vegetarian: Vegan**

Total time: 5 minutes
Serves: 2
Serving size: 1-1/2 cup
Exchange: 3/4 fat-free milk

1. Crush ice in blender.
2. Add all ingredients and blend on high.
3. Pour in two tall glasses and garnish with cinnamon sticks. Serve.

**Nutrition Information:**

CAL 75  CHO 9G  PRO 6G  FAT 2G  CHOL 0MG  CALCIUM 227MG  POTASSIUM 184MG  SODIUM 136MG  FIBER 2G

*Chlorine is often used in the process of removing caffeine from coffee. *Organic* usually means that a different process is used and may denote no chlorine.

# COLD CHAI TEA LATTÉ

*The phytonutrients in this beverage help reduce the risk of stroke.*

**Vegetarian: Vegan**

Total time: 2 minutes
Serves: 2
Serving size: 1 cup
Exchange: 1/2 fat-free milk, 1/2 fruit; reduced sugar version, 1/2 fat-free milk

1 cup Soy milk*, vanilla, 1 percent fat

1 cup Chai tea latte**

2 Cinnamon sticks

6 Ice cubes (or equivalent amount of crushed ice)

Divide all ingredients equally between two glasses, mix gently, and serve.

## Serving Suggestion

This latte can be served hot as well as cold by eliminating the ice cubes and heating the beverage for 1 minute in the microwave or 3 minutes in a saucepan on the stove.

**Nutrition Information:**

CAL 71  CHO 11G  PRO 4G  FAT 2G  CHOL 0MG  CALCIUM 154MG  POTASSIUM 156MG  SODIUM 92MG  FIBER 1G

**Reduced Sugar Version**

CAL 46  CHO 3G  PRO 4G  FAT 2G  CHOL 0MG  CALCIUM 154MG  POTASSIUM 156MG  SODIUM 92MG  FIBER 1G

*Usually contains 3 grams of soy protein. Twenty-five grams of soy protein with a low-fat diet may reduce heart disease. Be sure the soy milk brand is enriched with calcium.

**The Original Oregon Chai, available in the tea section of many supermarkets and health food stores. Try the caffeine-free version. A reduced sugar or sugar free version is available for diabetics.

# HOT SPICED APPLE CIDER

*This drink contains lots of cinnamon, which aids insulin performance.*

4 cup Apple cider, pasteurized
1/4 cup Orange juice (not concentrate)
1 medium Orange, sliced
1 tsp. Cloves, whole
1/4 tsp. Nutmeg, ground
4 Cinnamon sticks

**Vegetarian: Vegan**

Total time: 8 minutes
Serves: 4
Serving size: 1 cup
Exchange: 2 fruit

1. Place all ingredients in a 2-quart pot and simmer over medium heat for 10 minutes.
2. Strain liquid to remove oranges and cloves.
3. Serve mugs with cinnamon sticks as garnish.

**Tip:** People who are trying to lose weight or control diabetes should limit themselves to a 1/2-cup portion.

**Nutrition Information:**
CAL 133  CHO 33G  PRO 0G  FAT 0G  CHOL 0MG  CALCIUM 33MG  POTASSIUM 356MG  SODIUM 8MG  FIBER 1G

# OLD-FASHIONED HOT CHOCOLATE

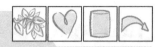

*This version of hot chocolate has less fat and more calcium than most instant forms. Calcium boosts bone density and reduces the risk of osteoporosis.*

**Vegetarian: Lacto-ovo**

Total time: 5 minutes
Serves: 1
Serving size: 1 cup
Exchange: With sugar substitute,
1 fat-free milk; with sugar, 1 fat-free
milk, 1 fruit

1 cup Fat-free milk
2 Tbsp. Cocoa powder, unsweetened
1 Tbsp. Raw sugar or brown sugar
  or
1 package Sugar substitute
To taste Cinnamon (optional, but it helps insulin action)

---

1. Stir together fat-free milk and cocoa powder in a saucepan over medium heat to desired temperature, approximately 4 minutes.
2. Pour the hot cocoa into a cup, add cinnamon and sugar or sugar substitute, and serve hot.

## Serving Suggestion

For a creamier texture and more protein, use the fat-free milk brands known as Plus Milk or Fit Milk, which are found in select supermarkets.

**Nutrition Information:**

**With Sugar**

CAL 147  CHO 23G  PRO 9G  FAT 1G  CHOL 4G  CALCIUM 330MG  POTASSIUM 614MG  SODIUM 133MG  FIBER 1G

**With Sugar Substitute**

CAL 109  CHO 16G  PRO 9G  FAT 1G  CHOL 4G  CALCIUM 320MG  POTASSIUM 571MG  SODIUM 129MG  FIBER 1G

# PEACH ICED TEA

*This iced tea includes cinnamon, which enhances insulin action, elevated calcium with mineral water, and antioxidants.*

**Vegetarian: Vegan**

2 tea bags Peach tea

12 oz. Mineral water

1 cup Ice, crushed

2 tsp. Sugar (or sugar substitute)

2 Cinnamon sticks

2 Mint sprigs, fresh (optional)

Total time: 6 minutes
Serves: 2
Serving size: 8 oz.
Exchange: With sugar substitute,
1/2 fruit; with sugar, 1 fruit

1. Boil mineral water and remove from heat.
2. Add tea bags and let stand 5 minutes.
3. Remove tea bags and pour into two glasses.
4. Add ice and sugar and then mix gently. Serve each glass with a cinnamon stick.

**Nutrition Information:**

**With Sugar**

CAL 73  CHO 18G  PRO 1G  FAT 0G  CHOL 0MG  CALCIUM 105MG  POTASSIUM 486MG  SODIUM 3MG  FIBER 0G

# SELTZER CITRUS SPLASH

*This is a refreshing way to boost your vitamin C.*

3/4 cup Seltzer, zero sodium

1/4 cup Orange juice (not from concentrate)

1/4 cup Cranberry juice

As needed Ice, crushed

3 Strawberries, sliced

**Vegetarian: Vegan**

Total time: 2 minutes
Serves: 1
Serving size: 1 cup
Exchange: 1 fruit

Blend liquids, pour over ice, add berries, and enjoy.

**Nutrition Information:**

CAL 73  CHO 18G  PRO 1G  FAT 0G  CHOL 0MG  CALCIUM 15MG  POTASSIUM 180MG  SODIUM 4MG  FIBER 1G

# SOOTHING CHAMOMILE ICE TEA

*If consumed three times a day, this tea provides significant anti-inflammatory activity. It also helps teething, stress, wound healing, gastric reflux, and upset stomach. In specialty food stores, you can buy chamomile root and make your own tea, which will have even more health benefits.*

1 Tbsp. Chamomile tea (dried flowers—bag or loose)

1 cup Hot water

1 Lemon wedge

1 Tbsp. Honey* or sugar substitute

2 Mint leaves, fresh

4 Ice cubes

**Vegetarian: Vegan**

Total time: 10 minutes
Serves: 1
Serving size: 1 cup
Exchange: With sugar substitute, free; with honey, 1 fruit

1. Place tea bag or loose tea in a strainer, then place in water and allow to steep for 4 minutes.
2. Remove tea bag or strainer, add honey or sugar substitute and stir. Cool 5 minutes.
3. Pour cooled tea over ice.
4. Squeeze in lemon juice and top with fresh mint.

**Nutrition Information:**

**Without honey**

| CAL 0** | CHO 17g | PRO 0g | FAT 0g | CHOL 0mg | CALCIUM 0mg | POTASSIUM 15mg | SODIUM 0mg | FIBER 0g |
|---|---|---|---|---|---|---|---|---|

*Warning: Pregnant women and children younger than 2 should avoid honey because it contains potentially harmful natural bacteria.

**With honey, 60 calories.

# SPICY VEGETABLE COCKTAIL

*This cocktail has two excellent phytonutrients: Beta-carotene, which will help your eyes, and lycopenes, which reduces the risk of prostate cancer.*

3/4 cup Vegetable juice, low-sodium

1 Tbsp. Lemon juice, fresh

Few drops Tabasco sauce

1/4 tsp. Horseradish, bottled

3 Ice cubes (or 1/2 cup crushed ice)

1 Celery stick (garnish)

To taste Pepper

**Vegetarian: Vegan**

Total time: 3 minutes
Serves: 1
Serving size: 1 cup
Exchange: 1 vegetable

Place all ingredients in a glass and stir or put in blender to crush the ice, then pour into a glass. Add celery stick garnish and serve.

### Serving Suggestion

When entertaining, make enough for a crowd by multiplying the amount of ingredients by the number you want to serve—and offer as a refreshing change to soda. For example, to serve five people, multiply each ingredient amount by five.

**Nutrition Information:**

CAL 31  CHO 8G  PRO 1G  FAT 0G  CHOL 0MG  CALCIUM 27MG  POTASSIUM 299MG  SODIUM 121MG  FIBER 1G

# TROPICAL SMOOTHIE

*This drink is great, even if you cannot get to a tropical island. It will help take the menace out of menopause, build strong bones, boost soy, calcium, and potassium. It may also reduce the number of hot flashes and help lower cholesterol.*

1-1/2 cup Pineapple, crushed

2 small Bananas, mashed

2 cups Soy milk, vanilla flavor, 1 percent fat, calcium-enriched

1 Tbsp. Maple syrup (or reduced sugar type)

1 cup Ice, crushed

**Vegetarian: Vegan**

Total time: 8 minutes
Serves: 6
Serving size: 1 cup
Exchanges: 1 fruit, 1/2 fat-free milk

Place all ingredients in a blender and purée on high until smooth. Serve immediately.

**Nutrition Information:**

CAL 110 CHO 24G PRO 3G FAT 1G CHOL 0MG CALCIUM 113MG POTASSIUM 288MG SODIUM 62MG FIBER 2G

# YOGIES TEA WITH MINT LEAVES

*This beverage contains herbs that will soothe and calm you. By using mineral water, you can boost your calcium intake. Yoga Tea is a brand that is caffeine-free and contains licorice root, peppermint, and other herbs that tend to be soothing. It makes a wonderful treat on a rainy day or at bedtime.*

1 cup Mineral water, boiling

1 Herbal tea bag, any type

1 tsp. Honey* or sugar substitute

3 Mint leaves, fresh

## QUICK BREAKFAST MENU

Peanut Butter on Whole
Wheat Toast

*Yummy Berry Smoothie*

**Vegetarian: Vegan**

Total time: 1 to 3 minutes
Serves: 1
Serving size: 1 cup
Exchange: Without honey, free; with honey, 1 fruit

1. Add tea bags to water and brew for 1 to 3 minutes.
2. Add honey or sugar substitute and mint and serve.

## Serving Suggestion

Diabetics may use sugar substitute instead of honey.

**Nutrition Information:**

**Without Honey**

CAL 0** CHO 17G PRO 0G FAT 0G CHOL 0MG CALCIUM 105 POTASSIUM 6MG SODIUM 3MG FIBER 0G

*Warning: Honey is not recommended for pregnant women or children under age 2; it contains natural bacteria that may be harmful.

**With honey, 60 calories.

# YUMMY BERRY SMOOTHIE

*Add fiber and antioxidants to your drinks. This one is great for young and old bones alike.*

1/4 cup Yogurt*, plain, fat-free

1 cup Berries, frozen, unsweetened

1/4 cup Nonfat dry milk powder

6 Ice cubes, crushed

2 Tbsp. Maple syrup (diet low = sugar
  type optional)

**Vegetarian: Lacto-ovo**

Total time: 5 minutes
Serves: 2
Serving size: 1 cup
Exchange: 1 fruit, 1 fat-free milk

---

Place all ingredients in a blender and purée until smooth.

**Nutrition Information:**

CAL 136  CHO 30G  PRO 5G  FAT 1G  CHOL 30G  CALCIUM 182MG  POTASSIUM 407MG  SODIUM 95MG  FIBER 3G

*Freeze plain yogurt a day ahead. Why freeze regular yogurt instead of buying frozen yogurt? Regular yogurt contains more magnesium, protein, and calcium as well as no added sugar and no fat. And excess sugar, calories, and additives in commercial products are best avoided.

# Chapter 6

# BREADS AND BREAKFAST

*Breakfast*

## BLUEBERRY CORN MUFFINS OR BREAD

*This is a great recipe for boosting calcium to create strong bones. Furthermore, blueberries contain a memory-enhancing phytonutrient.*

*Chef Brian MacMenamin*

1 cup Cornmeal, fine
1 cup Flour
1 Tbsp. Sugar
2 tsp. Baking powder
1/2 tsp. Baking soda
1/2 tsp. Salt
1 Egg, lightly beaten
2/3 cup Buttermilk, fat-free
2/3 cup Milk, fat-free
1/3 cup Apple sauce
1/2 cup Creamed corn, canned
1 cup Blueberries, fresh, rinsed

**Vegetarian: Lacto-ovo**

Total time: 35 minutes
Serves: 12
Serving size: 1 muffin or 1/2-inch slice
Exchange: 1 starch

Preheat oven to 375°F.

*(continues)*

# BLUEBERRY CORN MUFFINS
# OR BREAD (Continued)

## For Bread

1. Place a 9-inch or 10-inch cast iron skillet into the oven as it is preheating.
2. Remove preheated skillet from oven, spray with nonstick pan spray, and pour batter into prepared pan.
3. Bake for 30 minutes.

## For Muffins

1. In a 12-muffin pan, place paper liners or grease with nonstick spray.
2. In a large bowl, combine cornmeal, flour, sugar, baking powder, baking soda, and salt.
3. In a small bowl, mix the egg, buttermilk, fat-free milk, and apple sauce together.
4. Stir buttermilk mixture into dry ingredients.
5. Add corn and blueberries, mixing until just combined.
6. Pour batter into muffin pan.
7. Bake until the edges are golden brown and crisp; check for doneness by inserting a knife or toothpick in the center until it comes out cleanly (approximately 20 to 25 minutes).
8. Let cool for 5 minutes, then invert onto a cooling rack.

**Tip:** The increased natural Vitamin E in canola oil and eggs may help protect you from Alzheimer's disease and dementia.

**Nutrition Information:**

CAL 217   CHO 30G   PRO 4G   FAT 5G   CHOL 48MG   CALCIUM 248MG   POTASSIUM 61MG   SODIUM 138   FIBER 3G

# BUTTERMILK BLUEBERRY PANCAKES

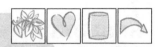

*Kids love these pancakes. As a bonus, flax boosts fiber and Omega-3 fatty acids, which aid heart health and increase attention span.*

**Vegetarian: Lacto-ovo**

Total time: 13 minutes
Serves: 4
Serving size: 2/4-inch rounds
Exchange: 2 starch, 1/2 fat

1 cup Pancake mix, oat or whole grain
1 cup Buttermilk, fat-free
1 Egg or Egg Beater
1 cup Blueberries, fresh
2 tsp. Canola oil

1. Place all ingredients except the canola oil and berries in a bowl and mix together. Once blended, add berries.
2. Place a drop of oil on an extra hot nonstick griddle. Pour 3 Tablespoons of mixture onto the griddle.
3. Cook until the pancake is brown on one side, then flip and brown the other side. Each pancake should be 4 inches wide.

## Serving Suggestion

Add flaxseed for more fiber and essential Omega-3 fatty acids. It can be purchased in a health food store ground as flaxseed meal.

**Nutrition Information:**

**Whole egg version**

CAL 216  CHO 19G  PRO 13G  FAT 10G  CHOL 40MG  CALCIUM 188MG  POTASSIUM 290MG  SODIUM 328MG  FIBER 2G

**Egg substitute**

CAL 153  CHO 19G  PRO 12G  FAT 4G  CHOL 0MG  CALCIUM 177MG  POTASSIUM 317MG  SODIUM 369MG  FIBER 3G

# BLUEBERRY-PECAN SCONE

*This is not your typical scone. It is designed to boost phytonutrients and can be easily substituted for a breakfast meal to hold you on long days.*

*Chef Brian MacMenamin*

2 cups All-purpose flour

1/2 cup Whole wheat flour

1/4 cup Bran, unprocessed

1-1/2 tsp. Baking powder

1/2 cup Sugar, granulated

1 tsp. Salt

1 stick Butter, sliced in pieces*

1/2 cup Applesauce

3/4 cup Buttermilk, fat-free

1/4 cup Pecans, chopped

1 Tbsp. Orange rind, ground

3 large Eggs, lightly beaten

1 cup Blueberries

Egg wash (beat together 1 egg white + 1 Tbsp. water)

1/2 cup Oats, quick cooking

1 Tbsp. Sugar

**Vegetarian: Lacto-ovo**

Total time: 55 minutes
Serves: 8
Serving size: 1/8
Exchange: 3 starch, 3 fat, 1/2 fruit

1. Preheat oven to 350°F and oil an 8-inch round pie dish.
2. Mix both flours, bran, baking powder, sugar, and salt in a mixing bowl. Add butter and mix until crumbly.
3. In a separate bowl, combine applesauce, buttermilk, pecans, orange rind, and eggs. Add to flour mixture and blend.
4. Add berries and mix together. Place in pie dish and brush with egg wash.
5. Sprinkle with sugar and oats and bake for approximately 45 minutes or until inserted toothpick in center comes out clean.

### Serving Suggestion

If you are trying to lose weight, this is not recommended as a complement to a meal. Instead, it would replace a meal or be a hearty between-meal snack.

**Nutrition Information:**

CAL 397  CHO 543G  PRO 9G  FAT 17G  CHOL 111MG  CALCIUM 106MG  POTASSIUM 216MG  SODIUM 445MG  FIBER 4G

*Use no trans-fat margarine to lower cholesterol.

# CHALLAH FRENCH TOAST WITH BERRIES

*By holding the maple syrup and adding fruit, this recipe boosts fiber and phytonutrients. The cinnamon aids insulin action.*

2 large Eggs, beaten (or 1/2 cup Egg Beaters)

2 tsp. Milk, fat-free

4 slices Challah bread

1 tsp. Canola oil

Cinnamon, ground (to garnish)

2 cups Berries, strawberries*, sliced

**Vegetarian: Lacto-ovo**

Total time: 14 minutes
Serves: 4
Serving size: 1 slice
Exchange: Without fruit,
1 starch, 1/2 high fat meat;
with fruit, add 1/4 fruit

1. Beat egg and milk together.
2. Dip bread into egg mixture.
3. Heat oil in a large skillet, then place bread in skillet and brown on both sides.
4. Serve French toast slices topped with cinnamon and berries.

**Nutrition Information:**

**Without fruit**

CAL 134  CHO 16G  PRO 6G  FAT 5G  CHOL 116MG**  CALCIUM 37MG  POTASSIUM 160MG  SODIUM 75MG  FIBER 1G

**With fruit**

CAL 142  CHO 18G  PRO 6G  FAT 5G  CHOL 116MG**  CALCIUM 40MG  POTASSIUM 206MG  SODIUM 75MG  FIBER 2G

*May substitute other berries or 2 Tablespoons of low-sugar fruit spread (but beware that fruit spread decreases fiber and phytonutrients).

**16 milligrams of cholesterol when Egg Beaters are used.

# CHILD-FRIENDLY GRANOLA

*This is a great snack to serve an hour before sporting events to help boost performance and energy.*

**Vegetarian: Lacto-ovo**

1/2 cup Mini chocolate chips, semisweet

1 cup Chex cereal, rice or bran

1 cup Barbara's Puffins cereal, cinnamon

1 cup Kashi Autumn Wheat cereal

1/2 cup Raisins

1/2 cup Banana chips, dried

1/2 cup Almonds, silvered

Total time: 10 minutes
Serves: 6
Serving size: 3/4 cup
Exchange: 2 starch, 1 fat, 1/2 fruit

Mix all ingredients and store in an airtight container until ready to use.

## Serving Suggestion

To children younger than 12, serve 1/2 cup. Do not serve to children younger than 2 because the granola requires teeth to chew and it may be hard to swallow.

**Nutrition Information:**

CAL 265  CHO 41  PRO 5G  FAT 8G  CHOL 0MG  CALCIUM 41MG  POTASSIUM 308MG  SODIUM 101MG  FIBER 5G

# CHOCOLATE CHIP PANCAKES

*Kids love these pancakes. As a bonus, flax boosts fiber and Omega-3 fatty acids for heart health and increased attention span.*

1 cup Pancake mix
1/2 cup Milk, fat-free
2 Tbsp. Mini chocolate chips, semisweet, dark
1 Egg
1/4 cup Flaxseed, ground*
2 tsp. Canola oil

**Vegetarian: Lacto-ovo**

Total time: 13 minutes
Servings: 4
Serving size: two 4-inch
round pancakes
Exchange: 1-1/2 starch, 1 fat

1. Place all ingredients except canola oil in a bowl and mix together.
2. Place a drop of oil on an extra hot nonstick griddle.
3. Pour 3 Tablespoons of mixture onto griddle and cook each pancake until brown on one side, then flip and brown other side. Each pancake should be 4 inches in diameter.

**Nutrition Information:**

CAL 193   CHO 23G   PRO 6G   FAT 5G   CHOL 59MG   CALCIUM 73MG   POTASSIUM 168MG   SODIUM 302MG   FIBER 3G

*Flaxseed can be purchased and ground in a coffee grinder or purchased ground as flaxseed meal.

# CINNAMON RICOTTA CHEESE DANISH

*Another bone pleasing recipe, this one includes cinnamon, which enhances insulin action.*

**Vegetarian: Lacto-ovo**

Total time: 6–10 minutes
Serves: 4
Serving size: 1 tortilla
Exchange: No sugar, 1 starch,
1 reduced fat dairy, 1/2 fat;
with sugar; 1-1/2 starch, 1 reduced
fat dairy, 1/2 fat

8 oz. Ricotta cheese, part skim

1 tsp. Cinnamon

1 Tbsp. Oat bran, unprocessed

1 Tbsp. Brown sugar (optional)

4 Flour tortillas, 5-inch round, whole wheat

1. Preheat toaster oven to 45°F.
2. Mix together first ricotta cheese, cinnamon, oat bran, and sugar and spread one-quarter of mixture on each tortilla.
3. Place in oven for 3 to 6 minutes and serve.

## Serving Suggestion

Serve these tortillas with fruit for a lasting, satisfying breakfast.

**Nutrition Information:**

**Without sugar**

CAL 218  CHO 26G  PRO 11G  FAT 8G  CHOL 17MG  CALCIUM 218MG  POTASSIUM 138MG  SODIUM 277MG  FIBER 3G

**With sugar**

CAL 242  CHO 33G  PRO 11G  FAT 8G  CHOL 17MG  CALCIUM 218MG  POTASSIUM 138MG  SODIUM 277MG  FIBER 3G

# CRUNCH AND MUNCH

*This recipe boosts lutein for your eyes and phytonutrients for your heart.*

**Vegetarian: Vegan**

1/2 cup Brazil nuts, chopped*

1/2 cup Almond slivers

1/2 cup Raisins, dark

1/2 cup Cranberries, dried

1 cup Wheat Bran Chex (General Mills)

1 cup Cheerios, multigrain (General Mills)

Total time: 5 minutes
Serves: 8
Serving size: 1/2 cup
Exchange: 1-1/2 starch, 2 fats

Mix all ingredients and store in an airtight container until ready to use. Stays fresh for approximately two weeks.

## Serving Suggestion

Use as a snack between meals. Take on a long trip as an alternative to airline food snacks or roadside options. This mix is much lower in sodium than many snacks.

**Nutrition Information:**

CAL 192  CHO 26G  PRO 4G  FAT 10G  CHOL 0MG  CALCIUM 61MG  POTASSIUM 224MG  SODIUM 111MG  FIBER 3G

*Brazil nuts are rich in selenium, which aids memory.

# GRANOLA MEDLEY

*This medley is high in fiber and antioxidants.*

1 cup Bran cereal

1 cup Grape-Nuts™ cereal (Post)

1 cup Rolled oats

1 cup Puffed rice cereal

1/4 cup Raisins

1/4 cup Sunflowers seeds

1/4 cup Cranberries, dried

1/4 cup Banana chips, dried

**Vegetarian: Vegan**

Total time: 10 minutes
Serves: 10
Serving size: 1/2 cup
Exchange: 2 starch, 1/2 fat

Mix all ingredients and store in an airtight container until ready to use.

## Serving Suggestion

For an added boost, sprinkle with 2 Tablespoons of flaxseed meal before eating. Place on top of yogurt or enjoy with milk as a cereal. If you are on a weight-loss diet, eat only a small portion (1/2 cup) because of calories and nutrient density.

**Nutrition Information:**

CAL 143  CHO 28G  PRO 4G  FAT 3G  CHOL 0MG  CALCIUM 27MG  POTASSIUM 192MG  SODIUM 100MG  FIBER 6G

# GREEK YOGURT PARFAIT

*This parfait is much higher in protein than regular yogurt and provides lots of calcium for bones. It also contains probiotics that boost beneficial bacteria for increased intestinal health.*

**Vegetarian: Lacto-ovo**

Total time: 2 minutes
Serves: 1
Serving size: 1-1/4 cup
Exchange: 1 fat-free milk,
1 starch, 1 very lean meat

1 cup Greek yogurt*, fat-free
1/4 cup Granola, low-fat
1 Strawberry, whole

Top yogurt with granola and strawberry, garnish and serve.

## Serving Suggestion

Make a parfait by topping with more fresh berries.

**Nutrition Information:**

CAL 175  CHO 26G  PRO 17G  FAT 1G  CHOL 0MG  CALCIUM 270MG  POTASSIUM 501MG  SODIUM 170MG  FIBER 1G

*Greek yogurt can be found in many specialty food stores. Substitute with plain, fat-free yogurt if necessary.

# QUICK WAFFLE SANDWICH

*This recipe is a great high-fiber option if you like waffles. It provides lots of calcium, too.*

**Vegetarian: Lacto-ovo**

Total time: 5 minutes
Serves: 1 to 2
Serving size: 1 whole sandwich for adults; 1/2 sandwich for children
Exchange: 2 starch, 1/2 fruit, 1 whole milk

2 High-fiber waffles
1/4 cup Ricotta cheese, part skim
2 Tbsp. Smucker's reduced sugar fruit
  spread*

1. Toast waffles.
2. Spread ricotta cheese and fruit spread on one waffle and top with the other waffle.
3. Cut in half and serve.

## Serving Suggestion

Choose high-fiber waffles such as Kashi, Multigrain Eggo, or Van's brands, but be sure to check labels and those with less than 3 grams of fat and more than 3 grams of fiber per serving.

**Nutrition Information:**

CAL 314  CHO 50G  PRO 13G  FAT 8G  CHOL 20MG  CALCIUM 276MG  POTASSIUM 233MG  SODIUM 532MG  FIBER 3G

*For optimal nutrition, use fresh berries instead of fruit spreads.

# TOMATO MOZZARELLA MELT

*This is a great calcium-rich choice.*

**Vegetarian: Lacto-ovo**

1 Italian bread, whole wheat, 8-inch loaf

1 large Tomato, chopped

1/4 cup Basil leaves, cleaned and chopped

1 clove Garlic, minced

8 oz. Mozzarella, part skim, shredded

Total time: 15 minutes
Serves: 4
Serving size: 1/4 loaf
Exchange: 1-1/2 starch, 1 fat,
1/2 medium fat milk

1. Slice bread lengthwise, and then cut each side in half. Place halves, open side up, on a sheet pan and toast in a toaster oven or under an oven broiler until light brown.
2. In a small bowl, combine tomato, basil leaves, and garlic.
3. Place 1 to 2 Tablespoons of tomato mixture on top of each slice of toasted bread. Top with mozzarella and place under broiler until cheese melts, approximately 60 seconds.
4. Remove immediately, cut into four portions, and serve.

## Serving Suggestion

This also makes a great party hors d'oeuvre. The tomato mixture can be made a day ahead and the bread can be toasted before the party starts.

**Nutrition Information:**

CAL 233  CHO 28G  PRO 8G  FAT 8G  CHOL 15MG  CALCIUM 265MG  POTASSIUM 233MG  SODIUM 435MG  FIBER 2G

# VEGETABLE CHEESE OMELETTE

*This recipe, a children's favorite, is a great way to add more calcium.*

1/2 tsp. Canola oil
1/2 Onion, small, chopped
4 large Eggs*, beaten
1/4 cup Spinach, raw, chopped
2 slices American cheese*
dash Pepper, black

**WEEKEND BRUNCH MENU**

Fresh Fruit Supreme
Vegetable Cheese Omelet
Herbed Biscuits
Spicy Vegetable Cocktail

**Vegetarian: Lacto-ovo**

Total time: 5–6 minutes per egg
Serves: 4
Serving size: 1 egg
Exchange: 1 medium fat meat, 1 fat

1. Heat oil in a skillet over medium heat and sauté onion.
2. Mix egg and spinach together and add to skillet and cook 1 to 2 minutes.
3. Add cheese and continue cooking until egg mixture reaches desired firmness.
4. Fold omelette in half. Cook 1 minute more and serve.

## Serving Suggestion

Serve with multigrain toast and a fresh fruit cup.

**Nutrition Information:**

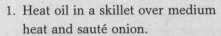

CAL 126  CHO 2G  PRO 9G  FAT 9G  CHOL 222MG**  CALCIUM 82MG  POTASSIUM 105MG  SODIUM 216MG  FIBER 1G

*To lower cholesterol, replace the eggs with Egg Beaters and use 50 percent reduced fat cheddar or American cheese.

**With Egg Beaters, cholesterol is 146 milligrams.

# YOGURT CRUNCH PARFAIT

*This recipe is so satisfying that you will not be hungry for hours.
It is rich in calcium, fiber, and phytonutrients.*

1 cup Yogurt, plain, fat-free

1 cup Fresh fruit or canned pineapple
chunks

1/2 cup Grape-Nuts™

4 Tbsp. Flaxseed, ground (meal)*

**Vegetarian: Lacto-ovo**

Total time: 5 minutes
Serves: 2
Serving size: 1 cup
Exchange: 1 reduced fat milk, 2 starch

Layer 1/4 cup of yogurt, then 1/2 cup of fruit followed by 1/8 cup Grape-Nuts
and 1 Tablespoon ground flaxseed. Repeat layers once more.

**Nutrition Information:**

CAL 286  CHO 48G  PRO 14G  FAT 6G  CHOL 2MG  CALCIUM 288MG  POTASSIUM 605MG  SODIUM 279MG  FIBER 8G

*Flaxseed is not digested. To obtain maximum benefit, including Omega-3 fatty acids, grind flaxseed in a coffee
grinder or buy it as meal in a health food store. Omega-3 fatty acids help your heart and have anti-aging
properties.

# CRUSTY GARLIC BREAD

*This bread is great with pasta and soup and makes excellent sandwiches.*

*Carla Arpino*

1 French baguette, 18 inches long
2 cloves Garlic, peeled
1 bunch Parsley, fresh, chopped

**Vegetarian: Vegan**

Total time: 4 minutes
Serves: 6
Serving size: 2 halves, 3 inches each
Exchange: 1 starch

1. Slice the baguette lengthwise and open. Place on a cookie sheet and broil until toasted to a golden brown.
2. Rub with fresh garlic and sprinkle with parsley. Enjoy!

## Serving Suggestion

Have a picnic, add some grapes and low-fat, part skim mozzarella cheese and have a terrific time.

**Nutrition Information:**
CAL 67  CHO 12G  PRO 2G  FAT 1G  CHOL 0MG  CALCIUM 22MG  POTASSIUM 37MG  SODIUM 141MG  FIBER 1G

# HERBED BISCUITS

*These biscuits boost phytonutrients and herbs.*

1-3/4 cups Bisquick, original
1/2 cup Flaxseed, ground*
3/4 cup Milk, fat-free
1/4 tsp. Garlic powder (optional)
1/2 tsp. Rosemary, dried and crushed, or mixed
  Italian seasonings (optional)

**Vegetarian: Lacto-ovo**

Total time: 14 minutes
Serves: 8
Serving size: 2 biscuits
Exchange: 1-1/2 starch, 1 fat

1. Heat oven to 450°F.
2. Mix Bisquick, flaxseed, and milk and blend into a soft dough. Place on a clean surface sprinkled with Bisquick and knead 12 times.
3. Roll out dough 1/2-inch thick and use a 2-1/2-inch cutter or cup to cut 16 circles of dough.
4. Place cut pieces on an ungreased cookie sheet and sprinkle with garlic powder and herbs.
5. Bake 8 to 10 minutes or until golden brown.

## Serving Suggestion

Use fresh rosemary and boost flavor even more.

**Nutrition Information:**

CAL 148  CHO 20G  PRO 4G  FAT 6G  CHOL 0MG  CALCIUM 70MG  POTASSIUM 45MG  SODIUM 336MG  FIBER 2G

*Flaxseed can be bought in health food stores. If you buy whole seeds, grind them in a coffee grinder or buy flaxseed meal, which is already ground. The Omega-3 and Omega-6 fatty acids in flaxseed are beneficial in protecting against heart disease and stroke. Flaxseed also adds fiber, which has been removed in processed flour mixes.

# LOW-FAT PUMPKIN BREAD

*This is a delicious alternative to higher fat pumpkin breads.*

1-1/2 cup All-purpose flour, sifted
1/4 tsp. Baking powder, double-acting
1 tsp. Baking soda
1/2 tsp. Salt
1 tsp. Cinnamon, ground
1/4 tsp. Cloves, ground
1-1/3 cup Sugar
1/4 cup Flaxseed meal*
1/3 cup Applesauce, unsweetened
1 Egg
2 Egg whites
1 cup Pumpkin, cooked or canned
2/3 cup Milk, 2 percent

**Vegetarian: Lacto-ovo**

Total time: 1 hour, 20 minutes
Serves: 12
Serving size: 3/4-inch slice
Exchange: 2 starch, 1/2 fat

1. Preheat oven to 350°F.
2. Sift together flour, baking powder, baking soda, salt, cinnamon, and cloves.
3. In a separate large bowl, blend together sugar, flaxseed meal, applesauce, and egg. Add pumpkin.
4. In three separate additions, add dry ingredients to pumpkin mixture, alternating with 1/3 cup fat-free milk. Do not overbeat between each addition.
5. Pour batter into greased 9-inch by 5-inch loaf pan and bake approximately 1 hour or until toothpick inserted in center comes out cleanly.

## Serving Suggestion

Serve with hot spiced apple cider or milk.

**Nutrition Information:**

CAL 179  CHO 38G  PRO 4G  FAT 2G  CHOL 18MG  CALCIUM 40MG  POTASSIUM 118MG  SODIUM 237MG  FIBER 3G

*Flaxseed can be purchased whole and ground in a coffee grinder or as meal. It can be found in health food stores. If unavailable, substitute with wheat bran or wheat germ. For more information on flaxseed, see Chapter 2.

# ONION AND SAUSAGE CORN PUDDING

*Paulette B. Schneider, Registered Dietitian*

2 cups Onion, diced
1/2 cup Green bell pepper, diced
1/2 cup Red bell pepper, chopped
2 Jalapeño peppers, seeded and diced
2 Tbsp. Olive oil
1-1/2 cups Yogurt, plain, fat-free
1/2 cup Egg substitute
17 oz. Creamed corn, low-sodium (1 can)
8 oz. Turkey sausage, bulk type, cooked
1 cup Cornmeal
1-1/2 Tbsp. Baking powder
8 oz. Cheddar cheese, low-fat, low-sodium, shredded
2 Tbsp. Sugar, granulated
1/4 tsp. Sage, ground

| |
|---|
| Total time: 1 hour, 30 minutes |
| Serves: 8 |
| Serving size: 1/2 cup |
| Exchange: 2 starch, 1 vegetable, 2 medium fat meat |

1. Preheat oven to 400°F.
2. In a large skillet over medium low heat, sauté the onion in 1 Tablespoon of olive oil for approximately 10 minutes or until onion is tender.
3. Remove from heat and add 1 cup of the yogurt and stir. Set aside until needed.
4. In another pan, sauté the jalapeños and green and red bell peppers in 1 Tablespoon of olive oil until tender, approximately 5 minutes.
5. Spray a large, shallow baking dish with nonstick cooking spray and place cooked sausage and one-half of the peppers in the bottom of the dish.
6. In a large mixing bowl, combine the egg substitute, cornmeal, 1/2 cup yogurt, creamed corn, baking powder, one-half of the cheddar cheese, sugar, sage, and the reserved peppers. Pour this mixture over the sausage and peppers.
7. Spoon the yogurt and onion mixture over the top of the pudding and sprinkle with the remaining cheese.
8. Bake for 25 to 30 minutes, then allow to cool for 15 minutes before serving.

*(continues)*

# ONION AND SAUSAGE CORN PUDDING (Continued)

## Serving Suggestion

If you do not care for hot spicy foods, the jalapeño peppers can be omitted. This dish works well as a brunch casserole or as a dinner casserole. Both fruit salads and crisp vegetable salads are great side dishes.

**Nutrition Information:**

CAL 312  CHO 36G  PRO 20G  FAT 10G  CHOL 23MG  CALCIUM 368MG  POTASSIUM 218MG  SODIUM 472MG  FIBER 3G

# QUICK AND EASY FLAX POPOVERS

2 Eggs, beaten
1 cup Flour, unbleached all-purpose
1/4 cup Flaxseed meal*
1 cup Milk, fat-free
1 Tbsp. Canola or vegetable oil
1/4 tsp. Salt

**Vegetarian: Lacto-ovo**

Total time: 40 minutes
Serves: 6
Serving size: 1 large popover
Exchange: 1 starch, 1 fat

1. Preheat oven to 475°F.
2. Beat eggs with flour, flaxseed meal, milk, oil, and salt until smooth.
3. Grease muffin tin cups or custard cups and fill half of each cup with batter.
4. Bake for 15 minutes, then lower heat to 350°F for 20 minutes or until popovers are crispy and golden brown. Serve hot.

**Nutrition Information:**

CAL 135  CHO 20G  PRO 3G  FAT 3G  CHOL 71MG  CALCIUM 71MG  POTASSIUM 143MG  SODIUM 339MG  FIBER 2G

*Flaxseed meal can be bought in health food stores. If you buy whole flaxseeds, grind them in a coffee grinder or buy flaxseed meal, which is already ground. The Omega-3 and Omega-6 fatty acids in flaxseed protect against heart disease and stroke. Flaxseed meal also adds fiber, which is often removed in processed flour.

# Chapter 7

# SALADS AND SOUPS

## *Salads*

## ASPARAGUS WITH HAZELNUTS AND TARRAGON VINAIGRETTE

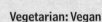

*Chef Brian MacMenamin*

**Vegetarian: Vegan**

Total time: 10 minutes
Serves: 4
Serving size: 1/4
Exchange: 1 vegetable, 3 fats

1 lb. Asparagus, fresh, trimmed
1/4 cup Shallots, minced
3 Tbsp. Tarragon white wine vinegar
4 tsp. Tarragon, fresh, minced (or 1-1/4 tsp. dried tarragon)
1 tsp. Dijon mustard
4 Tbsp. Walnut oil or olive oil
To taste Salt
To taste Pepper, black, ground
4 cups Baby lettuce leaves or inner leaves of curly endive
1/4 cup Hazelnuts, toasted, husked, and coarsely chopped

1. Pour water into a large pot to a depth of 2 inches and bring to boil.
2. Place asparagus in boiling water in pot and cook until crisp-tender, approximately 5 minutes.
3. Transfer asparagus to bowl of ice water. Once asparagus are cool, drain and place on paper towels.

*(continues)*

# ASPARAGUS WITH HAZELNUTS AND TARRAGON VINAIGRETTE (Continued)

4. Combine shallots, vinegar, tarragon, and mustard in mixing bowl.
5. Gradually whisk in oil. Once emulsion has formed, season to taste with salt and pepper.
6. Place baby lettuce leaves on large platter. Arrange asparagus atop lettuce leaves. Drizzle with vinaigrette and sprinkle with hazelnuts.

## Serving Suggestion

If you do not have hazelnuts, substitute sliced and toasted almonds.

**Nutrition Information:**

**With Walnut Oil**

| CAL 190 | CHO 5G | PRO 4G | FAT 19G | CHOL 0MG | CALCIUM 51MG | POTASSIUM 323MG | SODIUM 36MG | FIBER 3G |

**With Olive Oil**

| CAL 189 | CHO 5G | PRO 4G | FAT 18G | CHOL 0MG | CALCIUM 51MG | POTASSIUM 323MG | SODIUM 36MG | FIBER 3G |

# BABY SPINACH AND GORGONZOLA MEDLEY

*Dark greens boost brain power.\* This recipe is rich in antioxidants, folic acid, fiber, and other phytonutrients that help vision and reduce risks of heart disease and stroke.*

1 lb. Baby spinach, fresh

1/2 Red onion, small, sliced (optional)

2 Tbsp. Balsamic vinegar, red or white

1 Tbsp. Olive oil

1/4 cup Gorgonzola cheese, crumbled\*\*

1/4 cup Almonds, smoked, unsalted

1/4 cup Cranberries, dried

**Vegetarian: Lacto-ovo**

Total time: 7 minutes
Serves: 4
Serving size: 1 cup
Exchange: 1 starch, 1 fat,
1 medium fat meat

1. Wash spinach and drain thoroughly.
2. Add onion and toss with balsamic vinegar and oil.
3. Top with remaining ingredients and serve.

## Serving Suggestion

Serve with crusty Italian bread (see index for recipe).

**Nutrition Information:**

CAL 218  CHO 13G  PRO 9G  FAT 10G  CHOL 12MG  CALCIUM 219MG  POTASSIUM 763MG  SODIUM 308MG  FIBER 5G

\*Harvard Medical School and Swedish researchers, information presented at the Ninth International Conference on Alzheimer's Disease and Related Disorders.

\*\*Although Gorgonzola is rich in saturated fat, this recipe stresses portion control to show that any foods are manageable if eaten in balance with less fat-dense foods. By adding a higher fat cheese to a low-fat salad, your hunger will be satisfied longer. The need to add a high-fat dressing to this salad is unnecessary.

# BARLEY SALAD

*This salad provides a rich source of fiber and B vitamins.*

*Phyllis Schondorf*

**Vegetarian: Vegan**

1 cup Barley*
3 cups Broth or water, boiling
2 Tbsp. Olive oil
3 Tbsp. Wine vinegar
1 clove Garlic, peeled and halved
1/8 tsp. Mustard, dry
1/4 tsp. Pepper, black, ground
1 Carrot, diced
1 Red pepper, diced
1 Red onion, small, diced
1/2 cup Fennel tops, fresh, minced

> Total time: 45 minutes
> Serves: 6
> Serving size: 1/2 cup
> Exchange: 2 starch, 1 fat

1. Simmer barley in broth in covered saucepan until tender, approximately 40 minutes.
2. Combine olive oil, wine vinegar, garlic, mustard, and black pepper to make dressing.
3. Mix barley with diced vegetables.
4. Remove garlic from dressing and pour dressing over salad.

## Serving Suggestion

Serve warm or at room temperature.

**Nutrition Information:**

CAL 183  CHO 32G  PRO 4G  FAT 5G  CHOL 0MG  CALCIUM 27MG  POTASSIUM 220MG  SODIUM 33MG  FIBER 6G

*Buy whole hulled barley at a health food store to get the beta-glucans soluble fiber that are thought to help lower cholesterol along with protein and B vitamins that are often lost in pearled barley.

# BEAN SPROUT SALAD

*This salad helps reduce your risk of getting cancer and boosts isoflavones, lycopenes, and phytofats.*

**Vegetarian: Vegan**

1 lb. Soybean sprouts, fresh
8 Cherry tomatoes, fresh
1/4 cup Peanuts, crushed, unsalted
8 slices Cucumber
1 Scallion, fresh, chopped

Total time: 4 minutes
Serves: 4
Serving size: 1 cup
Exchange: 1 starch,
2 medium fat meat

1. Rinse all vegetables.
2. Place 1 cup of sprouts in four individual salad bowls and top each bowl with two tomatoes, 1 Tablespoon of peanuts, two cucumber slices, and one-fourth of the chopped scallion.

## Serving Suggestion

Serve with sesame dressing (see index for recipe).

**Nutrition Information:**

CAL 202  CHO 15G  PRO 18G  FAT 12G  CHOL 0MG  CALCIUM 91MG  POTASSIUM 719MG  SODIUM 20MG  FIBER 3G

# CANNELLINI (ALUBIAS) BEAN SALAD

*This dish makes a great summer salad.*

*Dorothy Court*

**Vegetarian: Vegan**

Total time: 10 minutes
Serves: 8
Serving size: 1/2 cup
Exchange: 2 starch, 1 lean meat

28 oz. Cannellini or alubias beans
  (1 large can)
2 stalks Celery, thinly sliced
1 Red onion, small, diced
1/2 cup Parsley, fresh, chopped
1 large Tomato, fresh, diced
2 Tbsp. Balsamic vinegar, white
2 Tbsp. Olive oil
1/4 tsp. Garlic powder (optional)
To taste Pepper, black, ground

1. Drain and rinse beans.
2. Cut all vegetables as noted, then mix together and add balsamic vinegar, olive oil, garlic powder, and black pepper. Mix well and chill for several hours, if possible, to allow flavors to absorb.

**Nutrition Information:**

CAL 179 CHO 28G PRO 10G FAT 4G CHOL 0MG CALCIUM 103MG POTASSIUM 672MG SODIUM 317MG FIBER 7G

# CHICKPEA AND TOMATO SALAD

*This salad is rich in fiber and lycopenes and will help with prostate function, regularity, weight loss, and blood sugar regulation.*

16 oz. Chickpeas (1 can)
4 large Tomatoes, ripe, cut into bite-sized
  wedges
1 Onion, small, chopped
5 Basil leaves, fresh, minced
2 Tbsp. Balsamic vinegar
1 Tbsp. Olive oil

**Vegetarian: Vegan**

Total time: 10 minutes
Serves: 6
Serving size: 3/4 cup
Exchange: 2 starch, 1 vegetable,
1 lean fat meat

Toss all ingredients together. Refrigerate for one hour before serving.

## Serving Suggestion

August is the best time for fresh tomatoes and basil. Enjoy the harvest!

**Nutrition Information:**
CAL 262 CHO 41G PRO 12G FAT 3G CHOL 0MG CALCIUM 70MG POTASSIUM 772MG SODIUM 177MG FIBER 11G

# COLORFUL COLESLAW

*This slaw is rich in antioxidants and low in fat.*

1/2 head Green cabbage, small, shredded
1/4 head Red cabbage, small, shredded
2 Carrots, 7 inches, shredded
1/2 cup Parsley, fresh, chopped
3 Tbsp. Light mayonnaise
2 Tbsp. Half sour pickle juice (from jar)
To taste Pepper, black, ground

**Vegetarian: Lacto-ovo**

Total time: 20 minutes
Serves: 10
Serving size: 1/2 cup
Exchange: 1 vegetable, 1 fat

1. Toss cabbage, carrots, and parsley together.
2. Blend mayonnaise and pickle juice until smooth in consistency. Season with black pepper, then pour on vegetables and mix thoroughly.
3. Serve immediately.

**Nutrition Information:**
CAL 34  CHO 5G  PRO 1G  FAT 2G  CHOL 2MG  CALCIUM 28MG  POTASSIUM 158MG  SODIUM 82MG  FIBER 1G

# CUCUMBERS IN SOUR CREAM DRESSING

*Chef Brian MacMenamin*

**Vegetarian: Lacto-ovo**

3 English cucumbers (regular cucumbers optional)
1/2 pint Sour cream, fat-free

| Total time: 70 minutes (preparation, 10 minutes; chilling, 1 hour) |
| Serves: 4 |
| Serving size: 1/2 cup |
| Exchange: 1 starch, 1 vegetable |

## Dressing

2 Tbsp. Champagne vinegar
1/2 tsp. Celery seeds
1/4 cup Scallions, chopped
1 tsp. Sugar
To taste Pepper, black, ground
To taste Salt
1/4 cup Arugula leaves, young, finely chopped

1. Wash, score, and thinly slice cucumbers. Lightly salt slices and let stand in a colander for 30 minutes to drain. Rinse and pat dry.
2. Whisk together the sour cream, vinegar, celery seeds, scallions, and sugar for the dressing. Season with salt and pepper.
3. Toss the arugula leaves with the dressing.
4. Add the cucumber slices and lightly combine with the dressed arugula.
5. Chill for one hour before serving.

## Serving Suggestion

An optional but elegant garnish for this dish are snipped chive blossoms.

**Nutrition Information:**

CAL 87  CHO 20G  PRO 4G  FAT 0G  CHOL 5MG  CALCIUM 123MG  POTASSIUM 437MG  SODIUM 91MG  FIBER 3G

# CURRIED WHEAT BERRY SALAD

*This salad provides a great way to boost fiber which aids in blood sugar regulation.*

1 cup Wheat berries, dry (also called *whole grain wheat*)

2 cups Water, low simmer

1 cup Apples, diced

1/4 cup Raisins

1/2 tsp. Curry powder

Dash Cinnamon, ground

1/4 tsp. Olive oil

**Vegetarian: Vegan**

Total time: 1 hour, 45 minutes
Serves: 4
Serving size: 3/4 cup
Exchange: 2 starch, 1 fat

1. Simmer wheat berries in water for approximately 90 minutes or until they are tender.
2. Drain and then chill in a large bowl.
3. Add apples, raisins, curry powder, cinnamon, and olive oil and toss lightly.
4. Serve chilled.

## Serving Suggestion

Cook wheat berries ahead of time and cut preparation time to just 7 minutes.

**Nutrition Information:**

CAL 165  CHO 33G  PRO 6G  FAT 4G  CHOL 0MG  CALCIUM 24MG  POTASSIUM 250MG  SODIUM 177MG  FIBER 5G

# FRUITY CHICKEN SALAD

*This dish is packed with phytonutrients and is low in sodium.*

*Michelle Jackson, Registered Dietitian*

2 cups Chicken or turkey breast, cooked
and diced

1 cup Seedless grapes,* washed and cut
in half

1/4 cup Chopped walnuts or slivered
almonds

1 stalk Celery, cleaned and diced

3 Tbsp. Light mayonnaise

1/4 tsp. Pepper, black, ground

> Total time: 12 minutes
> Serves: 4
> Serving size: 1/2 cup
> Exchange: 1/2 fruit, 1 vegetable,
> 3 very lean meat

1. Combine diced chicken or turkey with grapes, walnuts, and celery in a bowl and toss well.
2. Combine mayonnaise and pepper and then blend with the chicken mixture.

## Serving Suggestion

Serve over lettuce or on whole grain bread. Or, for an Indian flair, mix
2 Tablespoons of mango chutney and 1 teaspoon of curry powder into the
mayonnaise (omit the ground black pepper).

**Nutrition Information:**

CAL 221  CHO 10G  PRO 22G  FAT 10G  CHOL 60MG  CALCIUM 26MG  POTASSIUM 304MG  SODIUM 74MG  FIBER 1G

*Or use 1 cup chopped apples (skin on) or 1/2 cup raisins.

# GREEK PASTA SALAD

*This salad is high in antioxidants, fiber, calcium, and more.*
*The broccoli improves mental sharpness.*

**Vegetarian: Lacto-ovo**

8 oz. Tricolor spiral pasta, cooked

8 oz. Penne pasta, cooked

1 bunch Broccoli, fresh, chopped and steamed

12 oz. Chickpeas (1 can), drained

8 oz. Herb feta cheese

1 cup Greek olives, whole and pitted, or black olives, sliced

> Total time: 15 minutes
> Serves: 8
> Serving size: 1-1/2 cup
> Exchange: 2 starch,
> 1 medium fat meat

## Dressing

2 Tbsp. Balsamic vinegar

3 Tbsp. Olive oil

To taste Garlic powder (optional)

8 leaves Basil, fresh (or 1 tsp. dried) (optional)

To taste Pepper, black ground (optional)

1. Mix together pastas, broccoli, chickpeas, feta cheese, and olives and chill.
2. Mix olive oil with vinegar and herbs.
3. Pour dressing over salad and toss before serving.

**Nutrition Information:**

**Including Dressing**

CAL 256   CHO 32G   PRO 12G   FAT 9G   CHOL 25MG   CALCIUM 201MG   POTASSIUM 40MG   SODIUM 534MG   FIBER 6G

# ITALIAN TOMATO SALAD

*This recipe boosts lycopenes and reduces cancer risk. August tomato crops offer the best flavor.*

*Amodio Arpino*

**Vegetarian: Vegan**

4 Tomatoes, medium, vine-ripened, chopped

8 Basil leaves, fresh

1 Onion, small, diced

1 Tbsp. Olive oil, extra virgin

1 Tbsp. Red wine vinegar

To taste Pepper, black, ground

To taste Salt

> Total time: 5 minutes
> Serves: 4
> Serving size: 3/4 cup
> Exchange: 1 vegetable, 1 fat

Rinse and dice tomatoes and onions, mix with other ingredients, and Manga!*

## Serving Suggestion

Serve with crusty Italian bread (see index for recipe) and part skim mozzarella cheese to make a complete meal. Prepare a few hours ahead for added flavor.

**Nutrition Information:**

**Without Added Salt**

CAL 63 CHO 8G PRO 1G FAT 4G CHOL 0MG CALCIUM 12MG POTASSIUM 307MG SODIUM 226MG FIBER 2G

*Means *Eat!* in Italian.

# MANDARIN SALAD

*This dish is rich in antioxidants and folic acid and helps to protect your heart. Fiber helps regulate weight and blood sugar.*

1 lb. Baby spinach, fresh

6 oz. Mandarin oranges (1 can), drained well

6 oz. Water chestnuts (1 can), sliced, drained

1/4 cup Honey roasted peanuts, crushed

1/4 cup Cranberries, dried

1/2 cup Goat cheese, crumbled

**Vegetarian: Lacto-ovo**

Total time: 7 minutes
Serves: 4
Serving size: 1 cup
Exchange: 2 starch,
1 lean fat meat, 2 fats

1. Rinse spinach and drain, then place in bowl.
2. Add remaining ingredients and top with dressing.

### Serving Suggestion

Use sesame dressing (see index for recipe).

**Nutrition Information:**

CAL 250  CHO 27G  PRO 10G  FAT 12G  CHOL 14MG  CALCIUM 186MG  POTASSIUM 845MG  SODIUM 310MG  FIBER 5G

# MEDITERRANEAN CUCUMBER SALAD WITH YOGURT DILL DRESSING

1 large Cucumber, peeled, seeded, and sliced
2 Tbsp. White onion, fresh, diced
1 Tbsp. Dill, fresh, minced
1 Tbsp. Dill seeds
2 Tbsp. Yogurt dill dressing*
As needed Dill sprigs for garnish

**Vegetarian: Lacto-ovo**

Total time: 6 minutes
Serves: 3
Serving size: 1/2 cup
Exchange: With dressing,
1 vegetable

Mix all ingredients, including dressing, then chill. Garnish with dill.

**Nutrition Information:**

**With Dressing**

CAL 28  CHO 5G  PRO 2G  FAT 0G  CHOL 0MG  CALCIUM 68MG  POTASSIUM 206MG  SODIUM 12MG  FIBER 1G

*See index for dressing recipe.

# MESCLUN GREENS WITH APPLES AND WALNUTS

*Walnuts are rich in Omega-3 fatty acids, which are beneficial for your heart.*

**Vegetarian: Vegan**

1 lb. Mesclun greens

2 medium Delicious apples, cored and sliced

1/2 cup Walnuts, quartered

2 Tbsp. Red onion, diced

4 Tbsp. Carla's Dijon vinaigrette dressing*

Total time: 10 minutes
Serves: 4
Serving size: 1 cup
Exchange: 1/2 fruit,
2 vegetable, 2 fats

1. Rinse mesclun, drain, and place in serving bowl.
2. Add remaining ingredients and toss lightly. Serve immediately.

**Nutrition Information:**

**With Dressing**

CAL 169  CHO 16G  PRO 4G  FAT 11G  CHOL 0MG  CALCIUM 75MG  POTASSIUM 517MG  SODIUM 76MG  FIBER 5G

*See index for dressing recipe.

# PANZANELLA SALAD

*Chef Brian MacMenamin*

**Vegetarian: Vegan**

12 oz. Crusty peasant-style bread, day old, cut into
   1-inch cubes
1 large head Romaine lettuce, cleaned and cut into
   bite-sized pieces
4 large Tomatoes (about 1 pound), trimmed and
   cut into bit-sized pieces
3/4 cup Cucumber, unwaxed, diced
1/2 cup Red onion, sliced
1/4 cup Olive oil, extra virgin
2 Tbsp. Red wine vinegar
10 leaves Basil leaves, fresh, shredded

> Total time: 15 minutes
> Serves: 6
> Serving size: 1/6
> Exchange: 1 vegetables,
> 2 starch, 2 fat

In a serving bowl, stir together the bread, Romaine, tomatoes, cucumber, onion, oil, vinegar, basil, and salt and pepper to taste until the salad is combined well. Serve immediately.

## Serving Suggestion
Add an individual 4-oz. container of 1 percent fat cottage cheese to make this a great midweek lunch.

**Nutrition Information:**

CAL 278 CHO 38G PRO 7G FAT 12G CHOL 0MG CALCIUM 91MG POTASSIUM 604MG SODIUM 345MG FIBER 5G

# PASTA SALAD WITH SUN-DRIED TOMATOES

*Lycopenes in tomatoes help fight prostate cancer, while high fiber helps regulate surges in blood sugar. This salad is also a rich source of potassium.*

**Vegetarian: Lacto-ovo**

8 oz. Rigatoni, cooked

6 oz. Tomatoes, sun-dried, sliced (soak in
  1/2 cup water; reserve liquid)

1 tsp. Olive oil

1 Tbsp. Garlic, fresh, minced

4 Tbsp. Parsley, fresh, chopped

2 Tbsp. Basil, fresh, chopped

2 Tbsp. Parmesan cheese

1 package Peas, frozen (cook 1 minute in microwave)

> Total time: 1 hour, 15 minutes
> Serves: 4
> Serving size: 1 cup
> Exchange: 3 starch, 1 vegetable, 1 lean meat

1. Cook rigatoni following directions on the box. Remove from heat and drain, then rinse with cold water.
2. Mix cooked pasta with olive oil, then add garlic, parsley, basil, peas, and reserved liquid from soaked tomatoes. Toss lightly and chill one hour before serving.
3. Top with Parmesan cheese to serve.

### Serving Suggestion

Add Carla's Dijon vinaigrette dressing (see recipe index). To lower sodium content and fat, eliminate the Parmesan and substitute chopped tomato for sun-dried tomato. Eating less than 2,400 milligrams of sodium per day is suggested on a low-sodium diet.

**Nutrition Information:**

**Without Dressing**

CAL 284  CHO 47G  PRO 15G  FAT 4G  CHOL 2MG  CALCIUM 125MG  POTASSIUM 1,656MG  SODIUM 705MG  FIBER 11G

# RAINBOW NICOISE

*This recipe will help boost your immune system. It is a wonderful alternative to a all lettuce salad.*

1 cup Red cabbage, fresh, chopped

1/2 cup Celery, diced

1/2 cup Red bell pepper, fresh, diced

1 Carrot, fresh, sliced

1/2 large Cucumber, sliced

1/4 cup Jicama, peeled, diced

6 oz. Tuna, water-packed (1 can)

To taste Garlic powder

To taste Pepper, black, ground

1 Tbsp. Balsamic vinegar

1 Tbsp. Olive oil

1 tsp. Lemon juice

8 leaves Boston lettuce

Total time: 10 minutes
Serves: 2
Exchange: 1 starch, 3 lean meat

---

1. Place four Boston lettuce leaves each on two plates and set aside.
2. Combine remaining ingredients, toss lightly, place on top of lettuce leaves, and serve.

### Serving Suggestion

This salad goes great with Ak-Mak flatbread crackers.

**Nutrition Information:**

CAL 216 CHO 15G PRO 23G FAT 8G CHOL 23MG CALCIUM 87MG POTASSIUM 818MG SODIUM 320MG FIBER 5MG

# RED NEW POTATO SALAD

*This lower-fat version of potato salad is rich in phytonutrients.*

5 medium Red new potatoes, cooked, chilled,
  and quartered
1/2 cup Red cabbage, fresh, shredded
1/2 cup Carrot, fresh, shredded
3 Tbsp. Dill, fresh, chopped
1/8 cup Scallions, fresh, chopped
1/4 cup Parsley, fresh, chopped
1/2 cup Celery, fresh, diced
2 Tbsp. Light mayonnaise
1/4 cup Pickle juice (half from sour dills)
2 Tbsp. Yogurt, plain, fat-free
1 Tbsp. Pickle relish, sweetened
1 Tbsp. Dijon mustard

**Vegetarian: Lacto-ovo**

Total time: 25 minutes
Serves: 6
Serving size: 3/4 cup
Exchange: 1 starch, 1/2 fat

1. Mix potatoes with cabbage, carrot, dill, scallions, parsley, and celery in a bowl.
2. In a separate bowl, blend light mayonnaise, pickle juice, yogurt, pickle relish, and mustard until the consistency is smooth.
3. Add dressing to mixed vegetables and toss.
4. Chill 20 minutes before serving.

**Nutrition Information:**

CAL 100 CHO 19G PRO 2G FAT 2G CHOL 2MG CALCIUM 33MG POTASSIUM 360MG SODIUM 143MG FIBER 2G

# ROMAINE GARDEN SALAD

*This salad is rich in phytochemicals and antioxidants.*

1 lb. Romaine lettuce
1/2 Red bell pepper, small, diced
1 cup Red cabbage, shredded
8 Cherry tomatoes
2 Tbsp. Sunflower seeds

**Vegetarian: Vegan**

Total time: 15 minutes
Serves: 4
Serving size: 1-1/2 cup
Exchange: 1 vegetable, 1/2 fat

1. Rinse lettuce, drain, and place in serving bowl.
2. Add bell pepper, cabbage, tomatoes, sunflower seeds and your favorite dressing and toss lightly. Serve immediately.

### Serving Suggestion

Try a balsamic vinaigrette dressing if you are a vegan.

**Nutrition Information:**

**Without Dressing**

CAL 56 CHO 7G PRO 3G FAT 3G CHOL 0MG CALCIUM 60MG POTASSIUM 501MG SODIUM 15MG FIBER 3G

# ROMAINE SALAD WITH CARAMELIZED ONION TOPPING

*This dish is rich in folic acid for your heart.*

1 Tbsp. Olive oil
8 oz. Romaine lettuce
10 Baby onions, peeled
10 Baby carrots, sliced thin
1 c. Chickpeas
1/4 tsp. Thyme, dried, chopped
4 tsp. White balsamic vinegar

**Vegetarian: Vegan**

Total time: 15 minutes
Serves: 4
Serving size: 1/4
Exchange: 1 starch, 1/2 fat

1. Place oil in skillet with onions over medium high heat. Sauté approximately 6 minutes until translucent.
2. Add carrots, chickpeas, and thyme and cook 5 more minutes.
3. Wash and drain lettuce and place equal amounts in individual salad bowls.
4. Top lettuce with onion mixture and drizzle with vinegar. Serve.

**Nutrition Information:**

CAL 102   CHO 17G   PRO 5G   FAT 2G   CHOL 0MG   CALCIUM 57MG   POTASSIUM 375MG   SODIUM 82MG   FIBER 5G

# SPRING GREENS WITH ROASTED BEETS AND BLOOD ORANGES

*Blood oranges are packed with the phytochemical cyanidin-3-glucoside (C3G),\* which increases adoponectin and may help burn fat. Beets also boost brain power, while greens are rich in folic acid for your heart and lutein for your eyes.*

*Chef Brian MacMenamin*

**Vegetarian: Vegan**

4 medium Beets, whole, trimmed, skin on

3 Tbsp. Olive oil

2 Tbsp. Sherry wine vinegar or balsamic vinegar

1-1/2 Tbsp. Walnut oil or olive oil

To taste Salt

To taste Pepper, black, ground

8 cups Mixed baby greens

2 Blood oranges, peel and seeds removed, thinly sliced

1/2 cup Red onion, finely diced

1/4 cup Walnuts, toasted and chopped

| |
|---|
| Total time: 1 hour, 20 minutes |
| Serves: 8 |
| Serving size: 1-1/2 cup |
| Exchange: 2 vegetables, 1 fat |

1. Preheat oven to 450°F.
2. Wrap beets completely in foil and roast until tender when pierced with a skewer (approximately 1 hour, 15 minutes). Remove and cool.
3. Peel beets and cut into 1/2-inch pieces.
4. Whisk olive oil, vinegar, and walnut oil in small bowl to blend. Season to taste with salt and pepper.
5. Place mixed baby greens in large bowl and arrange blood orange slices, red onions, and beets on top.
6. Drizzle dressing over salad, sprinkle with toasted walnuts, and serve.

**Nutrition Information:**

CAL 90 CHO 10G PRO 2G FAT 5G CHOL 0MG CALCIUM 48MG POTASSIUM 373MG SODIUM 45MG FIBER 3G

\*Trial animal studies by researchers at Doshisha University in Japan showed that blood oranges contain high levels of C3G, which may help burn fat.

# TEX MEX BLACK BEAN AND CORN SALAD

*This is a delicious medley of antioxidants, fiber, and phytonutrients.*

15 oz. Black beans, canned, drained
8 oz. Corn, canned, drained
1 Red bell pepper, diced
1/4 cup Red onion, diced
1/4 cup Cilantro, fresh, chopped
2 Tbsp. Olive oil
2 tsp. Apple cider vinegar
2 tsp. Lemon juice, fresh
To taste Pepper, black, freshly ground
To taste Hot pepper flakes or Tabasco sauce (optional)

**Vegetarian: Vegan**

Total time: 8 minutes
Serves: 6
Serving size: 1/2 cup
Exchange: 2 starch,
1/2 medium fat meat

Place all ingredients in a bowl, toss lightly, and serve.

## Serving Suggestion

This is a great complement to a veggie burger.

**Nutrition Information:**

CAL 180 CHO 28G PRO 7G FAT 5G CHOL 0MG CALCIUM 56MG POTASSIUM 387MG SODIUM 355MG FIBER 6G

# TOMATO MOZZARELLA SALAD

*This dish is rich in calcium for bones and lycopenes for prostate health, and it also boosts potassium to help control blood pressure. August is the best time to enjoy freshly harvested tomatoes.*

8 oz. Mozzarella cheese, part skim, sliced

2 medium Tomatoes, vine-ripened

8 leaves Basil, fresh, chopped

1/2 tsp. Oregano, dried

1 Tbsp. Olive oil

1 Tbsp. Red wine vinegar

To taste Pepper, black, ground (optional)

**Vegetarian: Lacto-ovo**

Total time: 5 minutes
Serves: 4
Serving size: 2 oz. cheese, 1/2 tomato
Exchange: 1 vegetable, 1 medium fat meat

1. Slice mozzarella cheese into eight 1-ounce slices.
2. Slice tomatoes.
3. Layer tomato and cheese slices on a platter and top with basil, oregano, oil, and vinegar.

## Serving Suggestion

Serve with sliced Italian bread.

**Nutrition Information:**

CAL 203 CHO 5G PRO 16G FAT 13G CHOL 31MG CALCIUM 125MG POTASSIUM 719MG SODIUM 160MG FIBER 1G

# TUNA AND BEAN SALAD

*This recipe is rich in fiber and antioxidants, which help control blood sugar.*

6 oz. Light tuna (1 can), packed in water
15 oz. Navy beans (1 can)
15 Cherry tomatoes, halved
1/2 Red onion, small, diced
1/4 cup Parsley, Italian flat leaf, chopped
12 leaves Red leaf lettuce

Total time: 7 minutes
Serves: 3
Serving size: 1-1/2 cup
Exchange: 3 starch,
3 lean meat

## Dressing

6 tsp. Red wine vinegar
1/2 Lemon, fresh, juiced
2 Tbsp. Olive oil
To taste Pepper, black, ground

1. Place first tuna, navy beans, tomatoes, red onion, and parsley in bowl and toss lightly.
2. Mix vinegar, lemon juice, and oil.
3. Serve tuna and bean mixture over red leaf lettuce. Top with dressing and season with pepper to taste.

## Serving Suggestion

Use light instead of albacore tuna. Studies suggest albacore tuna contains more pollutants and may increase cancer risk.

**Nutrition Information:**

**With Dressing**

CAL 379 CHO 45G PRO 28G FAT 11G CHOL 17MG CALCIUM 133MG POTASSIUM 986MG SODIUM 753MG FIBER 11G

# TUSCAN WHITE BEAN SALAD

*This salad is packed with nutrients to protect your eyes, heart, and bones.*

*Chef Brian MacMenamin*

**Vegetarian: Lacto-ovo**

1-1/2 cups Navy beans, dried

2 Tbsp. Olive oil

1 Yellow onion, finely diced

4 cups Spinach, fresh, cleaned and firmly packed

1/2 cup Tomatoes, sun-dried, diced

10 oz. Mozzarella cheese, fresh, cut into 1/2-inch cubes

1/2 cup Black olives, pitted

To taste Pepper, black, ground

To taste Salt

Total time: 2 hours
Serves: 10
Serving size: 3/4 cup
Exchange: 1 starch, 1 reduced fat dairy, 1 medium fat meat

1. Place beans in a large pot and cover with 3 to 4 inches of water. Bring to a boil, lower heat and simmer, uncovered, for 45 minutes to 1 hour, or until beans are tender but still firm. Drain and rinse the beans thoroughly. Set aside to cool.
2. Heat the olive oil in a skillet over medium heat. Add the onion and stir until slightly brown, approximately 5 minutes.
3. Toss the beans, onions, spinach, sun-dried tomatoes, mozzarella, and olives in a large bowl with a vinaigrette of your choice. Season with salt and pepper and serve immediately or refrigerate in an airtight container until ready to use. If refrigerating, add the spinach just before serving. Top with the vinaigrette of your choice.

## Serving Suggestion

To reduce preparation time, use 3 cups of drained canned navy beans instead of dried beans.

**Nutrition Information:**

**Without Dressing**

CAL 266  CHO 28G  PRO 16G  FAT 11G  CHOL 15MG  CALCIUM 284MG  POTASSIUM 495MG  SODIUM 295MG  FIBER 7G

# WATERCRESS AND RADICCHIO SALAD

*This salad is so simple, so good, and great for weight loss.*

2 bunches Watercress, fresh, torn into small pieces
1 head Radicchio, torn into small pieces
1 bunch Endive (optional), torn into small pieces

**Vegetarian: Vegan**

Total time: 10 minutes
Serves: 8
Serving size: 1 cup
Exchange: Free

Wash and drain all lettuce. Place in bowl. Toss.

## Serving Suggestion

Use your favorite low-fat dressing (see index for recipe). Try a balsamic vinaigrette.

**Nutrition Information:**

CAL 5  CHO 1G  PRO 1G  FAT 0G  CHOL 0MG  CALCIUM 26MG  POTASSIUM 109MG  SODIUM 11MG  FIBER 1G

# WHEAT BERRY AND WILD RICE SALAD

*This is a refreshing change from high-fat mayonnaise-based salads.*

1/2 cup Wild rice, cooked

3/4 cup Wheat berries, dried, uncooked

4 cups Water

1 cup Red bell pepper, diced

2 Scallions, chopped

1 Tbsp. Teriyaki sauce

1 Tbsp. Sesame seed oil

**Vegetarian: Vegan**

Total time: 2 hours*
Serves: 4-8
Serving size: 1/2 cup or 1 cup
Exchange: 1/2 cup, 1 starch, 1/2 fat; 1 cup, 2 starch, 1fat

1. Precook wild rice according to box directions.
2. Place wheat berries and water in a pot. Bring to boil and simmer for approximately 90 minutes. Drain and cool.
3. Combine wheat berries and wild rice with bell pepper, scallions, teriyaki sauce, and sesame seed oil and toss lightly.
4. Chill before serving.

**Nutrition Information:**

**1 Cup Serving**

| CAL 145 | CHO 26G | PRO 5G | FAT 3G | CHOL 0MG | CALCIUM 19MG | POTASSIUM 254MG | SODIUM 142MG | FIBER 4G |
|---------|---------|--------|--------|----------|--------------|-----------------|--------------|----------|

*Precook wheat berries and rice ahead of time and reduce preparation by 9 minutes!

## Soups

## ABOUT BROTH

Fresh always tastes best. The broth recipes in this book were created to lower the amount of sodium and fat that is typically found in most store brands. Included are three basic broth recipes: beef, fish stock with herbs, and vegetable.

Broth can be used as the base for soup or for cooking vegetables, meat, and pasta. If you do not cook, take a shortcut and use low-sodium, low-fat types of bouillon. Avoid products with monosodium glutamate (MSG) or hydrolyzed vegetable protein. In *Excitotoxins: The Taste that Kills,* a book published in 1997, Russell Blaylock, M.D., states that these "substances added to foods and beverages literally stimulates neurons to death, causing damage of varying degrees."

Although we still have much to learn about our body's reaction to certain foods, there may be reasons other than too much sodium in commercially prepared broth to make your own. So enjoy the difference in flavor and health from your own homemade broths.

# BEEF BROTH

1-1/2 lbs. Lean beef sirloin, cut into 1-inch
  cubes

1 medium Onion, diced

3 cloves Garlic

2 to 3 Beef bones

1 Tbsp. Olive oil

1 tsp. Salt

7 cups Water

1 tsp. Pepper, black, whole

1 stalk Celery, diced

1/2 cup Parsley, chopped

2 Leeks or scallions (optional), diced

2 Carrots, diced

To taste Salt (optional)

Total time: 2 hours, 10 minutes
Serves: 6
Serving size: 1 cup
Exchange: Free (broth only)

1. In heavy large pot, brown lean beef, onions, and garlic.
2. Add remaining ingredients and simmer, covered, for 2 hours.
3. Remove from heat and cool, then drain broth through colander lined with cheesecloth.
4. Store broth up to three days in a sealed container in the refrigerator or in the freezer up to three months until used. Remember to remove any fat that solidifies on top before reheating.

**Nutrition Information:**

**Broth Only**

CAL 55  CHO 7G  PRO 0G  FAT 3G  CHOL 28MG  CALCIUM 30MG  POTASSIUM 376MG  SODIUM 78MG*  FIBER 1G

**With 3 oz. Beef and 1/2 cup Vegetables**

CAL 272  CHO 7G  PRO 23G  FAT 17G  CHOL 68MG  CALCIUM 36MG  POTASSIUM 428MG  SODIUM 106MG**  FIBER 1G

*Made with salt, sodium is 306 milligrams.

**Made with salt, sodium is 376 milligrams.

# FISH STOCK WITH HERBS

2 medium Onions, diced

2 cloves Garlic, diced

2 Tbsp. Olive oil

1/2 cup Parsley, fresh, chopped

8 cups Water

1-1/2 lbs. Whitefish (or environmentally safe haddock, cod, sea bass, or scrod)

1 Tbsp. Salt (optional)

To taste Pepper, black, ground

Total time: 50 minutes
Serves: 6
Serving size: 1 cup
Exchange: Free

1. Sauté onions and garlic for 10 minutes in oil in a 3-quart heavy pot.
2. Add parsley, water, fish, salt, and pepper. Bring water to boil, then simmer for approximately 40 minutes.
3. Remove from heat and pour broth through strainer and cool.
4. Place in container and store in refrigerator. Use within 24 hours or serve immediately without straining.

## Serving Suggestion

Use this stock as a base for fish chowder. Just add sliced and cooked celery, canned stewed tomatoes, oregano, and cooked and diced potato.

**Nutrition Information:**

**Without Salt**

CAL 48  CHO 3G  PRO 2G  FAT 4G  CHOL 3MG  CALCIUM 18MG  POTASSIUM 81MG  SODIUM 96MG*  FIBER 1G

*With salt, 896 milligrams.

# VEGETABLE BROTH

8 cups Water

2 medium Onions, diced

1/2 cup Parsley, fresh, chopped

1/2 cup Celery, diced

1/2 cup Carrots, fresh, sliced

1 cup Spinach or escarole, fresh, cleaned and chopped

1 cup Tomatoes, plum (fresh or canned), diced

4 cloves Garlic, diced

To taste Salt (optional)

To taste Pepper, black, ground

**Vegetarian: Vegan**

Total time: 1-1/2 hours
Serves: 8
Serving size: 1 cup
Exchange: Free (broth only)

1. Combine all ingredients in a pot and simmer for 1-1/2 hours.
2. To use as a clear broth, strain the broth through a strainer or colander; reserve the liquid and discard the vegetables.
3. Optional: Place the vegetables in a food processor or blender (or use immersion blender) and purée and then add to broth.

## Serving Suggestion

Add 1-1/2 cups of cooked pasta, rice, peas, or beans to make this complete meal. Serve immediately.

**Nutrition Information:**

**Without Salt**

CAL 24  CHO 5G  PRO 1G  FAT 0G  CHOL 0MG  CALCIUM 26MG  POTASSIUM 189MG  SODIUM 15MG*  FIBER 2G

*With salt, 815 milligrams.

# CHINESE CABBAGE SOUP

*This soup is rich in soy protein to help lower cholesterol and reduce menopausal symptoms.*

1 head Cabbage, Chinese or green, washed, shredded

8 oz. Whole baby corn (1 can), cut up

2 cloves Garlic, minced

1/4 tsp. Ginger, ground

1 quart Chicken broth, low-sodium

1/4 cup Rice vinegar

1 Tbsp. Sesame seed oil

12 oz. Tofu, firm, cut into 1/2-inch cubes

1 cup Mushrooms, straw or white, quartered

3 Scallions, diced

**Vegetarian: Vegan (without chicken broth)**

Total time: 50 minutes
Serves: 12
Serving size: 1 cup
Exchange: 1 vegetable, 1/2 fat, 1/4 starch

1. Place all ingredients in large saucepan, except tofu, mushrooms, and scallions. Bring to a boil and simmer for 45 minutes.
2. Add tofu and mushrooms. Simmer 3 minutes and serve.
3. Ladle soup into 12 bowls and top each bowl with scallions.

## Optional

To make a complete meal, add fine Japanese noodles to the soup and cook for approximately 1 minute or until tender.

## Serving Suggestion

Vegetarians can substitute vegetable broth for the chicken broth. For a tastier broth, try the broth recipes at the beginning of this section.

**Nutrition Information:**

CAL 65 CHO 8G PRO 5G FAT 3G CHOL 0MG CALCIUM 82MG POTASSIUM 440MG SODIUM 93MG FIBER 2G

# ASIAN-STYLE VEGETABLE SOUP

*This soup is rich in phytonutrients and is excellent for promoting a speedy recovery to good health. And, if you are going through menopause or have prostrate problems, then the ingredients in this soup are known to be helpful.*

**Vegetarian: Vegan**

3-1/2 cups Water

1 cube Vegetable bouillon, low-sodium

1 tsp. Teriyaki sauce

1 tsp. Mellow red miso,* organic

1 small Sweet potato with skin, cleaned

1/2 Red bell pepper, seeded, cleaned, and
 diced

3 Broccoli florets, fresh, cleaned and cut up

10 Green beans, fresh, cleaned and cut into 1-inch pieces

1 clove Garlic, diced

1/2 cup Tofu, firm, diced

1 cup Rice vermicelli (Chinese pasta)

1/4 tsp. Hot chili sauce (optional)

2 Scallions, cleaned, chopped

Total time: 20 minutes
Serves: 2
Serving size: 1-1/2 cup
Exchange: 3 starch, 1-1/2 very
lean meat

1. Clean and cut all vegetables except the sweet potato.
2. Place water, bouillon, teriyaki sauce, and red miso in a 2-quart pot and bring to a boil and then simmer.
3. Pierce the sweet potato with a fork and cook in a microwave oven for 1 to 2 minutes until the potato is tender but firm. Remove and slice into 1/2-inch pieces, leaving skin on.
4. Add the sweet potato, red bell peppers, broccoli, and green beans, then add the garlic and tofu and simmer on medium heat for 1 to 3 minutes or until vegetables are firm but tender.
5. Add vermicelli and cook an additional 2 to 3 minutes or until it is soft.
6. Add hot sauce as desired.
7. Split the soup between two bowls and top each with equal amounts of scallions as garnish. Serve hot.

*(continues)*

# ASIAN-STYLE
# VEGETABLE SOUP (Continued)

### Serving Suggestion

If pressed for time, use frozen prepared vegetables instead of fresh. Leftovers can be served cold for lunch the next day. Add 1 to 2 Tablespoons of rice vinegar for a tangy twist.

**Nutrition Information:**

| CAL 307 | CHO 48g | PRO 18g | FAT 6g | CHOL 1mg | CALCIUM 195mg | POTASSIUM 591mg | SODIUM 346mg | FIBER 5g |
|---|---|---|---|---|---|---|---|---|

*Miso or soybean paste can be found in most supermarkets and Asian food markets.

# BEEF BARLEY SOUP

*This easy, one-pot meal is complete in nutrient balance.*

1 tsp. Olive oil

1 lb. Center-cut beef shank, all visible fat removed

8 cups Water

1 medium Onion, peeled and diced

2 Carrots, peeled and sliced

6 tsp. Beef bouillon, low-sodium type (optional)

To taste Black pepper, freshly ground

1-1/2 cup Celery, thinly sliced

1 cup Pearled barley, uncooked

1 lb. Mushrooms, diced

## MENU

*Mescaline Greens with Apples and Walnuts*

*Beef Barley Soup*

*Herb Biscuit*

Total time: 3 hours, 15 minutes (preparation, 15 minutes; cooking, 3 hours)
Serves: 6
Serving size: 1-1/2 cup
Exchange: 3 starch, 1 vegetable, 3 very lean meat

1. In a large stockpot, braise the meat and onion in oil.
2. Add water and bring to a boil. Reduce heat to a simmer and cook for 2 hours, or until meat is tender.
3. Add bouillon, celery, carrots, and black pepper.
4. Remove meat from pot and cut meat into small pieces, then return to soup.
5. Add barley and cook for 15 minutes more.
6. Remove from heat, cool, and refrigerate 8 to 24 hours. When cooled, remove excess fat from top.
7. When ready to serve, add mushrooms. Reheat and simmer 15 minutes, then serve hot.

### Serving Suggestion

Use the beef stock recipe at the beginning of this section. Beef bouillon can be eliminated, and the flavor will be even better as well as cut the sodium to 123 milligrams.

**Nutrition Information:**

CAL 373  CHO 51G  PRO 31G  FAT 6G  CHOL 60MG  CALCIUM 71MG  POTASSIUM 785MG  SODIUM 323MG  FIBER 11G

# CARROT SOUP WITH BROCCOLI AND EDAMAME

*Lisa O'Gorman*

**Vegetarian: Vegan
(if vegetable broth used)**

2 Tbsp. Ginger, fresh, grated

4 sticks Celery, diced

5 cloves Garlic, diced

1 large Red onion, diced

2 lbs. Carrots, peeled and diced

1 Tbsp. Olive oil

1-1/2 qts. Chicken or vegetable broth (48-oz. can)

10 oz. Broccoli (1 package), frozen and chopped (thaw under lukewarm
  running water)

1-1/2 cups Edamame (green soybeans), frozen and shelled

1-1/2 cups Water

1/2 cup Cilantro, fresh, minced

2 Tbsp. Hot sauce (Frank's Red Hot or Tabasco)

Total time: 20 minutes
Serves: 13
Serving size: 1 cup
Exchange: 1 starch, 1/2 lean meat
(if chicken broth is used)

1. Heat olive oil in large saucepan.
2. Add celery, red onion, carrots, garlic, and ginger to oil and cover with
   lid. Cook on low heat, stirring occasionally until vegetables are softened,
   approximately 6 minutes.
3. Add water and chicken broth, increase heat, and simmer until carrots
   are tender when touched with a fork, approximately 5 minutes.
4. Remove soup from heat and purée in blender (or use immersion
   blender in saucepan). Add chopped cilantro, edamame, hot sauce, and
   thawed broccoli.
5. Return soup to high heat for 4 minutes, then remove, and serve hot.

**Nutrition Information:**

**With Chicken Stock**

CAL 98 CHO 13G PRO 6G FAT 3G CHOL 0MG CALCIUM 75MG POTASSIUM 514MG SODIUM 153MG FIBER 4G

**With Vegetable Stock**

CAL 89 CHO 14G PRO 4G FAT 3G CHOL 6MG CALCIUM 74MG POTASSIUM 455MG SODIUM 238MG FIBER 4G

# CAULIFLOWER CHEDDAR SOUP

*This dish is rich in calcium for bones and phytonutrients that may help fight cancer.*

**Vegetarian: Lacto-ovo**

1 small head Cauliflower, cut into
  bite-sized pieces
3 cups Water
2 cubes Vegetable bouillon
1 Tbsp. Cornstarch
1 envelope Milk, fat-free dried (Carnation brand)
3 slices American cheese
1 Tbsp. Parsley, dried (or 2 Tbsp. fresh)
To taste Pepper, black, ground (optional)

Total time: 15 minutes
Serves: 4
Serving size: 1 cup
Exchange: 1 starch, 2 lean meat

1. In a 2-quart pot, cook cauliflower in simmering water with vegetable bouillon for approximately 5 minutes or until soft.
2. Remove from heat and drain, but reserve cooking liquid.
3. Place cauliflower in blender, add cooking liquid and fat-free dried milk, and purée (or use immersion blender in pot).
4. Return purée to pot, add cheese, and simmer for 10 minutes until well blended.
5. Add pepper to season and garnish with parsley.

## Serving Suggestion

Use a bouillon with no MSG or hydrolyzed vegetable protein—or use the homemade broth at the beginning of this section. Another option is to use chicken-flavored broth.

**Nutrition Information:**
CAL 171  CHO 17G  PRO 13G  FAT 6G  CHOL 19MG  CALCIUM 381MG  POTASSIUM 521MG  SODIUM 368MG  FIBER 2G

# CREAM OF PUMPKIN SOUP

*For less fat and creamy taste, use Skim milk Plus instead of 2 percent. Reduce the risk of cancer and protect your eyes with this recipe.*

16 oz. Pumpkin puree,* canned or
   fresh
1-1/2 cups Milk, 2 percent
1/2 cup Skim milk powder (Carnation
   brand)
1 cup Chicken broth, homemade or
   low-sodium type
1 cup Applesauce
1 Tbsp. Onion powder
To taste Cinnamon, ground (optional)
To taste Nutmeg, ground (optional)

## LUNCH MENU

*Cream of Pumpkin Soup*
*Baby Spinach and Gorgonzola
   Medley*
*Crusty Garlic Bread*

**Vegetarian: Lacto-ovo
(if vegetable broth used)**

Total time: 25 minutes
Serves: 6
Serving size: 1 cup
Exchange: 1 dairy, 1/2 starch

1. If using fresh pumpkin, boil
   pieces in water until soft, then remove from water and peel off skin.
   Purée in blender (or use immersion blender).
2. Place puréed pumpkin in a 3-quart pot and add milk, skim milk powder,
   chicken broth, and onion powder and stir to blend. Let simmer 20
   minutes, stirring occasionally.
3. Sprinkle spices on top of soup before serving.

**Nutrition Information:**

CAL 115  CHO 19G  PRO 7G  FAT 2G  CHOL 6MG  CALCIUM 221MG  POTASSIUM 475MG  SODIUM 99MG  FIBER 3G

*Butternut squash or carrot purée can be used instead of pumpkin.

# ESCAROLE AND BEAN SOUP

*This dish provides a great boost of beta-carotene, folic acid, and fiber and helps the eyes, heart, and regularity and reduces the risk of cancer when made with vegetable broth.*

1 Tbsp. Olive oil

4 cloves Garlic, minced

1 head Escarole

30 oz. Water*

3 cubes Chicken or vegetable bouillon (low-sodium)*

15 oz. Cannellini beans (1 can), drained

To taste Pepper, black, ground

**Vegetarian: Vegan**

Total time: 35 minutes
Serves: 4
Serving size: 1-1/2 cup
Exchange: 2 starch, 1 lean meat

1. Sauté garlic in olive oil.
2. Add escarole and braise for 3 minutes.
3. Add water and bouillon and simmer for 15 to 20 minutes.
4. Add beans and pepper and continue to simmer for 15 to 30 minutes over low heat.

## Serving Suggestion

Serve with roast peppers and mozzarella on a baguette (see index for recipe).

**Nutrition Information:**

CAL 194  CHO 29G  PRO 11G  FAT 4G  CHOL 1MG  CALCIUM 125MG  POTASSIUM 690MG  SODIUM 570MG  FIBER 7G

*Or use 30 ounces of homemade chicken or vegetable broth for the water and bouillon.

# GRANDMA DOT'S FAMOUS CABBAGE SOUP

*Boost your immune system and decrease your appetite with this delicious dish.*

**Vegetarian: Vegan**

*Dorothy Court*

1 small Cabbage, green, shredded

16 oz. Crushed tomatoes (1 can)

2 medium Carrots, sliced

2 stalks Celery, sliced

1 medium Onion, sliced

2 cloves Garlic, crushed

4 Bay leaves, whole

1/2 tsp. Thyme, dried

1/2 cup Parsley, fresh, chopped

32 oz. Water

1 cup Barley, pearled

To taste Salt (optional)

To taste Pepper, black, ground (optional)

Total time: 1 hour
Serves: 10
Serving size: 1 cup
Exchange: 1 starch, 1 vegetable

Place all ingredients in a 1-gallon pot and simmer for 1 hour. Serve with flat bread or high-fiber crackers.

**Nutrition Information:**

CAL 111  CHO 24G  PRO 4G  FAT 1G  CHOL 0MG  CALCIUM 63MG  POTASSIUM 322MG  SODIUM 210MG  FIBER 6G

# GREENS AND ORZO IN BROTH

*This recipe is high in folic acid and beta-carotene to help boost your immune system.*

*Gemma Arpino*

**Vegetarian: Vegan (If made with vegetable broth)**

4 cups Chicken broth, low-sodium (optional) or the vegetable broth recipe from earlier in this section

4 cloves Garlic, fresh, whole

1/4 Lemon, juice from, freshly squeezed

1-1/2 cups Kale or escarole, fresh, cleaned and chopped

1 cup Orzo pasta, cooked

To taste Pepper, black, ground (optional)

Total time: 25 minutes
Serves: 4
Serving size: 1-1/2 cup
Exchange: 1 starch

1. In a large saucepan, combine chicken broth, garlic cloves, and lemon juice. Add vegetables and bring to a simmer.
2. In a separate pot, cook pasta following package directions and then drain.
3. When vegetables are cooked and tender (approximately 15 minutes), add orzo and pepper to taste.

## Serving Suggestion

Serve topped with Parmesan cheese.

**Nutrition Information:**

CAL 83  CHO 13G  PRO 5G  FAT 1G  CHOL 0MG  CALCIUM 40MG  POTASSIUM 208MG  SODIUM 60MG  FIBER 1G

# HEARTY VEGETABLE LENTIL SOUP

*This soup is high in fiber, antioxidants, and phytonutrients that may aid in digestion. It also protects your heart and reduces the risk of cancer.*

1 cup Lentils, dried
4 Carrots, peeled and sliced
1 medium Onion, diced
2 Tomatoes, fresh, diced
1/2 tsp. Olive oil
1/2 tsp. Rosemary, dried, crushed
4 cubes Beef bouillon, low-sodium
6 cups Water

Total time: 35 minutes soak time, 45 minutes cook time
Serves: 6
Serving size: 3/4 cup
Exchange: 1-1/2 starch, 1 very lean meat

1. Soften lentils by boiling for 35 minutes in a 3-quart pot, then drain.
2. Place lentils back in the pot with the carrots, onions, tomatoes, olive oil, rosemary, and beef bouillon. Cover and simmer until lentils are tender.
3. Serve hot.

## Option

Omit the water and beef bouillon cubes and instead use 5 cups of beef broth from the recipe earlier in this section on page 181.

Nutrition Information:

CAL 140  CHO 26g  PRO 9g  FAT 1g  CHOL 0mg  CALCIUM 45mg  POTASSIUM 547mg  SODIUM 309mg*  FIBER 9g

*If regular bouillon is used, 803 milligrams.

# QUICK LOW-FAT MUSHROOM SOUP

*Mushrooms may have anticancer properties.*

1 quart Portabello mushroom soup, Imagine
  brand*

4 Tbsp. Sherry (omit for children)

8 oz. Mushrooms, white, sliced

4 Tbsp. Chives, dried, minced

**Vegetarian: Vegan**

Total time: 3–5 minutes
Serves: 4
Serving size: 1 cup
Exchange: 1 starch

1. Empty container of soup into a 2-quart saucepan. Add sherry if desired. Simmer for 3 minutes over medium heat.
2. Add mushrooms. Stir frequently and heat until mushrooms are cooked, approximately 2 minutes.
3. Top each serving with chives.

## Serving Suggestion

Serve with herb biscuits (see index for recipe).

**Nutrition Information:**

CAL 98  CHO 13G  PRO 3G  FAT 2G  CHOL 2MG  CALCIUM 62MG  POTASSIUM 257MG  SODIUM 310MG  FIBER 1G

*Found in many grocery and health food stores.

# SIMPLE NAVY BEAN SOUP

*This version is richer in fiber and lower in sodium than canned soup.*

1-1/2 cup Navy beans, dried
6 cups Water
4 cloves Garlic, chopped
1/4 Lemon, juice of, freshly squeezed
1/2 cup Onions, diced
3 Carrots, peeled and sliced
1/2 tsp. Salt
To taste Pepper, black, ground

**Vegetarian: Vegan**

Total time: 14 hours (soaking, 12 hours; cooking, 1–2 hours)
Serves: 8
Serving size: 1 cup
Exchange: 2 starch, 1/2 very lean meat

1. Soak dried beans overnight or for 12 hours. Drain.
2. Place beans in a 3-quart pot. Add water, garlic, lemon juice, onions, salt, and pepper. Bring to a boil, then simmer for 1 to 2 hours. Add more water to achieve desired consistency.
3. Serve hot.

**Nutrition Information:**

CAL 142  CHO 27G  PRO 9G  FAT 1G  CHOL 0MG  CALCIUM 76MG  POTASSIUM 422MG  SODIUM 158MG  FIBER 7G

# SUMMER GAZPACHO SOUP

*A rich source of beta-carotene and fiber make this a terrific soup.*
*Loads of anti-aging phytonutrients help boost the immune system.*

6 large Tomatoes, cut in quarters, cored

1 large Cucumber, peeled, chopped

1 small Onion, diced

1/2 Green bell pepper, diced

1 Tbsp. Basil, fresh, chopped

3 cloves Garlic, minced

2 Tbsp. Parsley, fresh, chopped (or 1 tsp. dried)

2 Tbsp. Basil, fresh, minced

2 Tbsp. Red wine vinegar

2 cups V-8 vegetable juice

4 Tbsp. Scallion, fresh, diced

4–5 drops Tabasco sauce (optional)

**Vegetarian: Vegan**

Total time: 15 minutes
Serves: 4
Serving size: 1 cup
Exchange: 1 starch, 1 vegetable

1. Place first 10 ingredients tomatoes, cucumber, onion, bell pepper, basil, garlic, parsley, basil, red wine vinegar, and V-8 in blender and purée (or use immersion blender).
2. Chill and serve garnished with chopped scallions. Add Tabasco sauce if desired.

### Serving Suggestion

Create a great vegetarian lunch with hummus and olives with pita (see index for recipe).

**Nutrition Information:**

CAL 105  CHO 24G  PRO 4G  FAT 1G  CHOL 0MG  CALCIUM 54MG  POTASSIUM 1,045MG  SODIUM 271MG  FIBER 5G

# SUNCHOKE SOUP

*Sunchokes contain phosphorus, iron, and vitamin A. They are low in starch and calories.*

*Phyllis Schondorf*

1 lb. Sunchokes, peeled and cut into 1-inch pieces
1 bunch Scallions, green part only, cut into 1-inch pieces
3 cups Water
1 cup Milk, fat-free

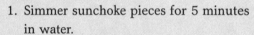

## Nutrition Nugget

Sunchokes or Jerusalem artichokes are the underground tuber of a wild sunflower that is easily grown in the northeastern United States. Look for it in the produce section, often in a 1-pound bag. Peeled and sliced, it is crunchy when eaten raw.

**Vegetarian: Lacto-ovo**

Total time: 18 minutes
Serves: 4
Serving size: 1 cup
Exchange: 1 starch

1. Simmer sunchoke pieces for 5 minutes in water.
2. Add green scallions to simmering sunchokes and cook 5 more minutes or until all are tender.
3. Remove and purée in blender or use immersion blender in pot.
4. Add milk to achieve desired consistency.
5. Soup can be served hot or chilled.

**Nutrition Information:**

CAL 86  CHO 18G  PRO 4G  FAT 0G  CHOL 1MG  CALCIUM 176MG  POTASSIUM 479MG  SODIUM 41MG  FIBER 2G

# TASTY LIMA BEAN SOUP

*The isoflavones, phytonutrients, and fiber in this soup may protect the heart, help regulate blood sugar, and stimulate the immune system.*

8 oz. Lima beans, large, dried
4 cups Chicken broth, canned
  (vegetable broth optional)*
1/4 tsp. Marjoram, crushed, dried
1/4 tsp. Rosemary, dried, crushed,
  dried
2 Tbsp. Parsley, fresh, chopped
1/2 tsp. Salt
To taste Pepper, black, ground

Before you say, "No, I don't like lima beans," try this recipe—it's a winner!

## MENU

*Romaine Garden Salad*
*Tasty Lima Bean Soup*
*Crusty Garlic Bread*

1. Soak dried lima beans overnight. Drain.
2. In a large pot, place beans in broth with marjoram, rosemary, parsley, salt, and pepper. Simmer 2 to 3 hours until beans are soft and tender. Add additional water as necessary to achieve desired consistency.

**Vegetarian: Vegan
(with vegetable broth)**

Total time: 13–15 hours (soaking, 12 hours; cooking, 1–3 hours)
Serving size: 1 cup
Serves: 8
Exchange: 1 starch, 1 very lean meat

## Serving Suggestion

Garnish with fresh rosemary sprig before serving.

**Nutrition Information:**

CAL 99  CHO 15G  PRO 8G  FAT 1G  CHOL 0MG  CALCIUM 19MG  POTASSIUM 459MG  SODIUM 661MG**  FIBER 5G

*Use low-sodium broth if you must follow a low-sodium diet or try our recipes for broth. Substitute vegetable broth if you are a vegetarian.

**Homemade broth lowers sodium to 234 milligrams. Omit salt to lower even more.

# TORTELLINI IN BROTH

*This dish provides a delicious way to get
your greens and add calcium to your diet.*

1 quart Chicken broth, homemade*
1 lb. Cheese tortellini, fresh (packaged)
3/4 cup Spinach, cooked, chopped
1/4 cup Parsley, fresh, chopped
4 tsp. Parmesan cheese

Total time: 15 minutes
Serves: 4
Serving size: 1 cup
Exchange: 1-1/2 starch,
1 high-fat meat

1. Place broth in a 2-quart pot and bring to a boil.
2. Add tortellini to broth and cook over medium heat until pasta is
   *al dente,*** approximately 10 minutes. Serve immediately.

## Serving Suggestion

Top with chopped fresh parsley and 1 teaspoon Parmesan cheese per serving.
Complement with sliced garlic bread and tomato salad.

**Nutrition Information:**

CAL 213  CHO 23G  PRO 13G  FAT 8G  CHOL 97MG  CALCIUM 178MG  POTASSIUM 330MG  SODIUM 173MG  FIBER 2G

*See recipe earlier in this section for broth or use a low-sodium store brand. For a vegetarian version, substitute chicken broth with vegetable broth.

**Literally, "to the tooth" in Italian; means that pasta should be cooked but not soft.

# Chapter 8

# GRAINS

## ABOUT GRAINS

### Nutrition Information

Whenever possible, use whole grains rather than refined, artificially fortified grains. Each kernel of a whole grain is made up of three major components: germ, endosperm, and bran. The *germ* is a tiny nutrient-packed seed that provides fat, protein, carbohydrates, and vitamins and is capable of sprouting into a new plant.

The *endosperm* comprises complex carbohydrates encased in protein that provides initial energy to the grain embryo.

The *bran* is a hard protective coat that provides important fiber, vitamins, and minerals.

Combined, the germ, endosperm, and bran are a source of long-lasting energy, a rich source of B vitamins, vitamin E, and minerals, especially calcium, phosphorous, and iron. Finally, they are low in calories, fat, and cholesterol and high in fiber.

Most Americans are familiar with corn (the only indigenous grain to the Americas), wheat, oats, and rice. As cultures and cuisines from around the world begin to mix, we are also introduced to others—quinoa, millet, polenta, teff, and spelt, to name a few.

A world of possibilities awaits your next meal. See Table 8-1 or try recipes in this cookbook or the many ethnic cookbooks that use different grains. Whether you want to improvise or sample a worldly tradition, this book can help you get started.

Starchy vegetables are also placed in this section to help you design balanced meals.

Some question grains such as corn which may be genetically modified (GMO). Many European countries ban GMO grains because long-term effects on health are unknown. Organic grains may protect you from unwanted pesticide residue but laws from state to state vary and do not guarantee protection from unwanted pollutants.

**TABLE 8-1 Great Grains**

| Grain | How to cook | Characteristics |
|---|---|---|
| Amaranth | 1 cup to 2-1/2 cups water for 20 minutes | Prized crop of the Aztecs; adds a crunchy texture to breads, cookies, and casseroles. |
| Barley, whole | 1 cup to 3 cups water for 60 minutes | Has a pleasant, chewy texture; can be substituted for brown rice. |
| Buckwheat | 1 cup to 2 cups water for 10 minutes | Toasted buckwheat (kasha) has a robust, hearty flavor; good cold weather fare. |
| Bulgur | 1 cup to 2 cups water for 10 minutes | Made by soaking and cooking the whole wheat kernel, then removing 5 percent of the bran and cracking the remaining kernel into small pieces. It can be used in salads, soups, breads, and desserts. |
| Corn | To make polenta, 1 cup coarse yellow or white cornmeal to 4 cups water for 30 minutes | Top polenta with yogurt or maple syrup for breakfast; layer with sauce and veggies for lasagna or pizza. |
| Couscous | 1 cup to 2-1/2 cups water for 10 minutes | Made from durum wheat, it tastes like pasta; often served as a pilaf, couscous is a good source of protein. |
| Millet | 1 cup to 3 cups water for 30 minutes | A welcome change to rice; light toasting gives it a pleasing aroma and almost nutty flavor. It adds texture and flavor to breads and can be ground and used like cornmeal. |
| Oats | 1 cup whole oats in 4 cups water for 60 minutes; rolled oats in 2 cups water for 10 minutes; steel cut oats in 3 cups water for 30 minutes | Oats are rich in protein and minerals; although oats have appeared on the breakfast table for many years, oat flour is a tasty addition to breads and baked goods. |
| Quinoa | 1 cup to 2 cups water for 15 minutes | Although not a true grain, this prize of the Incas is a superior source of protein, as well as calcium, iron, vitamins, and potassium. Tasty and quick |

| Grain | How to cook | Characteristics |
| --- | --- | --- |
| | | cooking, it is a welcome addition to almost any dish from salads to desserts. |
| Rice | 1 cup to 2 cups water; bring to a boil for 8 minutes, then reduce to low for 35 minutes | Many different varieties abound, each with unique flavor and texture characteristics. |
| Rye | 1 cup in 2 cups water for approximately 10 minutes | With a hearty flavor, rye can be eaten like rolled oats or added to bread for chewiness. |
| Spelt berries, ground | | Use in place of wheat in baked goods, cereals, and other recipes; related to wheat but frequently tolerated by those who have wheat allergies. |
| Teff | 1 cup to 3 cups water for 15 minutes | The smallest grain in the world, its size prohibits it from being hulled, thus retaining all the whole grain nutrients. It is delicious in combination with other grains. |

Achieve vital fiber in your diet with a different grain each day. They help lower cholesterol, regulate blood sugar and reduce the risk of colon cancer. Enjoy new varieties and break free of limited choices of the past.

Buying Tips: Unfortunately, "Quick" types of grains offer less fiber and more sodium, so compare labels.

Check for availability in these locations: general supermarket, health food stores, co-operative stores, and natural food–oriented markets (for example, Trader Joe's and Whole Foods).

*Source:* Information and chart prepared by Sundance Natural Foods, Inc. See http://www.sundancenaturalfoods.com/.

# ACORN SQUASH

*This vegetable is rich in beta-carotene.*

**Vegetarian: Vegan**

2 medium Acorn squash
2 Tbsp. Honey
1/2 tsp. Cinnamon, ground
1/2 cup Water

Total time: 55 minutes
Serves: 8
Serving size: 1/4
Exchange: 1 starch

1. Cut squash in quarters, remove seeds, and rinse clean.
2. Place squash quarters in a baking pan with a cover.
3. Drizzle honey over each piece and sprinkle with cinnamon.
4. Place 1/2 cup water in the pan, cover, and bake 45 to 60 minutes at 350°F or until tender.

**Nutrition Information:**

CAL 77   CHO 20G   PRO 1G   FAT 0G   CHOL 0MG   CALCIUM 50MG   POTASSIUM 474MG   SODIUM 5MG   FIBER 2G

# BROWN BASMATI

*Dr. Wahida Karmally, Registered Dietitian, CDE*

1 cup Brown basmati rice
2 Bay leaves, whole
1 Tbsp. Olive oil
2 cups Water
1/4 tsp. Salt

## Nutrition Nugget

Some brands of brown rice are higher in fiber than others, so check labels.

**Vegetarian: Vegan**

Total time: 30 minutes
Serves: 4
Serving size: 1/2 cup
Exchange: 2 starch, 1 vegetable

1. Place the water in a covered pot on the stovetop and bring to a boil.
2. Add the basmati rice, bay leaves, salt, and olive oil and stir. When the water begins to boil, stir again and cover. Lower the heat to simmer. Do not stir again. The basmati rice should be done in 20 to 30 minutes.

**Nutrition Information:**
CAL 210  CHO 38G  PRO 4G  FAT 4G  CHOL 0MG  CALCIUM 22MG  POTASSIUM 61MG  SODIUM 155MG  FIBER 3G

# BUTTERNUT SQUASH WITH APPLE BUTTER

1 large Butternut squash
1 cup Water
1/2 cup Apple butter
2 Tbsp. Pine nuts
To taste Cinnamon, ground

**Vegetarian: Vegan**

Total time: 15 minutes
Serves: 6
Serving size: 1/2 cup
Exchange: 1 starch, 1/4 vegetable

1. Pierce squash skin with a fork and place in a microwave oven for 3 minutes or until fork inserts easily. Remove and cut in half. Remove seeds and skin and cut into 2-inch pieces.
2. Boil water in a microwavable dish, add squash pieces, cover, and steam in microwave for 4 minutes or until soft enough to mash.
3. Drain water, place squash in a bowl, add apple butter, and mash or place in a blender or food processor to purée.
4. Serve topped with pine nuts and cinnamon.

**Nutrition Information:**

CAL 105  CHO 21G  PRO 1G  FAT 2G  CHOL 0MG  CALCIUM 46MG  POTASSIUM 348MG  SODIUM 7MG  FIBER 3G

# CHEDDAR-STUFFED BAKED POTATO

**Vegetarian: Lacto-ovo**

*Delicious way to get calcium and potassium! Great after school or work snack!*

1 small Idaho potato
1/4 cup Salsa, commercial
2 oz. Cheddar cheese (Cracker Barrel
  Light or reduced or low-fat cheddar)

Total time: conventional oven, 45 minutes; microwave, 5 minutes
Serves: 1
Serving size: 1 potato
Exchange: 1 starch, 1/2 nonfat dairy, 1-1/2 lean meat

1. Preheat oven to 350°F.
2. Pierce potato skin with fork, then bake whole potato until done (approximately 30 to 40 minutes in conventional oven, 5 to 8 minutes in microwave).
3. Remove potato from oven and slice lengthwise. Using a fork, mash the inside of each half leaving potato in skin.
4. Top each half with equal parts salsa and cheddar cheese.
5. Place potato halves under a broiler for a few minutes until the cheese is melted. Serve hot.

**Nutrition Information:**
CAL 186  CHO 21G  PRO 16G  FAT 4G  CHOL 12MG  CALCIUM 428MG  POTASSIUM 469MG  SODIUM 526MG  FIBER 3G

# CRANBERRY PECAN STUFFING

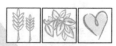

*High in fiber, this stuffing has better phytofats than traditional sausage stuffing, which is high in saturated fat. This recipe is also rich in vitamin E and Omega-3 fatty acids.*

1/2 cup Onion, yellow, diced

2 cloves Garlic, minced

1/2 cup Celery, diced

1 Tbsp. Olive oil

8 oz. Turkey gizzards

1 quart Water

1/2 cup Mushrooms, fresh, sliced

2 Tbsp. Butter (optional)

1/4 cup Pecans or almonds, chopped

16 oz. Bread, dried (mixed: pumpernickel, rye, whole wheat, multigrain, raisin), diced

1/2 cup Parsley, fresh, chopped

1/4 cup Flaxseed meal

1/2 cup Cranberries, fresh

1/2 tsp. Poultry seasoning, dried

1/2 cup Apples, fresh, peeled and diced

1/8 tsp. Thyme, dried

1 cup Wild rice, cooked

1/8 tsp. Sage, dried

3 Eggs, beaten

To taste Salt

To taste Pepper, black, ground

> Total time: 1 hour
> Serves: 10
> Serving size: 3/4 cup
> Exchange: 1-1/2 starch, 1 fat, 1 fruit, 1 medium fat meat

1  In a 2-quart pot, sauté onion, garlic, and celery in 2 teaspoons of olive oil, then add gizzards and sauté until gizzards are brown.

2. Add water, butter, salt, and pepper and simmer approximately 30 minutes.

3. Remove gizzards from broth and discard.

4. Add 1/2 cup to 1 cup broth to the dried bread. It should be moist but not soaked.

*(continues)*

# CRANBERRY PECAN STUFFING (Continued)

5. Place diced bread in a separate bowl. Mix remaining ingredients with bread—mushrooms, nuts, parsley, flaxseed meal, cranberries, poultry seasoning, apples, thyme, apples, wild rice, sage, and eggs—with bread.
6. Place mixture in a casserole dish lightly oiled with 1 teaspoon of olive oil. Bake at 350°F for approximately 30 minutes or until done.

**Nutrition Information:**

CAL 298  CHO 39G  PRO 11G  FAT 13G  CHOL 87MG  CALCIUM 81MG  POTASSIUM 363MG  SODIUM 531MG  FIBER 8G

# CRISPY HERB POTATO WEDGES

*These are great with a veggie burger.*

**Vegetarian: Lacto-ovo**

3/4 lb. or 3 large Baking potatoes, cut into thin
  wedges, skin on
1/4 tsp. Onion powder
1/8 tsp. each Garlic powder, dried oregano, dried
  basil
1 Tbsp. Parmesan cheese
1 Tbsp. Parsley, dried or fresh
1 Tbsp. Olive oil
To taste Pepper, black, ground (optional)

Total time: 25 minutes
Serves: 4
Serving size: 1/2 cup
Exchange: 1 starch

1. Preheat oven to 450°F.
2. Place potatoes and all herbs except black pepper in a plastic bag. Close
   bag and shake until potatoes are coated.
3. Coat a nonstick baking sheet with 1/2 Tablespoon of olive oil; arrange
   potatoes on sheet and drizzle top of potatoes with remaining oil. Bake 10
   minutes, then turn potatoes over and bake until edges are lightly
   browned, approximately 10 minutes longer.
4. Sprinkle potatoes with black pepper and serve.

**Nutrition Information:**

CAL 94  CHO 18G  PRO 2G  FAT 2G  CHOL 1G  CALCIUM 35MG  POTASSIUM 308MG  SODIUM 35MG  FIBER 2G

# CURRIED MILLET

*These tiny yellow kernels are a grain staple in many countries. The slightly chewy texture is enjoyable as a breakfast cereal or as a side dish at dinner.*

*Phyllis Schondorf*

**Vegetarian: Vegan
(with vegetable broth)**

Total time: 20 minutes
Serves: 6
Serving size: 1 cup
Exchange: 2 starch, 1 fat

1 Tbsp. Olive oil

1 medium Onion, diced

3 cloves Garlic, minced

1 Green bell pepper, seeded and thinly sliced

1 Apple, peeled, cored, and diced

2 Carrots, peeled and thinly sliced

2 Zucchini, cut into 1/2-inch slices

1 cup Millet

2 cups Broth, vegetable or chicken, boiling

1 tsp. Ginger, ground

1 tsp. Curry powder (adjust to taste)

To taste Black pepper, freshly ground

1. Heat the oil in a sauce pan, then lightly brown the onion and garlic.
2. Add the onion, garlic, green pepper, apple, carrots, and zucchini and cook, stirring often, approximately 5 minutes.
3. Add millet, hot broth, and seasonings. Mix well and simmer, covered, on low heat until liquid is absorbed, approximately 15 minutes.

**Nutrition Information:**

**With Chicken Broth**

CAL 208  CHO 36G  PRO 7G  FAT 4G  CHOL 0MG  CALCIUM 35MG  POTASSIUM 468MG  SODIUM 355MG  FIBER 6G

**With Vegetable Broth**

CAL 199  CHO 37G  PRO 5G  FAT 4G  CHOL 0MG  CALCIUM 34MG  POTASSIUM 414MG  SODIUM 346MG  FIBER 6G

# ESCAROLE AND BEANS

*This dish is rich in fiber and folic acid, which is especially important during pregnancy.*

1 Tbsp. Olive oil

3 cloves Garlic, minced

1 small head Escarole, fresh, washed

1-1/2 cups Water

29 oz. Cannellini beans (1 large can)

To taste Salt (optional)

To taste Pepper, black, ground
   (optional)

**VEGETARIAN MENU**

Tomato Mozzarella Salad

*Escarole and Beans*

Crusty Garlic Bread

Cherry Yogurt Parfait

**Vegetarian: Vegan**

Total time: 25 minutes
Serves: 4
Serving size: 1 cup
Exchange: 2 starch, 1 lean meat

1. Place oil in a 4-quart pot over medium heat.
2. Add garlic and lightly sauté.
3. Add escarole and sauté with garlic until leaves wilt.
4. Add water, cover pot, and simmer until escarole is tender and liquid is reduced by half (approximately 10 minutes).
5. Add beans and simmer 10 more minutes. Serve.

## Serving Suggestion

This makes a great side dish. You can also add a 12-oz. can of chicken or vegetable broth and serve 1 cup of the dish as a soup lunch with a slice of whole wheat bread and a glass of milk.

**Nutrition Information:**

CAL 198   CHO 31G   PRO 12G   FAT 4G   CHOL 0MG   CALCIUM 153MG   POTASSIUM 913MG   SODIUM 321MG   FIBER 10G

# GARLIC MASHED POTATOES

*This recipe offers a rich source of potassium.*

**Vegetarian: Lacto-ovo**

4 large Eastern potatoes, quartered, skin on
2 quarts Water
1 Tbsp. Butter
Pinch Garlic powder
1/4 cup Milk, fat-free
To taste Pepper, white, ground

Total time: 25 minutes
Serves: 6
Serving size: 1/2 cup
Exchange: 1-1/2 starch

1. Place potato quarters in a pot with cold water, bring to a boil, and cook for approximately 20 minutes or until quarters are soft.
2. Drain water and mash potato until smooth, then add remaining ingredients and mash again until blended and creamy. Serve hot.

## Serving Suggestion

For more flavor, sauté two freshly sliced garlic cloves and 3 Tablespoons of chopped fresh parsley in the butter instead of the garlic powder.

**Nutrition Information:**

CAL 126  CHO 25G  PRO 2G  FAT 2G  CHOL 5MG  CALCIUM 29MG  POTASSIUM 420MG  SODIUM 26MG  FIBER 3G

# GREEK-STYLE FAVA BEANS

*Chef Brian MacMenamin*

**Vegetarian: Vegan**

2 Tbsp. Olive oil

1 clove Garlic, thinly sliced

1 Onion, fine dice

1 lb. Fava beans (canned), drained

8 Tomatoes, skinned, seeded, and diced

2 Tbsp. Dry white wine

1 Tbsp. Parsley, fresh, chopped

1 Tbsp. Oregano, fresh, chopped

1 Tbsp. Tarragon leaves, chopped

1 Bay leaf, whole

To taste Pepper, black, ground

> Total time: 20 minutes
> Serves: 4–6
> Serving size: 2/3 cup
> Exchange: For 4, 1 vegetable, 2 starch,
> 1 fat, 1 lean meat

1. Heat the oil in a pan, add the garlic and onion, and sauté for 4 to 5 minutes over medium high.
2. Stir in the fava beans and toss well to coat in the oil.
3. Add the tomatoes, wine, parsley, oregano, tarragon, and bay leaf and season with pepper to taste. Cook on low heat for 5 minutes.
4. Remove the bay leaf and let the beans cool before serving.

## Serving Suggestion

Serve a side dish or a vegetarian entrée. Reduce portion to one-half cup for a side dish.

**Nutrition Information:**

**Four Servings**

CAL 289  CHO 44G  PRO 13G  FAT 8G  CHOL 0MG  CALCIUM 133MG  POTASSIUM 1,097MG  SODIUM 452MG  FIBER 11G

# GRILLED CORN ON THE COB

*No time to husk corn? Place it on an outdoor grill. Fresh local corn is not only great for you but also good for the environment because it requires less energy use and packaging.*

**Vegetarian: Vegan**

Total time: 10–12 minutes
Serves: 4
Serving size: 1 ear
Exchange: 1 starch, 1 vegetable

4 medium ears Corn, fresh

Husk and cook until tender, approximately 10 minutes; turn the ears every 3 to 4 minutes. Cover with the grill lid to cook evenly. Serve hot.

## Serving Suggestion

Let everyone husk their own. Leaving the husk on gives the corn great flavor and makes cooking incredibly easy.

**Nutrition Information:**

CAL 108  CHO 25G  PRO 3G  FAT 1G  CHOL 3MG  CALCIUM 2MG  POTASSIUM 249MG  SODIUM 17MG  FIBER 4G

# HOT AND SPICY BLACK-EYED PEAS

*Black-eyed peas are high in fiber and isoflavones and may help lower cholesterol.*

1 small Onion, diced
1 tsp. Olive oil
1 stalk Celery, diced
15-1/2 oz. Black-eyed peas (1 can), drained
1/2 cup Water
1/4 cup Red bell pepper, diced
1/4 tsp. Cumin, ground
1/4 tsp. Garlic powder

**MENU**

Mesclun Salad
Barbecue Chicken
*Hot and Spicy Black-Eyed Peas*
Collard Greens

**Vegetarian: Vegan**

Total time: 15 minutes
Serves: 4
Serving size: 1/3 cup
Exchange: 2 starch, 1 very lean meat

1. Sauté onion in oil until translucent and caramelized.
2. Add celery, black-eyed peas, water, bell pepper, cumin, and garlic powder and simmer covered for 10 minutes. Serve hot.

**Nutrition Information:**

CAL 181  CHO 32G  PRO 11G  FAT 2G  CHOL 0MG  CALCIUM 113MG  POTASSIUM 721MG  SODIUM 15MG  FIBER 8G

# LENTILS WITH PLANTAINS BRAZILIAN STYLE

*This dish is an excellent source of fiber.*

*Eva Cahvez and Juliana Maldanado*

**Vegetarian: Vegan**

Total time: 35 minutes
Serves: 4
Serving size: 1/4
Exchange: 4 starch, 2 vegetables

6 cups Water
1 cup Lentils, dried
1 medium Carrot, peeled and sliced
1 medium Potato, peeled and sliced
  diagonally into 1/2-inch pieces
1 large Plantain, yellow type turned black, sliced with skin on
1 small Apple, skin on, cored and diced
1 medium Tomato, quartered
2 cloves Garlic
1 small Onion, peeled and quarter
As needed Water

1. Boil lentils with oil and water.
2. When lentils are *al dente* (firm), add carrots, potato, plantain, and apple and cook until tender.
3. In a blender or food processor, chop garlic, onion, and tomato in 1 Tablespoon of water. Pour the resulting garlic mixture through a strainer to remove seeds.
4. Heat oil in a skillet, then remove the skillet from the heat and add the garlic mixture, then return to medium heat for approximately 4 minutes.
5. Add the lentil and vegetable mixture, stir to blend, and then heat for 1 more minute.
6. Optional: Remove skins from plantains before serving.

## Serving Suggestion

Serve this dish with rice to create a vegetarian meal or as a side dish. Serves eight if used as a side dish, so cut the exchange in half.

**Nutrition Information:**

CAL 314  CHO 68G  PRO 14G  FAT 1G  CHOL 0MG  CALCIUM 53MG  POTASSIUM 1,166MG  SODIUM 29MG  FIBER 12G

# OVEN-BAKED POTATO WITH VEGETABLES

*Dorothy Court*

16 medium Red potatoes, tennis ball-sized, skin on, small dice

1 Red or green bell pepper, fresh, cut into strips

1 large Onion, peeled and sliced into 1/4-inch rings

1 cup Italian flat-leaf parsley, fresh, minced

2 cloves Garlic, minced

2 tsp. Oregano or rosemary, dried

1 eight ounce package Mushrooms, fresh, white, thinly sliced

1 Tbsp. Butter, melted

1 Tbsp. Olive oil

To taste Pepper, black, ground

**Vegetarian: Lacto-ovo**

Total time: 35 minutes
Serves: 16
Serving size: 1/16 portion
Exchange: 1 starch, 2 vegetables

1. Preheat oven to 350°F.
2. Place all ingredients in a large baking pan and mix together to evenly coat with herbs.
3. Bake for approximately 15 minutes, then stir to give uniform color to all vegetables. Bake for another 15 minutes or until potatoes are golden.

**Nutrition Information:**

CAL 123  CHO 25g  PRO 3g  FAT 2g  CHOL 2mg  CALCIUM 18mg  POTASSIUM 511mg  SODIUM 14mg  FIBER 3g

# PORTABELLO MUSHROOM–STUFFED BAKED POTATO

*The anticancer properties of mushrooms help make this dish a winner. Eat the skin for fiber.*

**Vegetarian: Vegan**

4 small Russet potatoes

1 small Onion, yellow, finely diced

1/4 tsp. Garlic, fresh, minced

1 Tbsp. Olive oil

2 large Portabello mushrooms, small dice

1/4 cup Parsley, fresh, minced

> Total time: Conventional oven, 50 minutes; microwave, 15 minutes
> Serves: 4
> Serving size: 1 potato
> Exchange: 1-1/2 starch, 1 vegetable, 1/2 fat

## Conventional Oven

1. Preheat oven to 350°F.
2. Wash potatoes and prick with fork to pierce the skin once to allow steam to escape during baking. Place in a pan and bake whole for approximately 45 minutes or until soft in center. Test with a fork.
3. While potato is baking, sauté the onion and garlic in oil over medium heat until the onion is caramelized. Add parsley and mushrooms and cook until the mushroom is tender but not mushy.
4. Remove cooked potato from the oven and cut lengthwise in half. Leaving potato in the skin, mash the inside to soften, then top with the mushroom mixture.

## Microwave Oven

If you are pressed for time, this shorter version may be easier. The potato skin, however, will be less crispy.

1. Place potato in the microwave and cook for 2 to 3minutes (time may vary depending on the microwave).
2. Follow the instructions above to cook mushrooms and other vegetables, then stuff the split potatoes.

**Nutrition Information:**

CAL 127  CHO 21G  PRO 19G  FAT 4G  CHOL 0MG  CALCIUM 4MG  POTASSIUM 435MG  SODIUM 37MG  FIBER 3G

# QUINOA WITH APPLE

1 Tbsp. Olive oil
1 Onion, diced
1 cup Quinoa, well-rinsed
1/2 cup Apple, peeled, diced
3 cloves Garlic
2-1/2 cups Water, boiled
4 tsp. Vegetable base, low-sodium

Quinoa is technically not a grain, but the dried fruit from the Chenopodium herb family. The three main varieties of quinoa differ dramatically in texture, color, and flavor. The higher quality seeds will taste bittersweet, which I do not personally enjoy.

The shelf life of quinoa is approximately one month because the seed is rich in essential oils, which makes it a prime target for spoilage microorganisms. You will be able to keep quinoa longer if you store in the refrigerator.

1. Heat the oil in a large skillet and add the onion and sauté until translucent.
2. Add the quinoa, apple, and garlic and stir over medium heat for 3 minutes.
3. Pour in the hot water and vegetable base and bring to a boil. Reduce the heat, cover, and allow to simmer until tender, approximately 20 minutes.

**Vegetarian: Vegan**

Total time: 25 minutes
Serves: 4
Serving size: 1/2 cup
Exchange: 2 starch, 1/2 fat

## Serving Suggestion

Serve as main meal with vegetables or as a side dish.

**Nutrition Information:**

CAL 154  CHO 28G  PRO 6G  FAT 2G  CHOL 0MG  CALCIUM 60MG  POTASSIUM 420MG  SODIUM 65MG  FIBER 2G

# RICE WITH ALMONDS

*Almonds are rich in Omega-3 fatty acids and vitamin E, which may help your heart.*

*Dorothy Court*

| Total time: 25 minutes |
|---|
| Serves: 4 |
| Serving size: 2/3 cup |
| Exchange: 3 starch, 1 fat |

1 Tbsp. Butter, unsalted
1 cup Rice, white
1/2 small Onion, diced
1 stalk Celery, thinly sliced
2 tsp. Bouillon, granulated, chicken or vegetable, low-sodium*
2 cups Water
Pinch Thyme, dried
1/4 cup Slivered almonds

1. Melt butter in a skillet, then add rice and brown until golden. Add onion and celery and cook until translucent.
2. Add remaining bouillon, water, and thyme and then stir, cover, and simmer over low heat for 15 to 20 minutes or until fluffy.
3. Serve rice topped with almond slivers.

**Nutrition Information:**

CAL 265  CHO 43G  PRO 6G  FAT 7G  CHOL 8MG  CALCIUM 41MG  POTASSIUM 125MG  SODIUM 25MG  FIBER 2G

*Herb Ox brand claims "no MSG added" (or use equivalent).

# ROSEMARY NEW POTATOES

6 medium New red potatoes

1 quart Water

1 Tbsp. Rosemary, fresh, minced

1 Tbsp. Butter

To taste Garlic powder

To taste Pepper, black, ground

**Vegetarian: Lacto-ovo**

Total time: 10 minutes
Serves: 6
Serving size: 1 medium potato
Exchange: 1/2 starch

1. Cut potatoes in half, leaving skins on. Place in pot with 1 quart cold water and boil until soft but not mushy. Remove from heat and drain.
2. Add remaining ingredients and serve.

**Nutrition Information:**

CAL 56   CHO 9G   PRO 1G   FAT 2G   CHOL 5MG   CALCIUM 5MG   POTASSIUM 151MG   SODIUM 15MG   FIBER 1G

# SIMPLE PINEAPPLE SWEET POTATOES

8 small Sweet potatoes

1 cup Crushed pineapple, unsweetened with juice

1 tsp. Cinnamon, ground

1/4 tsp. Nutmeg, ground

**Vegetarian: Vegan**

Total time: 45 minutes
Serves: 8
Serving size: 1 small potato
Exchange: 1 starch, 1/2 fruit

1. Preheat oven to 350°F.
2. Cut washed potatoes in half and place in casserole dish. Sprinkle with cinnamon and top with pineapple. Cover and bake for 40 minutes.
3. Remove cover, use fork to check for softness, and continue baking until potatoes are fully cooked.

**Nutrition Information:**

CAL 81 CHO 20G PRO 1G FAT 0G CHOL 0MG CALCIUM 25MG POTASSIUM 323MG SODIUM 6MG FIBER 2G

# SUNDAY ITALIAN PASTA

*Who needs meat when you have the flavor of herbs?*

1 medium Onion, fresh, diced
1 Tbsp. Olive oil, extra virgin
4 cloves Garlic, fresh, peeled and sliced
1 lb. Mushrooms, fresh, sliced
4–5 Tomatoes, fresh (vine-ripened are best), diced
6 leaves Basil, fresh, minced
1/4 cup Parsley, fresh, minced
As needed Water for pasta
1 lb. Pasta (angel hair or vermicelli)
To taste Salt
To taste Pepper, black, ground
4 Tbsp. Parmesan cheese, grated or shaved (omit for vegan version)

## VEGETARIAN MENU

Baby Spinach and Gorgonzola
  Medley
*Sunday Italian Pasta*
Crusty Garlic Bread

**Vegetarian: Lacto-ovo or Vegan**

Total time: 25 minutes
Serves: 8
Serving size: 1 cup
Exchange: 3 starch, 1 fat, 1 vegetable

1. In a skillet over medium heat, sauté the onions and garlic in olive oil until translucent.
2. Add mushrooms, tomatoes, basil, and parsley. Simmer on low heat for an additional 15 to 20 minutes or until tomatoes are cooked through.
3. While tomatoes are simmering, boil water for pasta. Place pasta in boiling water; add 1 teaspoon of oil to prevent sticking. Cook until *al dente* (tender but not mushy). Remove from heat and drain well.
4. Mix pasta thoroughly with sautéed tomatoes and mushrooms.
5. Season with salt, pepper, and Parmesan cheese as desired and serve immediately.

**Nutrition Information:**
CAL 582  CHO 105G  PRO 23G  FAT 8G  CHOL 5MG  CALCIUM 139MG  POTASSIUM 900MG  SODIUM 435MG  FIBER 8G

# SWEET POTATO FRIES

*Sweet potatoes are rich in beta-carotene and vitamin A, which are great for skin and vision.*

**Vegetarian: Vegan**

1 lb. Sweet potatoes
1 Tbsp. White balsamic vinegar
1 Tbsp. Olive oil, light
3 Tbsp. Italian parsley, minced
1/2 tsp. Kosher salt (optional)
To taste Pepper, black, ground

Total time: 20 minutes
Serves: 4
Serving size: 4 oz. or 1/2 cup
Exchange: 1 starch, 1 fat

1. Preheat oven to 450°F.
2. Wash and cut sweet potatoes into french fry–style strips.
3. Coat a nonstick pan with 1/4 teaspoon olive oil.
4. Put sweet potato fries, vinegar, remaining oil, parsley, salt, and pepper into a plastic ziplock bag and shake to coat the sweet potato.
5. Arrange the fries evenly on a sheet pan and bake in oven for approximately 8 minutes, then turn the fries and bake another 8 minutes until golden brown.

**Nutrition Information:**

CAL 104  CHO 17G  PRO 1G  FAT 4G  CHOL 0MG  CALCIUM 28MG  POTASSIUM 361MG  SODIUM 305MG*  FIBER 2G

*Without salt, 5 milligrams.

# WHEAT BERRIES WITH PASTA

*Children will love this high protein grain, which not only adds fiber but also is satisfying. This makes a great vegetarian meal just a few hours before a sporting event.*

1 cup Wheat berries

2 cups Vegetable broth*

3 cups Water

8 oz. Tubettini pasta, uncooked

1–2 Tbsp. Parsley, fresh, minced (or to taste)

To taste Garlic powder

2 Tbsp. Parmesan cheese, shredded

---

### VEGETARIAN MENU

Italian Tomato Salad

*Wheat Berries with Pasta*

Spinach Sauté

**Vegetarian: Lacto-ovo**

Total time: 1 hour, 30 minutes
Serves: 4 as meal, 8 as side dish
Serving size: 3/4 cup, 1/3 cup
Exchange: Meal, 2 starch, 1 lean meat; side dish, 2 starch, 1/2 lean meat

1. Place wheat berries and broth in a 1-quart pot. Simmer for 90 minutes or until wheat berries are tender. Drain.

2. Add pasta to boiling water and cook until tender; approximately 15 minutes. Drain.

3. Mix pasta and wheat berries. Add fresh parsley, garlic powder, and Parmesan cheese.

### Serving Suggestion

Prepare wheat berries one or two days ahead and reduce meal preparation time to 15 minutes. Wheat berries will last three to four days in a sealed container in the refrigerator.

**Nutrition Information:**

**For 3/4 cup**

CAL 313  CHO 63G  PRO 13G  FAT 3G  CHOL 2MG  CALCIUM 71MG  POTASSIUM 300MG  SODIUM 152MG  FIBER 6G

**For 1/3 cup**

CAL 157  CHO 32G  PRO 7G  FAT 1G  CHOL 1MG  CALCIUM 36MG  POTASSIUM 150MG  SODIUM 76MG  FIBER 3G

*Use low-sodium broth if you are on a low-sodium diet.

# Chapter 9

# SANDWICHES AND WRAPS

## BARBECUE CHICKEN WEDGE

*This is a teen favorite.*

1 Baguette, 8 inches long
6 oz. Chicken breasts, cooked, sliced
  (not deli)
1 Tbsp. Barbecue sauce
4 leaves Romaine lettuce
4 slices Tomato, medium

### BAG LUNCH MENU

*Barbecue Chicken Wedge*
Tangerine or Clementine
  Orange
Low-Fat Chocolate Milk

1. Cut baguette in half lengthwise.
2. Place chicken on bread and top
   with lettuce and tomato.
3. Spread sauce on the other half of
   the bread and close to form a sandwich.
4. Cut in half and serve.

Total time: 6 minutes
Serves: 2
Serving size: 4-inch baguette
Exchange: 3 starch, 1 fruit, 3 lean meat

**Nutrition Information:**

CAL 446  CHO 62G  PRO 27G  FAT 10G  CHOL 72MG  CALCIUM 115MG  POTASSIUM 520MG  SODIUM 811MG  FIBER 4G

# CHICKEN AND BEAN BURRITO

*This burrito has lots of fiber, calcium, and great taste all in one.*

*Michelle Jackson*

4 Flour or corn tortillas, 6 inches
   round
1 cup Vegetarian refried beans
1 cup White meat chicken,* cooked
   and shredded
1 Tomato, cored and diced
1 cup Cheddar cheese, low-fat or light,
   shredded
2 Tbsp. Onion, diced
2 Tbsp. Cilantro leaves, cleaned and
   minced
1 cup Salsa
4 Tbsp. Sour cream, low-fat
1 Green onion, sliced (optional)

**MENU**

Black Olives and Celery Sticks
*Chicken and Bean Burrito*
Fresh Pineapple

Total time: 26 minutes
Serves: 4
Serving size: 1 burrito
Exchange: 2 starch, 2 lean meat,
1 reduced fat dairy

1. Wrap tortillas lightly in foil and heat in 350°F oven for 10 minutes.
2. Leave oven on, but remove tortillas and then top each one with 1/4 cup chicken (just below center). Spread 1/4 cup beans, 2 Tablespoons of diced tomato, 2 Tablespoons of shredded cheese, 1/2 Tablespoon of diced onion, and 1/2 Tablespoon of minced cilantro on each tortilla.
3. Fold bottom edge of each tortilla up and over filling. Fold left and right sides of each tortilla in until they meet. Roll tortilla up from the bottom and toward the open top to close and form a burrito.
4. Arrange burritos on a Teflon-coated baking sheet and bake in 350°F oven for 10 to 12 minutes or until heated thoroughly.
5. Cover each burrito with 1/4 cup salsa and 1 Tablespoon of low-fat sour cream. If desired, sprinkle with green onion.

**Nutrition Information:**

CAL 388  CHO 42G  PRO 27G  FAT 13G  CHOL 58MG  CALCIUM 324MG  POTASSIUM 582MG  SODIUM 859MG  FIBER 6G

*For a vegetarian meal, omit the chicken and substitute 1 cup of cooked vegetables.

# GRILLED ZUCCHINI AND CHEESE WRAP

*With the zucchini, this wrap is rich in the phytochemicals that help vision.*

1 large Flour tortilla
1 tsp. Honey mustard
4 slices Swiss or Jarlsberg cheese, reduced fat made from part skim milk
1 Carrot, peeled and shredded or cut lengthwise into strips
5 leaves Green leaf lettuce
4 slices Zucchini, grilled

> **BAG LUNCH MENU**
>
> *Tex-Mex Black Bean and Corn Salad*
> *Grilled Zucchini and Cheese Wrap*
> Fresh Grapes
> V-8 Juice

Spread mustard on tortilla and top with cheese and remaining vegetables. Roll and cut in half. Place a toothpick in the center to hold together—just remember to take out the toothpick before eating!

**Vegetarian: Lacto-ovo**

Total time: 10 minutes
Serves: 2
Serving size: 1/2 tortilla wrap
Exchange: 2 starch, 2 very lean meat, 1–2 vegetables

## Serving Suggestion

Serve as an appetizer by slicing wrap into 1-1/2 slices.

**Nutrition Information:**

CAL 195  CHO 19G  PRO 19G  FAT 5G  CHOL 20MG  CALCIUM 598MG  POTASSIUM 334MG  SODIUM 320MG  FIBER 2G

# MEDITERRANEAN PITA

*This pita sandwich is rich in phytonutrients and fiber to boost your immune system.*

1 tsp. Olive oil

4 slices Eggplant, sliced 1/8-inch thick

4 slices Zucchini, sliced thinly
  lengthwise

4 slices Red onion, oven-grilled

4 medium Mushrooms, sliced

To taste Oregano, dried

To taste Pepper, black, ground

4 oz. Goat cheese

2 Pitas, 6-inch round, whole wheat

## MENU

Fresh Grapes

Mediterranean Pita

Iced Soy Latte

**Vegetarian: Lacto-ovo**

Total time: 15 minutes
Serves: 2
Serving size: 1 pita
Exchange: 2 starch, 1 medium fat meat,
1 vegetable, 1 reduced fat dairy

1. To grill vegetables, preheat oven to 400°F.
2. Grease cookie sheet with 1 Tablespoon of olive oil. Place sliced vegetables on cookie sheet, keeping mushrooms in a separate area. Season with oregano and black pepper. Put cookie sheet in oven.
3. After 5 minutes, remove mushrooms if cooked, and turn all remaining vegetables.
4. Remove sheet from oven when vegetables are tender, 5 to 10 more minutes.
5. Stuff each pita with vegetables and 2 ounces of goat cheese and serve.

**Nutrition Information:**

CAL 375  CHO 49G  PRO 21G  FAT 11G  CHOL 45MG  CALCIUM 216MG  POTASSIUM 658MG  SODIUM 538MG  FIBER 9G

# MEXICAN FIESTA WRAP

*This vegetarian wrap is high in fiber and calcium.*

2 oz. Cheddar cheese, reduced fat, shredded
1/4 cup Kidney beans, canned, drained
2 Tbsp. Salsa, commercial
2 sprigs Cilantro, fresh
3 leaves Romaine lettuce, shredded
3 Black olives, chopped
1/2 small Tomato, diced
1 Flour tortilla, 6 inches round

Combine cheddar cheese, beans, salsa, cilantro, lettuce, olives, and tomatoes and put in the center of the tortilla. Fold in the bottom and roll to close before serving.

## BAG LUNCH MENU

Raw Carrots
*Mexican Fiesta Wrap*
Apple
Water or Milk

**Vegetarian: Lacto-ovo**

Total time: 3 minutes
Serves: 1
Serving size: 1 wrap
Exchange: 2 starch, 1 reduced fat dairy, 2 lean meat

## Serving Suggestion

Need more servings? Just multiply the ingredient amounts by the number needed.

**Nutrition Information:**

CAL 328  CHO 40G  PRO 23G  FAT 9G  CHOL 12MG  CALCIUM 498MG  POTASSIUM 482MG  SODIUM 589MG  FIBER 6G

# MINUTE CHEESE STEAK HOAGIE

*This is yummy and rich in calcium. Onions contain important phytonutrients.*

1 tsp. Olive oil
1 medium Onion, quartered and thinly sliced
2 Lean minute steaks, 4 ounces each, sliced less than 1/4 inch thick
4 slices American or cheddar cheese, reduced fat, shredded
2 Hoagie rolls, each 8 inches long, sliced lengthwise

### WINTER LUNCH MENU

*Romaine Garden Salad*
*Minute Cheese Steak Hoagie*
*Baked Apple with Cinnamon*
*Old-Fashioned Hot Chocolate*

Total time: 8 minutes
Serves: 4
Serving size: 1/2 hoagie
Exchange: 2 starch, 1 fat, 1-1/2 medium fat meat

1. Heat oil in a small skillet over medium heat. Add onions and sauté until they are caramelized and brown.
2. Remove onions from skillet and add steaks. Brown 30 seconds on each side. Remove steaks from skillet and set aside.
3. Place opened hoagie rolls on baking sheet. Place slice of cheese on top of each half. Place cheese hoagie under broiler until bubbly, approximately 1 minute.
4. Remove rolls from oven and add steak and onion. Close sandwiches and cut in half.
5. Serve immediately.

### Serving Suggestion

Garnish with sticks of raw carrots and celery.

**Nutrition Information:**
CAL 262  CHO 27G  PRO 14G  FAT 11G  CHOL 32MG  CALCIUM 149MG  POTASSIUM 194MG  SODIUM 299MG  FIBER 2G

# OPEN-FACED ITALIAN HERO MELT

*This makes a great Sunday afternoon treat.*

*Dorothy Court*

1 loaf Italian bread, 12 inches long
8 oz. Turkey pastrami, lean, thinly sliced
1 large Tomato, sliced
1 small Yellow onion, thinly sliced
1 can Artichoke hearts, water packed, large dice
1 small jar Roasted peppers
12 oz. Mozzarella cheese, part skim milk, shredded

**MENU**

*Eggplant Caponata*
*Open-Faced Italian Hero Melt*
*Fresh Fruit Cup*

Total time: 10 minutes
Serves: 4*
Serving size: 3 inches
Exchange: 4 high fat meat, 1 vegetable, 3-1/2 starch

1. Preheat oven to 375°F.
2. Cut bread lengthwise and layer both sides with pastrami, tomato, onion, artichoke hearts, and roasted peppers, then top with cheese.
3. Place on baking pan and heat in oven until cheese melts.
4. Cut into four equal pieces.

**Nutrition Information:**

CAL 606  CHO 55G  PRO 42G  FAT 24G  CHOL 76MG  CALCIUM 714MG  POTASSIUM 598MG  SODIUM 1685MG  FIBER 5G

*Overweight children less than 10 years of age need only one-half serving.

# ORIENT EXPRESS WRAP

*If you are tired of your usual lunch, then try this wrap. It is packed with isoflavones that help protect your heart and immune system.*

1 small Asian rice wrap or flour
  tortilla
1/2 tsp. Hoisin sauce
1/4 cup Iceberg lettuce, shredded
1/4 cup Bean sprouts
2 oz. Tofu, firm, low-fat, diced into
  1/2-inch cubes
3 Mushrooms, sliced
1/4 Red bell pepper, diced
1-1/2 tsp. Hot chili sauce with garlic

Spread Hoisin sauce on wrap or tortilla, top with remaining ingredients, fold in sides, then roll to close. Cut in half and serve.

## BAG LUNCH MENU

Baby Carrots
*Orient Express Wrap*
Almond Cookie
Sugar-Free Iced Tea

**Vegetarian: Vegan**

Total time: 4 minutes
Serves: 1
Serving size: 1 wrap
Exchange: With tortilla wrap, 2 starch, 1 lean meat, 1 vegetable, 1 fat; with rice wrap, 1 starch, 1 very lean meat, 1 fat

**Nutrition Information:**

**Rice Wrap**

CAL 144   CHO 17G   PRO 12G   FAT 5G   CHOL 0MG   CALCIUM 62MG   POTASSIUM 612MG   SODIUM 243MG   FIBER 4G

**Tortilla Wrap**

CAL 258   CHO 36G   PRO 15G   FAT 8G   CHOL 0MG   CALCIUM 114MG   POTASSIUM 660MG   SODIUM 443MG   FIBER 5G

# PEANUT BUTTER AND JELLY SANDWICH

*Reduce fat and gain phytonutrients in this classic favorite.*

2 slices Bread, whole wheat*
2 Tbsp. Peanut butter, reduced fat**
2 Tbsp. Smucker's reduced sugar fruit
  spread, strawberry

Spread peanut butter on one slice of bread and fruit spread on the other slice. Place bread slices together and slice in half.

## BAG LUNCH MENU

Celery sticks
*Peanut Butter and Jelly Sandwich*
Apple
Low-Fat milk

**Vegetarian: Vegan**

Total time: 3 minutes
Serves: 1
Serving size: 1 sandwich
Exchange: 2 starch, 1 fruit, 2 high
fat meat

**Nutrition Information:**

CAL 344   CHO 46G   PRO 15G   FAT 15G   CHOL 0MG   CALCIUM 57MG   POTASSIUM 396MG   SODIUM 494MG   FIBER 6G

*To lower fat and calories more, buy "Better N' Peanut Butter." It is defatted!
**Contains more than 2 grams of fiber per slice.

# ROASTED PEPPER AND MOZZARELLA ON A BAGUETTE

*This is a great and welcome change from the typical bag lunch.*

1 Baguette, 8 inches long

4 oz. Mozzarella cheese, fresh, whole milk, sliced

4 oz. Roasted peppers, fresh in water-packed jar

To taste Oregano, dried

To taste Pepper, black, ground

To taste Garlic powder

---

Cut baguette lengthwise and open. Place cheese and peppers on top and sprinkle with seasonings. Cut in half and *Manga!**

## VEGETARIAN BAG LUNCH MENU

Fresh fruit supreme

*Roasted Pepper and Mozzarella on a Baguette*

Almond Biscotti

**Vegetarian: Lacto-ovo**

Total time: 5 minutes
Serves: 2
Serving size: 4-inch baguette
Exchange: 2 starch, 1 vegetable, 1 fat, 2 medium fat meat

**Nutrition Information:**

CAL 342  CHO 35G  PRO 20G  FAT 14G  CHOL 31MG  CALCIUM 466MG  POTASSIUM 216MG  SODIUM 348MG  FIBER 2G

*Means *Eat!* in Italian.

# SMOKED GOUDA CHEESE MELT

4 slices Multigrain bread (1 oz. each slice)
4 oz. Smoked Gouda
1 Granny Smith apple
2 tsp. Honey mustard
As needed Nonstick pan spray

**Vegetarian: Lacto-ovo**

Total time: 6 minutes
Serves: 2
Serving size: 1 sandwich
Exchange: 2 whole milk, 1 starch

1. Place honey mustard, apple slices, then gouda cheese on two slices of bread.
2. Place bread in toaster oven or broiler for 2 to 3 minutes or until cheese melts and remove.
3. Place remaining bread on top of each cheese melt and return to toaster to brown the top.
4. Serve hot.

**Nutrition Information:**

CAL 364  CHO 35G  PRO 20G  FAT 17G  CHOL 65MG  CALCIUM 441MG  POTASSIUM 284MG  SODIUM 864MG  FIBER 5G

# SPICY CHEESE AND ONION QUESADILLAS

8 oz. Mexican cheese mix (cheddar,
  Monterey jack, queso), shredded
8 Burritos,* 6 inches round (1.5 oz. each)
1 medium Onion, fresh, diced
6 oz. Salsa, medium to hot, jarred or fresh
2 cups Kidney or white navy beans,
  cooked

**Vegetarian: Lacto-ovo**

Total time: 20 min.
Serves: 4
Serving size:1–2
Exchange for 2: 3 starch, 1 reduced
fat dairy, 3 medium fat meat

1. Place burritos on baking sheet. Spread 2 Tablespoons of salsa on each burrito.
2. In a separate skillet, sauté onion, then add salsa. Mash the beans into small pieces in the skillet.
3. Place 1/4 cup of bean mixture on each burrito and top each with 1 ounce of cheese. Roll to close and place in a baking pan or glass dish if you want to microwave it.
4. To bake, heat oven to 375°F. Place burritos in hot oven for 15 minutes or until cheese is melted.
5. To microwave burritos, heat for 1 minute or until cheese is melted.

## Serving Suggestion

Serve as an after-school snack. These also provide great energy one or two hours before a sport or as a meal.

**Nutrition Information:**

CAL 514 CHO 61G PRO 36G FAT 14G CHOL 88MG CALCIUM 474MG POTASSIUM 854MG SODIUM 1,166MG FIBER 22G

*I do not usually recommend specific brands, but Joseph's Oat Bran and Whole Wheat Tortillas are popular. They contain 70 calories and 6 grams fiber per tortilla.

# SPINACH AND FETA PITA

*This pita is packed with vitamins and minerals to help your vision, bones, heart, and more.*

1 cup Baby spinach leaves, fresh, washed

1-1/2 oz. Feta cheese

3 Black olives, chopped

1 slice Red onion

2 slices Tomato, 1/8-inch thick

1 large Egg, hard-boiled, sliced

1 Tbsp. Balsamic vinaigrette dressing (see index for recipe)

1 small  Pita, garlic or whole wheat pita, 6 inches round

## VEGETARIAN BAG LUNCH MENU

Mediterranean Cucumber Salad

*Spinach and Feta Pita*

Fresh Apple

Low-Fat or Fat-free Milk or Soy Milk

**Vegetarian: Lacto-ovo**

Total time: 4 minutes
Serving size: 1 pita
Serves: 1
Exchange: 1-1/2 starch, 2 medium fat meat, 1 vegetable, 1 fat

Mix all ingredients except pita bread. Open pita pocket on one side and insert ingredients.

**Nutrition Information:**

CAL 356  CHO 23G  PRO 17G  FAT 15G  CHOL 252MG  CALCIUM 299MG  POTASSIUM 408MG  SODIUM 770MG  FIBER 4G

# TURKEY PASTRAMI AND CHEESE SANDWICH

*To lower cholesterol, hold the mayonnaise and bring on the mustard or cranberry sauce.*

1 tsp. Honey mustard
  or
1 Tbsp. Cranberry sauce
2 slices Pumpernickel bread
2 oz. Turkey pastrami
1 oz. Cheddar cheese, reduced fat
1 leaf Romaine lettuce

Spread mustard on bread, then add remaining ingredients in order listed. Cut in half and serve.

## BAG LUNCH MENU

Raw carrots
Turkey Pastrami and Cheese Sandwich
Small Box Raisins
Low-Sodium Vegetable Juice

Total time: 5 minutes
Serves: 1
Serving size: 1 sandwich
Exchange: With mustard, 2 starch, 3 medium fat meat; with cranberry sauce, 2 starch, 3 medium fat meat, 1 vegetable

**Nutrition Information:**

**With Mustard**

CAL 318  CHO 28G  PRO 29G  FAT 9G  CHOL 43MG  CALCIUM 457MG  POTASSIUM 317MG  SODIUM 935MG  FIBER 3G

**With Cranberry Sauce**

CAL 341  CHO 34G  PRO 29G  FAT 9G  CHOL 42MG  CALCIUM 453MG  POTASSIUM 313MG  SODIUM 882MG  FIBER 3G

# Chapter 10

## MEATLESS ENTREES

## ABRUZZI-STYLE SPAGHETTI WITH FRESH PLUM TOMATOES AND HERBS

*Chef Brian MacMenamin*

2 lbs. Plum tomatoes, vine-ripened, room temperature
1/4 cup Olive oil, extra virgin
~1/2 cup Basil leaves, fresh, coarsely chopped
1/2 cup Parsley, flat leaf, coarsely chopped
4 oz. Ricotta cheese, part skim milk
12 oz. Spaghetti, fresh or dried
4 Tbsp. Parmigiana reggiano cheese
To taste Black pepper, freshly ground

### MENU

*Vegetable Broth*
*Abruzzi-Style Spaghetti with Fresh Plum Tomatoes and Herbs*
*Fresh Fruit Supreme*

**Vegetarian: Lacto-ovo**

Total time: 10–20 minutes
Serves: 4
Serving size: 1/4
Exchange: 4 starch, 2-1/2 vegetable, 1 fat

1. Bring a large pot of salted water to a boil. Drop in the tomatoes, cook for 15 seconds, and then transfer them to a large bowl of cold water. Slip off the skins and cut through the middle. Poke out the seeds with your finger, and roughly dice the flesh.

*(continues)*

# ABRUZZI-STYLE SPAGHETTI WITH FRESH PLUM TOMATOES AND HERBS (Continued)

2. Warm a large ceramic or glass mixing bowl by rinsing it with hot water. Toss the tomatoes in the bowl with the olive oil, mixed herbs, parsley, and ricotta cheese.
3. Bring the large pot of water back to a rolling boil, add the spaghetti, and cook until tender but still firm, approximately 6 minutes for fresh pasta and 14 minutes for dried. Drain and add immediately to the tomato mixture in the bowl.
4. Sprinkle with the parmigiana cheese. Toss with tongs or two wooden spoons until the pasta is evenly coated.
5. Add freshly ground pepper to taste.

### Serving Suggestion

If you are trying to lose weight or watch your total carbohydrate consumption, have a small portion. Another option is to reduce the olive oil to 2 Tablespoons. This could also serve as a side dish.

**Nutrition Information:**

CAL 566   CHO 78g   PRO 19g   FAT 20g   CHOL 14mg   CALCIUM 217mg   POTASSIUM 672mg   SODIUM 504mg   FIBER 8g

# ASPARAGUS CREPES

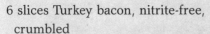

6 slices Turkey bacon, nitrite-free, crumbled

2 cups Pancake mix, unbleached type

3 Tbsp. Flaxseed, ground (meal)

2 medium Eggs, beaten

2 cups Milk, fat-free

As needed Nonstick pan spray (canola)

1 lb. Asparagus, fresh, steamed and chopped

8 oz. Mozzarella cheese, part skim milk, shredded

**Vegetarian: Lacto-ovo**

Total time: 15–20 minutes
Serves: 6
Serving size: 2
Exchange: 1 starch, 1 vegetable, 1 reduced fat milk, 2 high fat meat

1. Preheat oven to 350°F.
2. Place turkey bacon on a microwavable dish and cover with a paper towel. Place in microwave and heat on high for 2 to 4 minutes until crisp. Remove from microwave and crumble, then set aside.
3. Blend pancake mix, flaxseed meal, eggs, and milk for 2 minutes.
4. Heat nonstick 7-inch skillet on medium heat and spray with nonstick spray.
5. Pour pancake mixture in the skillet, then pick up skillet to evenly coat pan with batter, and cook until bubbles form and the crepe is cooked (approximately 70 seconds), then flip to the other side to continue cooking for 30 more seconds. Remove from heat.
6. Divide the asparagus into six portions, then add one portion of asparagus and 1 ounce of mozzarella and 1 Tablespoon of bacon bits in the center of each crepe. Roll to form a wrap.
7. Place rolled crepes on a baking sheet and heat in the oven for 5 minutes or until the cheese melts. Serve immediately.

## Serving Suggestion

Garnish with parsley. This is a great and healthy option for a brunch or appetizer. If you do not like asparagus, then try mushrooms instead. Dislike veggies? Then try your favorite fruit such as apples. If you are always rushed, then crepes can be made and frozen and only stuffed and rolled on the day you plan to eat them.

**Nutrition Information:**

CAL 383  CHO 36G  PRO 25G  FAT 15G  CHOL 98MG  CALCIUM 534MG  POTASSIUM 454MG  SODIUM 106MG  FIBER 4G

# BLACK BEANS OVER RICE

*This dish is rich in protein and fiber for lasting satiety and health.*

1 small Onion, diced
2 tsp. Olive oil
16 oz. Black beans (1 can)
4 cups White rice, cooked
1/4 cup Cilantro, fresh, minced
   (optional)

**VEGETARIAN MENU**

*Summer Gazpacho Soup*
*Black Beans over Rice*
*Herbed Biscuit*

**Vegetarian: Vegan**

Total time: 15 minutes
Serves: 4
Serving size: 1-1/2 cup beans,
1 cup rice
Exchange: 3 starch—or 2 starch,
1 protein

1. In a medium skillet over medium heat, sauté the onion in oil until slightly browned.
2. Add beans and simmer 10 minutes; add the cilantro the last 3 minutes.
3. In a separate pot, cook rice following directions on the box.
4. Serve beans over rice.

**Nutrition Information:**

CAL 393   CHO 76G   PRO 14G   FAT 3G   CHOL 0MG   CALCIUM 99MG   POTASSIUM 500MG   SODIUM 1,040MG   FIBER 8G

# CRUSTLESS SPINACH PIE

*This pie is rich in folic acid to protect your heart, and the beta-carotene may reduce your risk of cancer.*

*Michelle Jackson, Registered Dietitian*

10 oz. Spinach (1 package), frozen, chopped, thawed, squeezed dry
3/4 cup Cottage cheese, low-fat
1 clove Garlic, minced
1/4 tsp. Nutmeg, ground
1/4 tsp. Salt
1/4 tsp. Pepper, black, ground
2 Red tomatoes, thinly sliced
1 Tbsp. Parmesan cheese, grated

**VEGETARIAN MENU**

*Spicy Vegetable Cocktail*
*Quick Low-Fat Mushroom Soup*
**Crustless Spinach Pie**
*Greek Pasta Salad*

**Vegetarian: Lacto-ovo**

Total time: 40 minutes
Serves: 4
Serving size: 1/4 casserole
Exchange: 1 lean meat

1. Preheat oven to 350°F.
2. In mixing bowl, thoroughly blend spinach with cottage cheese, garlic, nutmeg, salt, and pepper. Spread one-third of the mixture in a casserole dish. Cover with tomato slices and sprinkle with one-third of the mozzarella cheese. Repeat layering until all ingredients are used.
3. Put the casserole dish in the oven and bake for 20 to 30 minutes or until cooked through and cheese is melted.

**Nutrition Information:**
CAL 73  CHO 7G  PRO 9G  FAT 2G  CHOL 5MG  CALCIUM 124MG  POTASSIUM 324MG  SODIUM 394MG  FIBER 2G

# EASY HOMEMADE PIZZA

*This delicious vegetarian meal boosts calcium and uses less fat than most pizzas.*

1 package Pizza dough
4 oz. Tomato sauce
1 cup Spinach, chopped, fresh or frozen (defrosted)
1/2 small Onion, raw, thinly sliced
8 oz. Mozzarella cheese, part skim, shredded
To taste Garlic powder (optional)

### VEGETARIAN MENU

*Mesclun Greens with Apples and Walnuts*

*Easy Homemade Pizza*

*August Fresh Fruit with Ginger Snap Cookies*

**Vegetarian: Lacto-ovo**

Total time: 20 minutes
Serves: 4
Serving size: 1/4 pie
Exchange: 1 reduced fat dairy, 1 vegetable, 3 starch, 1 fat

1. Heat oven to 400°F.
2. Spread dough in a 16-inch round pie pan and cover with tomato sauce. Add spinach, onion, cheese, and garlic powder.
3. Place in oven and bake for approximately 15 minutes or until dough is golden and cheese is melted.

## Serving Suggestion

Use low-sodium tomato sauce to lower sodium content.

**Nutrition Information:**

CAL 502  CHO 56g  PRO 28g  FAT 16g  CHOL 43mg  CALCIUM 441mg  POTASSIUM 309mg  SODIUM 576mg  FIBER 3g

# EGGPLANT PARMESAN

*Let your taste buds be the judge if you like this vegetable recipe. Check out the calcium you get in this. No frying, no spattering— and streamlined.*

1 medium Eggplant, peeled and sliced

1/4 cup Olive oil

2 Eggs, beaten

1-1/2 cups Italian seasoned bread crumbs

2 cups Marinara sauce, 1 gram fat or less

1 lb. Mozzarella cheese, part skim milk, shredded

4 Tbsp. Parmesan cheese

## MENU

*Baby Spinach Greens*
*Eggplant Parmesan*
*Crusty Garlic Bread*

**Vegetarian: Lacto-ovo**

Total time: 35 minutes
Serves: 6 or 8
Serving size: 1/6 or 1/8
Exchange: Six servings: 1 vegetable, 2 high fat diary, 2 fat, 1 bread, eight servings: 1 vegetable, 3 fat, 1 bread, 2 reduced fat milk

1. Preheat oven to 375°F.
2. Brush two cookie sheets with olive oil.
3. Pat eggplant slices with a paper towel, then dip the slices in egg and then bread crumbs, then place on cookie sheets in a single layer. Bake 5 to 7 minutes; turn each slice, then bake until brown on each side. Remove from oven.
4. Increase oven heat to 400°F. Place a small amount of sauce on the bottom of a casserole dish, add eggplant and cheeses in alternating layers. Bake for 10 minutes or until cheese is melted.

## Serving Suggestion

Use nonstick pan spray and cut the fat to 4 to 7 grams per serving.

**Nutrition Information:**

**Six Portions**

CAL 576  CHO 45G  PRO 29G  FAT 25G  CHOL 115MG  CALCIUM 681MG  POTASSIUM 540MG  SODIUM 896MG  FIBER 4G

**Eight Portions**

CAL 408  CHO 35G  PRO 22G  FAT 18G  CHOL 86MG  CALCIUM 511MG  POTASSIUM 405MG  SODIUM 822MG  FIBER 4G

# HOMEMADE VEGGIE BURGERS

*This is a great Saturday lunch for using up the week's leftover vegetables. Best of all, it will boost your well-being because it is packed with phytonutrients.*

1 medium Potato, boiled with skin

4 oz. Creamed corn (small can)

1/2 cup Unbleached flour

1/2 cup Italian-flavored bread crumbs

2 Tbsp. Flaxseed, ground (meal)

1/2 tsp. Garlic, minced

1cup Peas and carrots, frozen but defrosted

4 medium Mushrooms, diced

1 Tbsp. Canola or flaxseed oil

4 oz. Mozzarella cheese, part skim milk, shredded

## MENU

*Homemade Veggie Burgers*

*Multigrain Bread*

*Lettuce and Tomato*

*Cold Broccoli Salad*

**Vegetarian: Lacto-ovo**

Total time: 20 minutes
Serves: 4
Serving size: 1
Exchange: 2 starch, 2 vegetable,
1 lean meat, 1 fat

---

1. Preheat oven to 375°F.
2. Place potato, creamed corn, flour, bread crumbs, flaxseed, and garlic in a blender or food processor and blend for 2 minutes until smooth; add 1 or 2 teaspoons of water if more moisture is needed.
3. Remove mixture from blender and place in bowl, blending with peas and carrots, mushrooms, oil, and mozzarella. Form 3-inch wide patties.
4. Grease a nonstick baking pan with oil, place patties on the sheet, and bake for 8 minutes. Flip the patties over and bake another 8 minutes.

**Nutrition Information:**

CAL 326  CHO 42G  PRO 15G  FAT 12G  CHOL 15MG  CALCIUM 262MG  POTASSIUM 545MG  SODIUM 338MG  FIBER 5G

# HOMEMADE MANICOTTI

8 Manicotti shells, cooked

16 oz. Ricotta cheese, part skim milk

4 oz. Mozzarella cheese, small dice

2 Tbsp. Parsley, dried

1-1/2 cup Tomato sauce, fat-free, less than 8 grams sugar

1/2 cup Basil, fresh, minced

## MENU

*Escarole and Bean Soup*

**Homemade Manicotti**

*Steamed Asparagus with Lemon*

*Baked Apple*

**Vegetarian: Lacto-ovo**

Total time: 40 minutes
Serves: 4–8
Serving size: 1–2
Exchange: For four: 2 whole milk, 2 starch, 2 vegetables; For eight: 1 whole milk, 1 starch, 1 vegetable

1. Preheat oven to 350°F.
2. Cook manicotti in boiling water for approximately 5 minutes. It should be firm, not soft. Remove from heat and drain.
3. Mix cheese and parsley. Stuff each manicotti with cheese mixture and place in a baking pan. Top with tomato sauce. Bake for 25 minutes or until pasta is soft and cheese is melted.
4. Serve topped with fresh basil.

## Serving Suggestion

Serve one manicotti as a side dish with soup or to a small child; serve two manicotti if it is an entrée alone.

**Nutrition Information:**

**Four Servings**

CAL 405  CHO 40G  PRO 26G  FAT 16G  CHOL 51MG  CALCIUM 552MG  POTASSIUM 585MG  SODIUM 431MG  FIBER 4G

**Eight Servings**

CAL 202G  CHO 20G  PRO 13G  FAT 8G  CHOL 25MG  CALCIUM 276MG  POTASSIUM 293MG  SODIUM 216MG  FIBER 2G

# ITALIANO PASTA PRIMAVERA

*Alexandra Gaudio*

3 Carrots, small dice
1 cup Peas, frozen or fresh
1 medium Green bell pepper, small
  dice
1 medium Red bell pepper, small dice
1 medium Yellow bell pepper, small
  dice
1 medium Red onion, quartered, then
  thinly sliced
6 oz. Spinach, fresh
2 medium Zucchini, diced
3 Tbsp. Organic extra virgin olive oil
1/4 cup Parsley, fresh, chopped
1 Tbsp. Parmesan cheese
8 oz. Barilla penne pasta (made with flaxseed optional)

## MENU

*Mesclun Greens with Apples and
  Walnuts*
**Italian Pasta Primavera**
*Low-Fat Lemon Mousse*

**Vegetarian: Lacto-ovo**

Total time: 35 minutes
Serves: 5
Serving size: 1/5
Exchange: 3 starch, 2 vegetables, 1 fat

1. Prepare a nonstick pot on a medium heat, add oil, heat 1 minute, and
   add the onion. Brown, then add remaining vegetables bell peppers,
   spinach, zucchini, and parsley. Let cook on a medium heat until tender,
   approximately 6 minutes. Add salt and pepper.
2. Boil water for pasta, following the directions on the box. When pasta is
   *al dente* (cooked firm but not mushy), drain water from pasta and add
   vegetables.
3. Serve topped with cheese.

**Nutrition Information:**

CAL 344   CHO 55G   PRO 11G   FAT 7G   CHOL 0MG   CALCIUM 96MG   POTASSIUM 516MG   SODIUM 130MG   FIBER 7G

# MOROCCAN SEITAN OVER WHOLE WHEAT COUSCOUS

*Paulette B. Scheider, Registered Dietitian, Irving Center for Clinical Research at Columbia University, Bionutrition Unit*

12 oz. Seitan, diced

1/2 tsp. Salt (optional)

1 Tbsp. Olive oil

1 medium Onion, diced

2 cloves Garlic, minced

2 Carrots, peeled and diced

2 stalks Celery, chopped

1 medium Sweet potato or yam, peeled and diced

1 Tbsp. Ginger root, grated

1/2 tsp. Hot paprika

3/4 tsp. Cumin, ground

1/2 tsp. Oregano, dried

1/4 tsp. Cayenne pepper, ground

1/4 tsp. Turmeric powder

1-1/2 cup Vegetable stock, low-sodium

1 cup Tomatoes, low-sodium

1 cup Chickpeas, low-sodium, canned, rinsed and drained

1 medium Zucchini, sliced

1 Tbsp. Lemon juice, freshly squeezed

## MOROCCAN FEAST

Spinach Salad

Topped with Orange Slices and Black Olives

*Moroccan Seitan Over Whole Wheat Couscous*

**Vegetarian: Vegan**

Total time: 1 hour

Serves: 4

Serving size: 1/4

Exchange: 2 medium fat meat, 2 vegetables, 2 starch

1. Season seitan if desired with salt or omit salt, depending on your taste preference.
2. Spray a large pot with nonstick spray and lightly sauté the seitan over medium heat to lightly brown its surface. Remove the seitan from the pot and set aside until needed.
3. Place the pot back over medium head and add the olive oil. Sauté the onion, garlic, carrots, celery, and sweet potato. When these are tender, add the ginger, paprika, cumin, oregano, cayenne pepper, and turmeric; stir-fry for approximately 1 minute, then mix in the broth and tomatoes.

*(continues)*

# MOROCCAN SEITAN OVER WHOLE WHEAT COUSCOUS (Continued)

4. Return the seitan to the pot and reduce the heat to low and simmer for approximately 10 minutes.
5. Add the chickpeas and zucchini to the pan and bring back to a simmer; cover the pan and cook for 15 minutes.
6. Serve over whole wheat couscous.

**Nutrition Information:**

CAL 305  CHO 42G  PRO 16G  FAT 10G  CHOL 0MG  CALCIUM 198MG  POTASSIUM 1,099MG  SODIUM 188MG  FIBER 9G

# PASTA AND TOMATOES IN LIGHT CREAM

*Give yourself a treat even if you are on a low-fat diet. This recipe contains only 5 grams of fat and is rich in phytonutrients.*

1 quart Water
4 oz. Vermicelli
1 tsp. Canola or olive oil
2 cloves Garlic, sliced
1 small Yellow onion, quartered and sliced
2 Tomatoes, vine-ripened, diced
As needed Water
2 Tbsp. Crème fraiche or half-and-half
To taste Pepper, black, ground
6 leaves Basil, fresh, minced

Seitan is a protein derived from wheat gluten. In some supermarkets and natural food stores, a variety of different flavors are available—for example, chicken and barbecued. Seitan's texture is similar to chicken.

## VEGETARIAN MENU

*Colorful Coleslaw Salad*

**Pasta and Tomatoes in Light Cream**

*Sliced Cantaloupe*

**Vegetarian: Lacto-ovo**

Total time: 30 minutes
Serves: 2 (side dish or entrée)
Serving size: 1 cup
Exchange: 3 starch, 1 reduced fat milk

1. Boil 1 quart of water.
2. Place pasta in boiling water, add 1 teaspoon oil, and stir occasionally to prevent pasta from sticking together. Drain when *al dente* (cooked firm but not mushy).
3. In a medium skillet, sauté garlic in oil. Add onion and sauté until translucent.
4. Add tomatoes and simmer, adding water as needed until sauce is partially reduced and tomatoes have softened, 10 to 15 minutes.
5. Add crème fraiche, blend, and simmer sauce 1 to 3 more minutes.
6. Place pasta in a serving dish, add sauce to the pasta, and gently toss to blend thoroughly.
7. Top pasta with fresh basil and pepper and serve.

**Nutrition Information:**
CAL 329  CHO 56G  PRO 10G  FAT 5G  CHOL 6MG  CALCIUM 58MG  POTASSIUM 418MG  SODIUM 23MG  FIBER 4G

# QUICK PASTA PRIMAVERA

1 medium Onion, diced

2 tsp. Olive oil

1 package Peas and carrots, frozen

1 package Broccoli, frozen, chopped

1 cup Vegetable broth, low-sodium

2 Tbsp. Cold water

2 Tbsp. Cornstarch

12 oz. Bow tie pasta (farfalle)

**Vegetarian: Vegan**

Total time: 20 minutes
Serves: 4 or 8
Serving size: 1 or 2 cups
Exchange: 1 cup: 2 starch, 1 vegetable, 1/2 very lean meat
2 cups: 4 starch, 2 vegetables, 1 very lean meat

1. In a 2-quart pot, sauté onion in olive oil until translucent.
2. Add chicken broth and vegetables and bring to a boil.
3. Mix cold water and cornstarch until blended, then add to vegetable mixture. Simmer 5 more minutes.
4. In a separate pot, boil 1 quart water, add pasta, and cook 10 minutes or until soft, but not mushy.
5. Drain pasta and add to vegetable mixture.
6. Serve in small bowl.

**Nutrition Information:**

**Four Portions (entrée)**

CAL 395  CHO 72G  PRO 16G  FAT 6G  CHOL 73MG  CALCIUM 73MG  POTASSIUM 314MG  SODIUM 498MG  FIBER 7G

**Eight Portions (side dish)**

CAL 197  CHO 36G  PRO 8G  FAT 3G  CHOL 37MG  CALCIUM 36MG  POTASSIUM 157MG  SODIUM 249MG  FIBER 4G

# SPINACH QUICHE

*This recipe tastes great and is high in beta-carotene.*

*Michelle Jackson, Registered Dietitian*

1 Pie crust, 9-inch deep dish
10 oz. Spinach (1 package frozen),
  thawed, squeezed dry*
1/2 cup Onion, diced
1/4 tsp. Salt
1/4 tsp. Pepper, black, ground
Dash Nutmeg, ground
1 Egg Beater
8 oz. Fat-free evaporated milk (1 can)
1 tsp. Basil leaves, dried
1/4 tsp. Red pepper, crushed (optional)
1 Tbsp. Flour
3/4 cup Swiss cheese, light or low-fat,
  shredded or chopped

## VEGETARIAN MENU

*Delicious Stuffed Mushrooms*
**Spinach Quiche**
*Asparagus Salad with Dijon*
*  Vinaigrette*

**Vegetarian: Lacto-ovo**

Total time: 65 minutes
Serves: 8
Serving size: 1/8 pie
Exchange:

1. Preheat oven to 400°F.
2. Prick bottom of pastry crust lightly with a fork and bake 5 minutes until soft but not brown. Set aside. Reduce oven temperature to 350°F.
3. Combine spinach, onion, salt, black pepper, and nutmeg and spoon into prepared crust.
4. In a bowl, combine Egg Beaters, evaporated milk, basil leaves, and red pepper. Whisk together until well blended.
5. Toss together shredded cheese and flour and add to egg mixture; mix well.
6. Pour egg mixture over spinach mixture in pie shell.
7. Bake 40 to 45 minutes or until a knife inserted in the center comes out clean.
8. Let stand 10 to 15 minutes before serving.

**Nutrition Information:**

CAL 185  CHO 167G  PRO 10G  FAT 9G  CHOL 8MG  CALCIUM 218MG  POTASSIUM 263MG  SODIUM 326MG  FIBER 2G

*Any type of defrosted frozen vegetables or 1 cup of lightly cooked fresh vegetable can be substituted for spinach in this recipe.

# VEGETABLE LASAGNA

1 large Onion, diced

2 cloves Garlic, minced

1 Tbsp. Olive oil

1 lb. Mushrooms, white, sliced

1 cup Spinach, cooked, drained well

1/4 cup Basil, fresh, minced

4 cups Tomato sauce, chunky style

4 Tbsp. Tomato paste

1 lb. Lasagna noodles

16 oz. Mozzarella cheese, part skim milk

8 oz. Ricotta cheese, part skim milk

3 Tbsp. Parmesan cheese

To taste Pepper, black, ground

## MENU

Mesclun Greens

*Vegetable Lasagna*

*Crusty Garlic Bread*

Fresh Grapes

Chianti (Optional)

**Vegetarian: Lacto-ovo**

Total time: 60 minutes
Serves: 8
Serving size: 1/8 (2 inches by 3 inches)
Exchange: 2 starch, 1 vegetable, 1 fat,
2 reduced fat milk, 1 very lean meat

1. Sauté onion and garlic in olive oil until translucent, then add mushrooms and sauté 1 more minute. Do not overcook mushrooms.
2. Remove from heat and add spinach and basil.
3. In a separate bowl, place ricotta cheese and swirl in 1/4 cup tomato sauce. It does not have to be completely blended.
4. Blend tomato sauce and tomato paste in a bowl. Next, in a large baking pan, spread tomato sauce on the bottom and layer with noodles, ricotta cheese, spinach mixture, tomato sauce, and mozzarella cheese. Repeat until all ingredients are used. The top layer should only have noodles and mozzarella, parmesan cheese, and pepper.

## Serving Suggestion

Make ahead and freeze. It comes out great, although you may have to add another 10 minutes to cook after thawing.

**Nutrition Information:**

CAL 466  CHO 51G  PRO 25  FAT 18G  CHOL 42MG  CALCIUM 605MG  POTASSIUM 916MG  SODIUM 873MG  FIBER 6G

# Chapter 11

# FISH

## ABOUT FISH

Fish have always been a great source of both protein and oils that protect the heart. However, in January 2001, the U.S. government started to warn women to limit their consumption of fish during pregnancy because of high levels of methylmercury fish that posed dangers for unborn children.

Since 2001, the Food and Drug Administration (FDA) has recommended that most people restrict their consumption of king mackerel, swordfish, and tilefish to 12 ounces or less per week.

The Environmental Protection Agency (EPA) recommends that pregnant women restrict fish in their diets to 8 ounces or less per week.

Studies show that these restrictions need to be tighter. Although not every serving of fish contains dangerous levels of methylmercury, many experts, including myself, believe that a safer option would be to restrict consumption of the fish listed below—especially by pregnant women, nursing women, and women who are considering pregnancy.

Limit consumption of the following to once or twice a month or less until further safety is known:

| | |
|---|---|
| Atlantic salmon and some farm-raised fish | Atlantic tuna steaks |
| blue crab (from the Gulf of Mexico) | halibut |
| king mackerel | lake whitefish |
| large-mouth bass | mahimahi |
| marlin | pike |
| pollack | sea bass |
| shellfish | swordfish |
| tuna, canned (especially albacore) | white croaker |

This cookbook does not contain shellfish due to exceedingly high levels of cadmium, a toxic heavy metal found in some shellfish such as oysters that may increase the risk of cancer and/or neurological problems. Shellfish is also high in cholesterol if you are concerned about the amount in your diet.

It is wise to keep abreast of reports on areas from which fish are safe to consume, and you often can go to your state's environmental protection agency for details. Web sites are devoted to listing the levels in fish (for example, the FDA's www.cfsan.fda.gov/~frf/seamehg2.html).

Unfortunately, many available reports are outdated. Many freshwater lakes and rivers are polluted, and the fish are not safe to consume. Smaller fish are more likely to be safer than large fish because they have less stored fat, which is where pollutants accumulate. Neurological damage and cancer are the main health concerns for humans. Methylmercury toxicity may be linked as a contributing factor in autism.

Currently, the fish below appear to be safe, but always check to stay abreast of our changing environment.

Safer options are the following:

| | |
|---|---|
| croaker (not white) | fish sticks |
| flounder (summer) | haddock |
| hake | red snapper |
| salmon (only wild Pacific)* | sardines |
| tilapia | wild Pacific trout |
| Other seafood not from the Gulf of Mexico | |

*Atlantic farm-raised fish have been known to contain high levels of polychlorinated biphenyls (PCBs), which may cause cancer.

# BAKED SALMON WITH CAPER DILL SAUCE

*Salmon contains Omega-3 fatty acids and docosahexaenoic acid, which help protect the heart.*

1 lb. Salmon fillets, fresh (four 4-oz. pieces)

2 Lemons, cut in half

### Caper Dill Sauce

3/4 cup Yogurt, fat-free

3 Tbsp. Capers, drained and rinsed

3 Tbsp. Dijon mustard

2 Tbsp. Dill, fresh, minced (or 1 tsp. dried)

1 Lemon, cut in half

## MENU

*Baked Salmon with Caper Dill Sauce*

*Watercress and Radicchio Salad*

*Crispy Herb Potato Wedges*

Total time: 25 minutes
Serves: 4
Serving size: 1 salmon filet*
Exchange: 3 very lean meat

1. In a small bowl, combine yogurt, capers, mustard, and dill. Squeeze juice from the lemon into the yogurt mixture. Blend and chill.
2. Preheat oven to 350°F.
3. Place fish fillets in baking pan. Squeeze juice from lemons over fish. Bake approximately for 15 to 20 minutes or until fish flakes.
4. Cut into four equal servings and serve warm with caper dill sauce.

**Nutrition Information:**

**With Sauce**

CAL 213  CHO 8G  PRO 26G  FAT 8G  CHOL 64MG  CALCIUM 123MG  POTASSIUM 763MG  SODIUM 534MG  FIBER 1G

*Wild pacific suggested

# DOT'S FAMOUS FISH TOPPING

*Dorothy Court*

**Vegetarian: Lacto-ovo**

1/2 cup Italian parsley, fresh, minced
1/2 Red bell pepper, fine dice
1/4 cup Onion, fine dice
2 cloves Garlic, minced
1/2 medium Tomato, fine dice
1/4 cup Light mayonnaise
1 tsp. Dry mustard
1 Tbsp. Butter
To taste Black pepper, freshly ground

Total time: 15 minutes
Serves: 6
Serving size: 1/3 cup
Exchange: 1 fat, 1/2 vegetable

Mix all ingredients together and heat for 30 seconds in a microwave or for 2 minutes on the stovetop. Stir and spread on your favorite fish fillet.

## Serving Suggestion
Serve with rice.

**Nutrition Information:**

CAL 61  CHO 3G  PRO 1G  FAT 5G  CHOL 3MG  CALCIUM 14MG  POTASSIUM 93MG  SODIUM 85MG  FIBER 1G

# GRILLED BLUEFISH WITH VEGETABLES

*Peppers contain phytonutrients that may help reduce joint inflammation.*

1 lb. Bluefish\*, filletted, washed
1 medium Onion, sliced
1 medium Green bell pepper, sliced
1 medium Tomato, sliced
1 medium Lemon, sliced
3 drops Tabasco sauce
To taste Pepper, black, freshly ground

> ### MENU
> *Summer Gazpacho Soup*
> **Grilled Bluefish with Vegetables**
> *Tuscan White Bean Salad with Spinach*

1. Preheat grill or preheat oven to 350°F.
2. Place washed bluefish on a sheet of aluminum foil, then alternate slices of onion, pepper, tomato, and lemon on top of the fish.
3. Add Tabasco and ground black pepper as desired.
4. Close the foil to create a sealed package then place on grill or in oven for 20 minutes or until fish flakes.

> Total time: 25 minutes
> Servings: 4
> Serving size: 4 oz.
> Exchange: 3 meat, 1 vegetable

**Nutrition Information:**

CAL 160  CHO 7G  PRO 21G  FAT 5G  CHOL 63MG  CALCIUM 24MG  POTASSIUM 643MG  SODIUM 66MG  FIBER 2G

\*Any white fish may be used with this recipe.

# GRILLED WASABI TUNA

*Dr. Gray Federici*

1 lb. Pacific tuna, fresh, cut into 1-1/2
  inch by 2 inch cubes

**Marinade**

1/2 tsp. Wasabi powder
1/2 tsp. Ginger, ground
2 Tbsp. Brown sugar
To taste White pepper, ground
4 tsp. Soy sauce, light

**MENU**

*Grilled Wasabi Tuna*
*Rice with Scallions*
*Green Beans Almandine*

Total time: 15–30 minutes
Serves: 4
Serving size: 4 oz.
Exchange: 4 lean meat, 1 vegetable

1. Combine marinade ingredients in a bowl, add tuna, and coat each piece with marinade. Marinate for 10 to 20 minutes in refrigerator.
2. When ready to cook, grill or broil for 5 to 10 minutes per side, depending on thickness.

**Nutrition Information:**

CAL 193  CHO 7G  PRO 27G  FAT 6G  CHOL 43MG  CALCIUM 17MG  POTASSIUM 324MG  SODIUM 226MG  FIBER 0G

# HAKE ORIENTAL

*Hake is a mild-flavored, white-fleshed fish.*

2 Parsnips, peeled and grated

2 Carrots, peeled and grated

2 Scallions, both green and white parts, diced

1 Onion, sliced

2 Tbsp. Sesame or roasted peanut oil

1 lb. Hake*

1 tsp. Dry sherry

To taste Ginger, ground

1/2 tsp. or less Soy sauce, reduced sodium

**MENU**

*Asian-Style Vegetable Soup*

*Hake Oriental*

*Swiss Chard with Tomatoes*

*August Fresh Fruit with Gingersnap Cookies*

Total time: 20 minutes
Serves: 4
Serving size: 4 oz.
Exchange: 3 lean meat, 1 starch

1. Sauté vegetables in oil, stirring frequently.
2. Arrange vegetables around outside of cook-and-serve pan. Place hake in center of pan then sprinkle with sherry, ginger, and soy sauce to taste.
3. Simmer gently over low heat or bake at 350°F until done, approximately 10 minutes.
4. Serve from pan.

**Serving Suggestion**

Serve with other greens and winter squash.

**Nutrition Information:**

CAL 241  CHO 16G  PRO 24G  FAT 8G  CHOL 62MG  CALCIUM 55MG  POTASSIUM 675MG  SODIUM 247MG  FIBER 4G

*Other firm, thick fillets such as haddock or cod can be substituted. Cook fish gently on low heat to prevent the delicate proteins from toughening.

# MEDITERRANEAN BAKED COD

*Antioxidants in this recipe will help boost your immune system and heart health.*

1 lb. Cod fillets
2 Plum tomatoes, diced
15 large Olives, black, chopped
1 Tbsp. Capers, small, drained
  and rinsed
1 Tbsp. Olive oil
1 clove Garlic, minced
1/2 medium Onion, sliced

## MENU

*Mediterranean Baked Cod*
*Wheat Berries with Pasta*
*Cold Lemon Broccoli Salad*

Total time: 30 minutes
Serves: 4
Serving size: 4 oz.
Exchange: 3 very lean meat

1. Preheat oven to 375°F.
2. Wash fish and place in baking dish. Top with tomatoes and olives.
3. In a separate pan, sauté garlic and onion in oil over medium high heat. When onion caramelizes and turns light brown, remove from heat and pour over cod.
4. Bake 20 minutes or until cod is thoroughly cooked through.

**Nutrition Information:**

CAL  CHO 163  PRO 4G  FAT 6G  CHOL 60MG  CALCIUM 35MG  POTASSIUM 394MG  SODIUM 283MG  FIBER 1G

# PAN-FRIED TILAPIA

1 tsp. Olive oil
1 lb. Tilapia fillets
1/2 cup Bread crumbs
1/2 tsp. Garlic powder
1/2 tsp. Italian seasoning
1/2 tsp. Old Bay seasoning
1 Egg, beaten

## LOW-FAT FISH AND CHIPS DINNER

*Italian Tomato Salad*
**Pan-Fried Tilapia**
*Herb Roasted Potatoes*
*Peach Iced Tea*

1. Heat olive oil in a large skillet over medium heat.
2. In a shallow bowl, mix bread crumbs with garlic powder, Italian seasoning, and Old Bay seasoning.

Total time: 12 minutes
Serves: 4
Serving size: 3 oz.
Exchange: 3 very lean meat, 1/2 starch

3. Beat egg in a shallow bowl.
4. Dip each fillet in the egg and then the bread crumb mixture.
5. Place breaded filets in skillet and sprinkle any remaining bread crumbs on top. Cook filets for approximately 5 minutes on each side or until each side is golden brown and the fish flakes easily. Serve immediately.

**Nutrition Information:**
CAL 188  CHO 10G  PRO 25G  FAT 5G  CHOL 113MG  CALCIUM 49MG  POTASSIUM 352MG  SODIUM 207MG  FIBER 1G

# RED SNAPPER WITH CAPERS

*This easy and delicious recipe is rich in nutrients for the heart and brain.*

1 Whole snapper, cleaned, or 2 8-oz. fillets

1 medium Lemon, quartered

2 Tbsp. Capers, drained, rinsed

1 Tbsp. Olive oil

1/4 tsp. Pepper, black, ground

2 tsp. Garlic powder

2 Tbsp. Parsley, fresh, minced

**MENU**

*Spring Greens with Beets and
 Blood Oranges*

**Red Snapper with Capers**

*Broccoli with Garlic*

*Rice with Almonds*

1. Arrange fish in baking dish with cavity open if the fish is whole. Squeeze lemon juice over fish.

Total time: 18 minutes
Serves: 2
Serving size: 4 oz. edible fish
Exchange: 3 lean meat, 1 vegetable

2. Mix capers, olive oil, pepper, and garlic powder and pour over fish. Top with fresh chopped parsley.

3. Bake at 350°F until fish flakes easily, approximately 15 minutes.

**Nutrition Information:**

CAL 185   CHO 6G   PRO 22G   FAT 8G   CHOL 60MG   CALCIUM 30MG   POTASSIUM 404MG   SODIUM 320MG   FIBER 1G

# SESAME TERIYAKI SALMON

*Yes, a little teriyaki sauce can be used sparingly on a low-sodium diet. Omega-3 fatty acids and phytonutrients may enhance memory and brain power.*

4 Pacific salmon filets, 4 oz. each, fresh
1 Tbsp. Teriyaki sauce
1 tsp. Garlic, fresh, minced
1 Tbsp. Ginger, fresh ground
2 Scallions, diced
1 Tbsp. Sesame seeds
1 Tbsp. Honey

**MENU**

*Chickpea and Tomato Salad*
*Sesame Teriyaki Salmon*
*Steamed Yellow Squash*

Total time: 24 minutes
Serves: 4
Serving size: 4 oz. edible fish
Exchange: 4 medium fat meat

1. Preheat oven to 350°F.
2. Place fillets in baking dish.
3. Mix teriyaki sauce, garlic, ginger, scallions, sesame seeds, and honey and top each fillet.
4. Bake for approximately 20 minutes or until thoroughly cooked through.

## Serving Suggestion

Because farm-raised fish may contain excessive amounts of cancer-causing PCBs, buy wild Pacific Salmon or other known safe sources.

**Nutrition Information:**

CAL 199  CHO 6ᴳ  PRO 25ᴳ  FAT 8ᴳ  CHOL 75ᴹᴳ  CALCIUM 25ᴹᴳ  POTASSIUM 618ᴹᴳ  SODIUM 243ᴹᴳ  FIBER 1ᴳ

# STEAMED SALMON IN GINGER MARINADE

*Besides tasting great, this recipe also boosts Omega-3 fatty acids.*

*Barbara Lewis*

1 lb. Salmon fillet, Pacific (wild, not farm-raised)
2 Scallions, chopped
To taste Hot chili sauce

## Marinade

1/2 cup Sake (Japanese rice wine)
4 shaved slices Ginger, fresh, 2 inches long

**MENU**

*Bean Sprout Salad*
*Steamed Salmon in Ginger Marinade*
*Basmati Brown Rice with Scallions*
*Spinach Sauté*

Total time: 24 minutes
Serves: 4
Serving size: 3 oz.
Exchange: 3 medium fat meat

1. Marinate salmon in wine and ginger in covered container in the refrigerator for 4 to 24 hours.
2. Place salmon on a poaching rack in a pan on top of stove. Pour water enough to cover bottom of pan below the rack. Pour marinate liquid over salmon. Cover and steam on medium heat until cooked through, 15 to 20 minutes. Add one-half of the scallions the last 5 minutes.
3. Remove from pan and place on serving dish. Sprinkle with chili sauce and remaining scallion. Serve immediately.

**Nutrition Information:**

CAL 215  CHO 8G  PRO 23G  FAT 7G  CHOL 63MG  CALCIUM 27MG  POTASSIUM 752MG  SODIUM 114MG  FIBER 1G

# STUFFED SOLE FLORENTINE

*This recipe is rich in folic acid to help protect the heart and iron to reduce fatigue.*

4 small Sole filets (approximately 5 oz. each), fresh
10 oz. Spinach (1 package frozen), thawed, chopped
1/2 cup Onions, diced
1/2 cup Italian-flavored bread crumbs
1/2 Lemon juice, freshly squeezed
2 Tbsp. Parmesan cheese

**Topping**

1/2 tsp. Dry mustard
3 Tbsp. Mayonnaise, light or low cholesterol type
1 Tbsp. Lemon juice
To taste Pepper, black, ground

## MENU

*Tomato Mozzarella Salad*
***Stuffed Sole Florentine***
*Crusty Garlic Bread*

Total time: 34 minutes
Serves: 4
Serving size: 5 oz.
Exchange: 1/4 starch, 4 low fat meats, 1/2 fat

1. Preheat oven to 350°F.
2. Sauté onions and set aside.
3. Wash fillets and place in baking dish.
4. Steam spinach until tender, drain well, and mix with onions, bread crumbs, lemon juice, and Parmesan. Place 2 Tablespoons in the center of each fillet and roll.
5. Mix topping ingredients until smooth and pour over fillets.
6. Bake for 20 minutes or until thoroughly cooked through (do not overcook).
7. Place under broiler for 3 minutes or until top browns. Serve immediately.

**Nutrition Information:**

CAL 276  CHO 17G  PRO 33G  FAT 8G  CHOL 86MG  CALCIUM 171MG  POTASSIUM 632MG  SODIUM 413MG  FIBER 2G

## Chapter 12

# POULTRY

# BADAMI CHICKEN

*This recipe requires a few more steps to prepare, but the taste of all of these spices and herbs is fabulous—just like the health benefits.*

*Dr. Wahida Karmally PHD, Registered Dietitian, CDE, Irving Center for Clinical Research, Columbia University Medial Center*

2 tablespoons Olive oil

2 each Cinnamon sticks

6 each Cloves

1 Tbsp. Cardamom pods

1 large Onion (3–4 inches in diameter), diced

2 cloves Garlic, crushed

1-1/2 inch piece Ginger root, fresh, peeled, and minced

4 large Chicken legs with thighs, skinless

2/3 cup Yogurt, plain, fat-free

1 tsp. Saffron threads soaked in
  2 Tbsp. Boiling water

1/4 tsp. Chili powder

1/2 cup Almonds, puréed in a blender with water to make a paste

### MENU

*Badami Chicken*
*Brown Basmati Rice*
*Simple Carrots with Parsley*
*Fat-Free Lemon Mousse*

Total time: 1 hour
Serves: 4–8
Serving size: 1/4
Exchange: For 4, 1 starch, 6 lean meat, 1 fat; for 8, 1/2 starch, 3 lean meat, 1/2 fat

*(continues)*

# BADAMI CHICKEN (Continued)

1/3 tsp. Salt
1/2 cup Evaporated fat-free milk
2 Hot chili peppers, dried
2 Tbsp. Cilantro, fresh, minced

1. Cut chicken, separating leg from thighs, or buy already separated pieces.
2. Heat oil in a saucepan. When hot, add cinnamon, cloves, and cardamom and fry for 1 minute.
3. Add diced onion and continue frying, stirring occasionally, until onion is translucent.
4. Add the garlic and ginger and fry for 3 minutes, stirring frequently.
5. Add the chicken pieces and fry until they are evenly browned.
6. Beat the yogurt, saffron mixture, and chili powder together, then stir mixture into chicken. Cook for 1 minute.
7. Stir the almond paste and salt into the chicken mixture. Simmer for 15 minutes.
8. Stir in milk and chilis and reduce the heat to low. Simmer for 30 minutes, or until the chicken is cooked through and tender. Uncover the pan for last 10 minutes of cooking.
9. Remove cinnamon sticks and cloves and transfer to a serving dish.
10. Garnish with chopped cilantro and serve with brown basmati rice (see index for recipe) and tomato and cucumber salad.

Suggestion: Begin cooking rice prior to starting this recipe. Have ready to serve. Eight Servings: reduce in half.

**Nutrition Information:**

**Four Servings**

| CAL 474 | CHO 16G | PRO 46G | FAT 25G | CHOL 111MG | CALCIUM 274MG | POTASSIUM 821MG | SODIUM 373 MG | FIBER 3G |

# BAKED CHICKEN PARMESAN

*This dish offers a great way to get calcium for bone health.*

1/2 cup Tomato sauce

1 lb. Chicken breast (4-oz. cutlets), free range

1 medium Egg, beaten (Egg Beaters Equivalent Optimal)

1-1/2 cups Bread crumbs, Italian-flavored

8 oz. Mozzarella cheese, part skim, shredded

2 Tbsp. Parmesan cheese

## MENU

*Oven-Roasted Peppers*

*Baked Chicken Parmesan*

*Crusty Garlic Bread or Escarole and Beans*

Total time: 26 minutes
Serves: 4
Serving size: 5–6 oz.
Exchange: 4 medium fat meat, 1 reduced fat dairy

1. Place 1/4 cup tomato sauce in the bottom of a 2-quart casserole dish and set aside.
2. Heat oven to 375°F.
3. Wash cutlets and pat dry, then dip them in egg and then bread crumbs and place in the casserole dish.
4. Bake approximately 15 minutes or until cooked.
5. Pour remaining tomato sauce over cutlets, then top with cheese.
6. Turn off heat and let casserole sit in oven 5 minutes or until cheese melts.
7. Serve immediately.

### Serving Suggestion

Place on a crusty fat-free garlic bread and serve with a side of roasted peppers. To boost fiber and lower calories, hold the bread and add a salad.

**Nutrition Information:**

CAL 352  CHO 11G  PRO 41G  FAT 16G  CHOL 148MG  CALCIUM 490MG  POTASSIUM 398MG  SODIUM 695MG  FIBER 1G

# BARBECUED CHICKEN

4 Chicken half breasts on bone

4 oz. Tomato sauce (canned)

2 Tbsp. Tomato paste

3 Tbsp. Brown sugar

1 Tbsp. Cider vinegar

1 small Onion, diced

**MENU**

*Quick and Easy Portabello*
  *Mushrooms*

*Barbecued Chicken*

*Crispy Herb Potato Wedges*

1. Preheat oven to 350°F.
2. Wash chicken and place in casserole dish.
3. Mix remaining ingredients in a small bowl, then pour over chicken.
4. Bake for 30 minutes or until tender and serve.

Total time: 35 minutes
Servings: 4
Serving size: 4-1/2 oz. with bone
Exchange: 3 meats, 1 starch

## Serving Suggestion

Serve with crispy potato wedges (see index for recipe).

**Nutrition Information:**
CAL 191  CHO 15g  PRO 24g  FAT 4g  CHOL 64mg  CALCIUM 31mg  POTASSIUM 434mg  SODIUM 299mg  FIBER 1g

# CHICKEN CACCIATORE

*This great one-pot meal can boost lycopenes, which are known to reduce the risk of prostate cancer. It can be made a day ahead and kept in the refrigerator in a covered microwavable dish. When ready to heat, place in the microwave on high for 5 to 8 minutes or until the meat is hot.*

1-1/4 lb. Chicken, whole, cut up, skin removed

1 Tbsp. Olive oil

5 cloves Garlic, fresh, minced

1 medium Onion, diced

1 Green bell pepper, diced

1/4 cup Basil leaves, fresh, whole stems removed

15-1/2 oz. Whole tomatoes (1 can)

8 oz. Tomato sauce (canned or homemade)

1/2 cup Red wine (burgundy, merlot, or Chianti)

### MENU

*Romaine Salad with Caramelized Onion*

*Chicken Cacciatore*

*Crusty Garlic Bread*

Fresh Grapes

Total time: 60 minutes
Serves: 4
Serving size: 1/4
Exchange: 2 lean meat

1. Brown chicken pieces in olive oil in a 1-gallon pot with garlic until lightly browned.
2. Add onions and bell pepper and sauté for 5 more minutes.
3. Add basil, tomatoes, tomato sauce, and wine and simmer for 40 to 60 minutes.

**Nutrition Information:**

CAL 170  CHO 15G  PRO 15G  FAT 4G  CHOL 39MG  CALCIUM 69MG  POTASSIUM 711MG  SODIUM 59MG  FIBER 3G

# CHICKEN FAJITAS

1 lb. Chicken breast strips, boneless
1 Tbsp. Canola oil
3 medium Green bell peppers,
 quartered and sliced
1 large Onion, quartered and sliced
2 Tbsp. Fajita sauce
4 Flour tortillas, 7-inch round

**MENU**

*Chickpea and Tomato Salad or
Tex-Mex Black Bean and
Corn Salad*
***Chicken Fajitas***
Fresh Pineapple

1. Brown chicken in 1 teaspoon of oil in a skillet, then remove and set aside.
2. Sauté bell pepper and onion in 2 teaspoons of oil. Place chicken and fajita sauce in skillet and sauté for 1 minute.
3. Heat tortillas for 2 minutes in hot oven.
4. Top each warm tortilla with chicken and vegetables and roll tortilla to enclose filling.
5. Serve immediately.

Total time: 25 minutes
Servings: 4
Serving size: 1 fajita
Exchange: 2 starch, 4 meat

## Serving Suggestion

To boost fiber, use Joseph's Oat Bran and Whole Wheat Tortilla instead of the flour tortilla.

**Nutrition Information:**

CAL 350   CHO 33G   PRO 30G   FAT 10G   CHOL 68MG   CALCIUM 84MG   POTASSIUM 489MG   SODIUM 306MG   FIBER 4G

# CHICKEN KABOBS WITH RICE AND PEANUT SAUCE

### Chicken

1lb. Chicken breast, cubed

2 Red bell peppers, sliced into 1/2-inch squares

4 Wooden skewers, soaked in water

### Peanut Sauce

1/2 cup Peanut butter, chunky style, reduced fat

1/2 cup Yogurt, fat-free

1/4 tsp. Teriyaki sauce

1/4 tsp. Soy sauce

To taste Chili peppers, dried (optional)

### MENU

*Bean Sprout Salad*

**Chicken Kabobs with Rice and Peanut Sauce**

*Brown Rice with Scallions*

*Thai Green Beans*

*Almond Cookies*

Total time: 15 minutes
Serves: 4
Serving size: 3 oz. chicken, 2 oz. sauce
Exchange: 4 medium fat meat,
1-1/2 starch

### Chicken

1. On each of four skewers, alternate one piece of chicken breast with one piece of red pepper until they are full.
2. Grill skewers over medium heat, turning as needed to brown all sides.

### Peanut Sauce

1. Place all ingredients in a saucepan over low heat. Stir to blend and cook until smooth.
2. Serve as dipping sauce with chicken kabobs.

### Serving Suggestion

Serve over Basmati brown rice with scallions (see recipe in index).

**Nutrition Information:**

CAL 368  CHO 21G  PRO 37G  FAT 16G  CHOL 69MG  CALCIUM 89MG  POTASSIUM 666MG  SODIUM 471MG  FIBER 4G

# CHICKEN MARSALA WITH SWEET POTATOES

*This dish is so tasty and so great for you.*

1/4 cup Porcini mushrooms, dried
1/4 cup Hot water
1 lb. Chicken breast, free range, whole, boneless and skinless
1/2 tsp. Basil, dried
1/16 tsp. Sea salt
1/4 tsp. Garlic, minced
To taste Pepper, black, ground
1 tsp. Olive oil
1/4 cup Marsala wine
3 medium Sweet potatoes, large cubes

Total time: 20–25 minutes
Serves: 4
Serving size: 3 oz. meat,
2/3 cup potato
Exchange: 3 very lean meat, 2 starch

1. Soak dried mushrooms in 1/4 cup of hot water and set aside.
2. Butterfly chicken breasts (lay each breast flat and cut parallel to the cutting surface through most of the breast to open it up).
3. Heat a nonstick skillet over high heat. When hot, add butterflied chicken breasts and cook for approximately 10 minutes. Season with basil, salt, garlic, and pepper.
4. Drizzle oil over top of breasts. When bottom is seared and brown, turn breasts over, seasoned side down. Cook on high another 5 minutes.
5. Reduce heat to medium and add mushrooms with water, marsala, and sweet potato cubes and cover skillet. Simmer until potatoes are tender, approximately 10 minutes.
6. Serve hot.

**Nutrition Information:**
CAL 317  CHO 36G  PRO 28G  FAT 5G  CHOL 68MG  CALCIUM 61MG  POTASSIUM 972MG  SODIUM 143MG  FIBER 5G

# CHICKEN, PEAS, AND BOW TIE NOODLES

8 oz. Bow tie pasta, dried

7 cloves Garlic, coarsely chopped

1 Tbsp. Oregano

1 tsp. Basil

1-1/2 tsp. Olive oil

1 lb. Chicken breasts, boneless and
  skinless, cut into 2-inch strips

8 oz. Peas, frozen

1/2 cup Chicken broth, low-fat,
  low-sodium

1/2 tsp. Lemon juice

## MENU

*Baby Spinach and Gorgonzola
  Medley*

*Chicken, Peas, and Bow Tie
  Noodles*

*Light Country Apple Pie or Apple*

Total time: 25 minutes
Serves: 6
Serving size: 1-1/2 cups
Exchange: 2 starch, 3 very lean meat

1. Cook pasta until slightly firm,
   according to package directions. When done, drain and set aside.
2. In a large skillet over medium high heat, sauté garlic, oregano, and
   basil in oil until brown.
3. Add chicken strips to herbs and cook 10 to 15 minutes.
4. Add peas, cooked pasta, chicken broth, and lemon juice to chicken
   mixture. Simmer 10 minutes over low heat, stirring after 5 minutes to
   keep ingredients from sticking.

## Serving Suggestion

Add a salad to make a complete meal and add more fiber and phytonutrients.

**Nutrition Information:**

CAL 268  CHO 31G  PRO 24G  FAT 5G  CHOL 79MG  CALCIUM 46MG  POTASSIUM 242MG  SODIUM 119MG  FIBER 3G

# CHICKEN PICCATA

4 Chicken breast cutlets, 4 oz. each
1/4 cup All-purpose flour
2 Tbsp. Olive oil
1 small Onion, diced
8 oz. Mushrooms, white, presliced, fresh
1/2 cup White wine
2 Tbsp. Parsley, fresh, minced
4 Lemon halves, fresh
To taste Pepper, black, freshly ground

> **MENU**
>
> *Eggplant Caponata*
> **Chicken Piccata**
> *Broccoli with Garlic*
> Orzo
> Fresh Cantaloupe

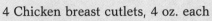

Total time: 25 minutes
Serves: 4
Serving size: 1 cutlet
Exchange: 3-1/2 lean meat, 1 starch

1. Coat chicken cutlets lightly with flour. Sprinkle with freshly ground pepper.
2. In a large skillet, heat 2 Tablespoons of oil. Sauté cutlets over medium heat for approximately 5 to 8 minutes on each side, until brown and tender. Remove and set aside.
3. In same skillet, add onions and mushrooms and sauté until translucent. Remove and set aside.
4. Add white wine to skillet to deglaze pan by stirring.
6. Add chicken back to skillet and cover. Cook 5 to 10 minutes longer, or until liquid is reduced to a thin glaze.
7. Add mushrooms and onions; mix thoroughly to coat with sauce.
8. Garnish with chopped parsley and lemon halves and serve.

**Nutrition Information:**

CAL 227   CHO 13G   PRO 28G   FAT 11G   CHOL 68 MG   CALCIUM 32MG   POTASSIUM 485MG   SODIUM 68MG   FIBER 2G

# CHICKEN STIR-FRY OVER CLEAR NOODLES

*This is a wonderfully flavorful way to get phytonutrients and fiber.*

2 Tbsp Water

1/4 tsp. Thai chili sauce

1 Tbsp. Cornstarch

1 tsp. Sesame seed oil

1/2 lb. Chicken breast, free range, skinless, sliced

1 tsp. Garlic, minced

1/2 lb. Pea pods, fresh, raw

8 oz. Baby corn (canned), cut into small pieces

4 oz. Water chestnuts (canned), sliced

1/4 cup Peanuts, unsalted, dry roasted

1/2 lb. Clear noodles

3 cups Water

**MENU**

*Bean Sprout Salad*

*Chicken Stir Fry over Clear Noodles*

*Fat-Free Lemon Mousse*

Total time: 16 minutes
Serves: 4–5
Serving size: 8 oz. chicken stir-fry, 1/2 cup clear noodles
Exchange: For 4, 1 lean meat, 4 starch,* 2 vegetables

1. Place 2 Tablespoons of water, Thai chili sauce, and cornstarch in a mixing bowl and blend, then set aside.
2. In a skillet or wok over high heat, heat oil and then add chicken slices and garlic to stir-fry.
3. In a separate pot, bring water to a boil.
4. Add Thai chili sauce and cornstarch mixture, pea pods, baby corn, water chestnuts, and peanuts to stir-fry in skillet or wok and toss every minute to cook evenly. Remove from heat when pea pods are cooked but remain crisp.
5. Place noodles in boiling water and cook for 3 minutes or until soft but not mushy. Drain and then place on serving dish.
6. Place stir-fried chicken, vegetables, and sauce over noodles and serve immediately.

## Serving Suggestion

If someone is allergic to peanuts, simply remove them from the recipe.

**Nutrition Information:**

CAL 459  CHO 74G  PRO 20G  FAT 9G  CHOL 34MG  CALCIUM 56MG  POTASSIUM 433MG  SODIUM 171MG  FIBER 6G

*To cut one starch, omit clear noodles.

# HERB-ROASTED CHICKEN

1 small Chicken, whole, free range, cleaned
  (approximately 2 lbs.)
4 cloves Garlic, sliced
5 sprigs Parsley, fresh
1 Tbsp. Herbs de Provence*
To taste Pepper, black, ground

Total time: 35 minutes
Serves: 4
Serving size: 4 oz.
Exchange: 3 very lean meat

1. Preheat oven to 350°F.
2. Place chicken on a roasting pan. Separate and lift skin over breast and insert parsley and garlic. Sprinkle Herbs de Provence over the skin and add pepper. Bake for 30 minutes or until cooked and tender (meat should not be pink).

**Nutrition Information:**

CAL 173  CHO 1G  PRO 26G  FAT 7G  CHOL 78MG  CALCIUM 21MG  POTASSIUM 234MG  SODIUM 77MG  FIBER 0G

*Found in specialty food stores; may be substituted with equal amounts of dried thyme and rosemary.

# LIME CHICKEN PITA PIZZAS

*Chef Brian MacMenamin*

18 oz. Chicken breasts, boneless
1/4 cup White wine
1/4 cup Lemon juice, fresh
1 cup Water
1 tsp. Garlic, minced
2 tsp. Flat leaf parsley, chopped fine
To taste Pepper, black, ground
1/2 cup Red onions, diced
1/2 cup Red bell peppers, cut into strips
1/2 cup Mozzarella cheese, fresh, diced
2 Tbsp. Cilantro, fresh, minced
6 Pita bread, whole wheat

> Total time: 25 minutes
> Serves: 6
> Serving size: 1
> Exchange: 2 starch, 2 vegetables,
> 3 very lean meat

## Sauce
2 Tbsp. Soy sauce, light
1/2 Orange, juice of
2 Tbsp. Lime juice
To taste Cayenne pepper
3 Tbsp. Brown sugar
2 Tbsp. Cornstarch

1. Over medium heat in a large skillet, cook chicken breasts in white wine, lemon juice, water, garlic, parsley, and ground pepper until meat is white and tender. Cool 5 minutes and then cube into bite-sized pieces.
2. Place six whole pitas on a cookie sheet and sprinkle the tops with cubed chicken, red onions, bell peppers, mozzarella cheese, and cilantro.
3. Heat broiler to 500°F and cook until cheese begins to melt (approximately 5 minutes).
4. In a saucepan over medium heat, combine soy sauce, orange juice, lime juice, cayenne pepper, and brown sugar and bring to a boil.
5. Whisk in cornstarch to thicken sauce then drizzle over pitas. Serve hot.

**Nutrition Information:**
CAL 319  CHO 39G  PRO 27G  FAT 6G  CHOL 57MG  CALCIUM 113MG  POTASSIUM 358MG  SODIUM 530MG  FIBER 4G

# MOROCCAN CHICKEN WITH LEMONS AND GREEN OLIVES

*Chef Brian MacMenamin*

4 Chicken breast halves, boneless and
  skinless (4 oz. each)
To taste Pepper, black, ground
2 Tbsp. Olive oil
2 med. Onions, sliced 1/4-inch thick
2 cloves Garlic, thinly sliced
1/2 tsp. Turmeric
8 pieces Preserved lemons
1/2 cup Chicken broth
1/4 cup Dry white wine
16 Green olives, pitted, halved
2 Tbsp. Cilantro, fresh, coarsely chopped

Total time: 35 minutes
Serves: 4
Serving size: 3 oz.
Exchange: 3 medium fat meat,
1 vegetable

1. Pat chicken dry, then season with pepper.
2. Heat 1 Tablespoon of oil in a 12-inch nonstick skillet over moderately high heat until hot but not smoking, then sauté chicken until golden brown, approximately 3 minutes on each side. Transfer chicken to a plate and keep warm and covered.
3. Add remaining Tablespoon of oil to skillet and reduce heat to moderate. Cook onions and garlic, stirring frequently, until softened but not browned, 8 to 10 minutes.
4. Add turmeric and black pepper and cook, stirring, for 1 minute.
5. Scrape pulp from preserved lemon, reserving for another use. Cut rind into thin strips and add to onions with broth, wine, and olives.
6. Return chicken, with any juices accumulated on the plate, to the skillet. Braise, covered, until chicken is cooked through, approximately 12 minutes. Serve sprinkled with cilantro.

**Nutrition Information:**

CAL 265   CHO 9G   PRO 26G   FAT 13G   CHOL 68MG   CALCIUM 42MG   POTASSIUM 360MG   SODIUM 286MG   FIBER 2G

# ROSEMARY TURKEY DRUMS

*Dr. Gary Federici*

4 small Turkey drum sticks
2 Tbsp. Rosemary leaves, fresh
To taste Pepper, black, freshly
  ground

---

Place rosemary under turkey skin and then sprinkle with freshly ground black pepper. Bake at 350°F for 30 minutes or until cooked through and tender.

## MENU

*Rosemary Turkey Drums*
*Pineapple Baked Sweet Potatoes*
*Brussels Sprouts*
*New Pumpkin Pie with*
  *Old-Fashioned Flavor*

Total time: 31 minutes
Servings: 4
Serving size: 1 drum
Exchange: 3 medium fat meats

**Nutrition Information:**

CAL 266  CHO 1G  PRO 35G  FAT 13G  CHOL 102MG  CALCIUM 41MG  POTASSIUM 360MG  SODIUM 91MG  FIBER 0G

# SESAME-HONEY CHICKEN BITES

*Sesame, garlic, and ginger may aid in reducing cancer and heart disease.*

4 Chicken breasts, boneless (4 oz. each)
1/2 cup Honey*
2 tsp. Ginger, fresh, crushed
2 tsp. Rice vinegar
1 tsp. Garlic powder
1 Tbsp. Teriyaki sauce
2 Tbsp. Sesame seeds

> **MENU**
>
> *Sesame-Honey Chicken Bites*
> *Colorful Coleslaw*
> *Simple Carrots with Parsley*
> *Low-Fat Pumpkin Bread*

1. Cut chicken into 1-inch cubes and place in mixing bowl.
2. Mix honey, ginger, rice vinegar, garlic powder, and teriyaki sauce and pour over chicken pieces.
   Marinate covered for 24 hours in refrigerator.
3. Preheat oven to 350°F.
4. Place cubes in baking pan and bake for 15 minutes or until tender.
5. Sprinkle with sesame seed before serving.

> Total time: 20 minutes (excludes 24 hours marinating time)
> Servings: 4
> Serving size: 3-1/2 oz.
> Exchange: 3-1/2 very lean meat, 2 fruit, 1 vegetable

**Nutrition Information:**

CAL 303   CHO 37G   PRO 27G   FAT 6G   CHOL 68MG   CALCIUM 23MG   POTASSIUM 264MG   SODIUM 238MG   FIBER 1G

*Honey should not be consumed by pregnant women or children less than 2 years of age. It contains natural bacteria that may be harmful to them.

# SKILLET CHICKEN WITH ONIONS AND PEPPERS

*John Arpino*

1-1/4 lbs. Chicken thighs, bone in, skinless
8 Italian green peppers, fresh, halved and sliced
1 large Onion, quartered, sliced
2 cloves Garlic
1/4 tsp. Thyme, dried
To taste Pepper, black, ground

**MENU**

*Skillet Chicken with Onion and Peppers*
*Wheat Berries with Pasta*
*Frozen Berry Dessert*

Total time: 30 minutes
Serves: 4
Serving size: 4 oz. with bone
Exchange: 3 very lean meat

1. Place chicken in a large skillet and sauté over medium heat. Add a few drops of water if the chicken sticks to the pan and continue cooking for 10 minutes.
2. Remove chicken and drain excess fat, leaving approximately 2 Tablespoons of liquid in pan.
3. Add peppers, onions, garlic, thyme, and pepper and cook, covered, 10 to 15 minutes, turning as needed.
4. Remove cover and cook another 5 to 10 minutes until chicken meat is no longer pink and peppers are tender.

**Nutrition Information:**

CAL 202  CHO 6G  PRO 28G  FAT 7G  CHOL 8MG  CALCIUM 47MG  POTASSIUM 390MG  SODIUM 77MG  FIBER 1G

# TURKEY CHILI

*Red tomatoes are high in lycopene, which may reduce the risk of cancers of the lung, breast, and prostate.*

*Michelle Jackson, Registered Dietitian*

1 Tbsp. Olive oil
12 oz. Turkey meat, ground
1 cup Onion, diced
1/2 cup Green bell pepper, diced
2 small or 1 large clove Garlic, minced
16 oz. Tomatoes (canned with liquid), diced (or 2 cup fresh tomato, cored and diced)
16 oz. Dark red kidney beans (1 can), drained
8 oz. Tomato sauce (1 can)
1 tsp. Chili powder
2–3 tsp. Basil, dried, crushed
1/4 tsp. Salt
1/4 tsp. Pepper, black, ground

## MENU

*Asparagus Salad with Dijon
    Vinaigrette*
*Turkey Chili*
*Brown Rice with Scallions*
*Whole Grain Bread Pudding*

Total time: 30 minutes
Serves: 4 main dish
Serving size: 1-1/2 cup
Exchange: 2 starch, 2 vegetables,
3 lean meat

1. In a large saucepan, cook ground turkey, onion, green pepper, and garlic in oil until meat is browned. Drain fat.
2. Stir in tomatoes, kidney beans, tomato sauce, chili powder, basil, salt, and pepper. Bring to a boil, then reduce heat. Cover and simmer for 20 minutes.
3. Serve hot.

## Serving Suggestion
Serve on a cold winter day after having fun outdoors.

**Nutrition Information:**
CAL 354   CHO 40ɢ   PRO 31ɢ   FAT 10ɢ   CHOL 57ᴍɢ   CALCIUM 76ᴍɢ   POTASSIUM 1,139ᴍɢ   SODIUM 826ᴍɢ   FIBER 11ɢ

# Chapter 13

# MEAT

## BRACIOLI

*Dr. Gary Federici*

1 lb. Beef filets, pounded thin,
   90 percent lean top round sliced
   lengthwise
1 Tbsp. Butter
1/4 cup Red wine
1 cup Tomato sauce

### Stuffing

10 oz. Frozen spinach (1 package),
   thawed
4 cloves Garlic, minced
4 Tbsp. White raisins, soaked in warm
   water
1/2 cup Bread crumbs
4 oz. Mozzarella cheese, part skim, shredded
1 Egg, beaten
2 Tbsp. Parmesan cheese
1/2 cup Parsley, fresh, minced
2 Tbsp. Pine nuts (optional)

### MENU

*Romaine Salad with Caramelize
   Onion Topping*
*Bracioli*
*Ali's Veggie Gratinati*

Total time: 30 minutes
Serves: 4
Serving size: 1
Exchange: 3 medium fat meat, 1
reduced fat dairy, 1 starch, 1 fat

*(continues)*

# BRACIOLI (Continued)

1. Preheat oven to 350°F.
2. In a skillet over medium high heat, sauté fillets in butter for 1 minute per side.
3. Add wine and simmer a few more minutes, then remove skillet from heat.
4. To make stuffing, combine spinach with garlic, raisins, bread crumbs, mozzarella cheese, egg, Parmesan cheese, and parsley together in a mixing bowl.
5. Place beef in a baking dish. Add equal amounts of stuffing to each fillet and roll them up, holding each one together with a toothpick.
6. Pour tomato sauce over rolls and bake 15 minutes or until cheese melts.

## Serving Suggestion

Serve with a side of your favorite pasta.

**Nutrition Information:**

**Without Pine Nuts**

| CAL 460 | CHO 20G | PRO 34G | FAT 22G | CHOL 138MG | CALCIUM 399MG | POTASSIUM 787MG | SODIUM 465MG | FIBER 4G |
|---------|---------|---------|---------|------------|----------------|------------------|---------------|----------|

# CHILI CON CARNE

*Phytonutrients may help your memory, heart, and immune system. They also will boost fiber and may improve insulin action.*

1/2 tsp. Olive oil

1 cup Onion, diced

1 cup Green bell pepper, diced

1lb. Ground beef or turkey, 90 percent lean

1 tsp. Jalapeño peppers, diced (optional)

2 tsp. Garlic, minced

2 tsp. Chili powder

14.5 oz. Tomatoes with green chilis (canned), diced (optional)

1/2 cup Ketchup

16 oz. Red kidney beans (1 can), drained

> **MENU**
>
> *Romaine Garden Salad*
> **Chili con Carne**
> *Basmati Brown Rice with Scallions*
> *Roasted Carrots and Onions*

> Total time: 30–40 minutes
> Serves: 6
> Serving size: 1 cup
> Exchange: 3 very lean meat, 2 starch

1. In a skillet, sauté onions in oil, add diced bell pepper and continue cooking until onions are translucent. Remove vegetables from skillet and set aside.
2. Add meat to skillet and brown with jalapeño peppers, garlic, and chili powder.
3. Drain excess liquid from cooked meat and add diced tomatoes and ketchup, stirring until blended. Cook for 5 to 10 minutes over low heat.
4. Add red kidney beans and reserved onions and pepper. Mix thoroughly and simmer 20 minutes or until hot.

## Serving Suggestion

Serve over steamed rice or corn bread. Make one day ahead and just reheat for 1 to 2 minutes in the microwave.

**Nutrition Information:**

**With Beef**

CAL 280  CHO 33G  PRO 23G  FAT 7G  CHOL 47MG  CALCIUM 61MG  POTASSIUM 802MG  SODIUM 649MG  FIBER 7G

# CRUSTY HONEY MUSTARD LAMB CHOPS

*Nuts enhance the phytofats that may help your heart. If you must, red meat is all right to eat once in awhile, but if you are concerned about cholesterol, then keep portion sizes to the amounts noted.*

8 Lamb chops, baby loin, cut 1-inch thick, fat removed (weight approximately 3 oz. each with bone)
As needed Garlic powder
As needed Pepper, black, freshly ground
1 tsp. Anise seeds, ground
6 Tbsp. Almonds, ground
3 Tbsp. Flaxseed meal
3/4 cup Honey mustard

**MENU**

*Greek Pasta Salad*

*Crusty Honey Mustard Lamb Chops*

*Carrots with Ginger and Sesame Seeds*

Total time: 38 minutes
Serves: 4
Serving size: 2 chops
Exchange: 1 starch, 2-1/2 high fat meat

1. Preheat oven to 500°F.
2. Lightly sprinkle both sides of lamb chops with garlic powder and freshly ground black pepper.
3. Combine anise seeds, almonds, flaxseed meal, and honey mustard and mix thoroughly. Spread mustard mixture evenly over the lamb chops.
4. Place lamb chops in baking dish in the center of the preheated oven for 4 minutes. Turn the oven off, but do not open the door for 30 minutes.
5. Serve chops medium rare, with some pink showing in the center of each chop.

**Nutrition Information:**

CAL 303  CHO 16G  PRO 18G  FAT 19G  CHOL 59MG  CALCIUM 51MG  POTASSIUM 290MG  SODIUM 226MG  FIBER 3G

# FLANK STEAK WITH GINGER GARLIC SAUCE

*No, butter is not forbidden—just used less frequently.*

*Brian MacMenamin*

3 Tbsp. Butter

12 oz. Flank steak, cut into 4 pieces (each approximately 1-inch thick)

To taste Salt

To taste Pepper, black, ground

2 Tbsp. Garlic, minced

3 Tbsp. Ginger, minced

1/2 cup Soy sauce

1/4 cup Lemon juice, freshly squeezed

2 Scallions, thinly sliced diagonally

**MENU**

*Flank Steak with Ginger Garlic Sauce*

*Quick and Easy Portabello Mushrooms*

*Asparagus with Mint*

Total time: 15 minutes
Serves: 4
Serving size: 3 oz.
Exchange: 3 high fat meat

1. Melt butter in large skillet over medium high heat.
2. Season steaks with salt and pepper then cook them to desired doneness, approximately 4 minutes per side for medium rare. Transfer steaks to plate to rest.
3. In same skillet, add chopped garlic and ginger and sauté for 2 minutes in juices from steaks. Remove from heat and add soy sauce and lemon juice.
4. Slice steaks against the grain, then spoon sauce from skillet over steaks.
5. Serve garnished with scallions.

**Nutrition Information:**

CAL 197 CHO 4G PRO 12G FAT 15G CHOL 57MG CALCIUM 21MG POTASSIUM 228MG SODIUM 90MG FIBER 0G

# GREEK-STYLE LAMB WITH ORZO

*Dr. Gary A Federici*

**Lamb**

5 lbs. Leg of lamb, boneless

10 cloves Garlic

1/2 tsp. Coriander, dried and crushed

1/4 cup Basil, fresh leaves

1/16 tsp. Salt

To taste Pepper, black, ground

2–3 Tbsp. Tomato paste (optional)

1Tbsp. Oregano, dried

1 large Onion, thinly sliced

1 cup Water

3 Lemons, juice of

As needed Basil leaves, whole (for garnish)

4 cups Orzo, cooked

**MENU**

*Mediterranean Cucumber Salad*

*Greek-Style Lamb with Orzo*

*Fresh Berries over Lemon Sorbet*

Total time: 2–5 hours
Serves: 8
Serving size: 5 oz. lamb, 1/2 cup orzo
Exchange: 2 bread, 4 lean meat, 1 starch

**Lamb**

1. Place washed lamb in roasting pan. Using the tip of a sharp knife to cut small pockets, insert garlic cloves into the surface of the lamb.
2. Mix coriander, basil, salt, and pepper together. Rub lamb with mixture, then let sit 1 to 4 hours in the refrigerator.
3. Preheat oven to 450°F before cooking, then place lamb in oven. Maintain high heat for 20 minutes to make crust on bottom of roasting pan.
4. Remove pan from oven and reduce temperature to 325°F.
5. Add 1/2 cup to 3/4 cup of water to bottom of pan, return lamb to pan, and squeeze fresh lemon juice over lamb. Return to oven and roast for approximately 1 to 1-1/2 hours. Baste with water and lemon juice every 20 minutes. The crust at the bottom of the pan will turn black.
6. Remove lamb from pan when done, cover with aluminum foil, and set aside to rest.

*(continues)*

# GREEK-STYLE LAMB
# WITH ORZO (Continued)

7. Add water to bottom of pan and scrape to loosen thick crust, then mix in 1 Tablespoon of tomato paste to create a dark burgundy-colored sauce.
8. Cut lamb into 1/4-inch slices.

## Orzo

Follow cooking directions on box.

## Serving Suggestion

Cook orzo while lamb is marinating, then place in a microwavable bowl and set aside to reheat once the lamb is ready to be served. Place warmed orzo on a serving platter and top with sliced lamb. Drizzle sauce over cooked orzo and lamb and garnish with fresh basil leaves before serving.

**Nutrition Information:**

Lamb and Orzo

| CAL 377 | CHO 27G | PRO 38G | FAT 13G | CHOL 127MG | CALCIUM 46MG | POTASSIUM 639 | SODIUM 268MG | FIBER 3G |

Orzo

| CAL 99 | CHO 20G | PRO 3G | FAT 0G | CHOL 0MG | CALCIUM 5MG | POTASSIUM 22MG | SODIUM 99MG | FIBER 1G |

# NUT-CRUSTED RACK OF LAMB

*This dish contains large amounts of phytonutrients to help guard against cancer.*

*Chef Brian MacMenamin*

1/4 cup Canola oil
6 Tbsp. Hoisin sauce
1/2 cup Plum wine or sherry
2 Tbsp. Garlic, fresh, minced
1/2 tsp. Red pepper, dried, crushed
  (optional)
2 Racks of lamb (1-3/4 lb.), trimmed
7 Tbsp. Chili sauce, bottled
1 cup Almonds, roasted, finely chopped

**MENU**

*Nut-Crusted Rack of Lamb*
Steamed New Potatoes
*Asparagus with Mint*

Total time: Marinating, 4–12 hours;
cooking, 35 minutes
Serves: 6
Serving size: Two 3-oz. chops with bone
Exchange: 2 medium fat meat, 1 fat,
1 starch

1. Mix oil, 2 Tablespoons of Hoisin sauce, plum wine or sherry, garlic, ginger, and red pepper flakes in a medium saucepan. Stir over low heat until warm, approximately 4 minutes, then set aside and cool.
2. Place lamb racks in glass baking dish, then pour cooled marinade over lamb to coat. Cover and chill at least 4 hours or overnight.
3. When ready to cook racks, preheat oven to 375°F.
4. Drain lamb and pat dry.
5. Heat large, heavy skillet over high heat. Add one lamb rack and turn to sear on all sides, approximately 6 minutes. Transfer to baking pan. Repeat with remaining rack.
6. Mix chili sauce and 4 Tablespoons Hoisin sauce in small bowl, then brush over lamb. Press chopped nuts onto lamb, coating it completely. Put baking dish into oven and bake at 350°F until meat thermometer registers 130°F for medium rare, approximately 20 minutes. Remove racks from oven and transfer to platter to let rest covered with foil for 15 minutes.
7. Cut lamb between ribs into two-chop portions.
8. Bring reserved marinade to a boil over medium high heat and reduce by half.
9. Serve lamb with reduction sauce.

**Nutrition Information:**

CAL 303  CHO 16G  PRO 18G  FAT 15G  CHOL 59MG  CALCIUM 84MG  POTASSIUM 290MG  SODIUM 474MG  FIBER 4G

# OLD-FASHIONED CORNED BEEF AND CABBAGE

6 cups Water

15 oz. Corned beef, uncooked, trimmed

1/2 cup Cilantro, minced

4 Bay leaves, whole

1/2 tsp. Coriander seeds, whole

1 small Cabbage, quartered

4 medium Potatoes, Eastern or new, cut
  in half

Total time: 1 hour
Serves: 4
Serving size: 1/4
Exchange: 1 starch, 2 high fat meat,
1 vegetable

1. Place water in a large pot and bring to boil over high heat. Add corned beef and spices and simmer for 30 minutes.
2. Add cilantro, bay leaves, coriander seeds, cabbage, and potatoes and simmer for 30 more minutes or until all vegetables are tender.
3. Remove meat and let sit 5 to 10 minutes before slicing.
4. Remove bay leaves from pot.
5. Serve sliced corned beef with vegetables.

## Serving Suggestion

This great one-pot meal can be made a day in advance and kept in the refrigerator. Serve a good quality mustard on the side as a dip for the meat.

**Nutrition Information:**

CAL 275  CHO 20G  PRO 17G  FAT 15G  CHOL 74MG  CALCIUM 112MG  POTASSIUM 713MG  SODIUM 899MG  FIBER 5G

# STUFFED CABBAGE

2 cups Brown rice
8 Cabbage leaves
1 tsp. Olive oil
1 small Onion, fine dice
1/2 lb. Ground beef, 90 percent lean
15 oz. Stewed tomatoes (canned)
 (reserve half)
1/2 cup Ketchup
To taste Pepper, black, ground
2 Tbsp. Parmesan cheese, grated

**MENU**

*Tortillini in Broth*
Stuffed Cabbage
Fat-free Lemon Mousse

Total time: 60 minutes with advanced preparation
Serves: 4–8
Serving size: 1–2
Exchange: One cabbage roll, 1 starch, 1 vegetable, 1 medium fat meat; two cabbage rolls, 2 starch, 1 medium fat meat, 1 vegetable

1. Make rice following the directions on the container.*
2. Remove eight leaves from a cabbage head and steam in a covered pan with 1/2 cup of water for 10 minutes or until the leaves are wilted. Set aside.
3. In a skillet over medium heat, sauté onion in olive oil. When onion is translucent, add ground beef and cook until brown.
4. Reserve 1 cup of stewed tomatoes but add the rest of the tomatoes, ketchup, black pepper, and Parmesan cheese and blend over medium heat until the liquid reduces.
5. Add rice and mix evenly with meat.
6. Place equal amounts of meat mixture in the center of each cabbage leaf, then wrap by folding in sides and then rolling the leaf up.
7. Put the finished cabbage rolls in a microwavable container with a lid, then top with reserved tomatoes. Cover and heat in a microwave 5 minutes or until hot. Serve immediately.

## Serving Suggestion

For busy people, this dish can be made ahead and frozen or saved for a day in the refrigerator and served as a quick heat-it-up for a dinner or lunch.

**Nutrition Information:**

**One Serving (one cabbage roll)**

CAL 148  CHO 22G  PRO 8G  FAT 4G  CHOL 18MG  CALCIUM 41MG  POTASSIUM 274MG  SODIUM 200MG  FIBER 3G

**Two Servings (two cabbage rolls)**

CAL 296  CHO 43G  PRO 16G  FAT 7G  CHOL 36MG  CALCIUM 81MG  POTASSIUM 548MG  SODIUM 400MG  FIBER 6G

*If you do not have time the day of preparation to make the brown rice, you can make it a day ahead and store it in the refrigerator.

# STUFFED ZUCCHINI

*This delicious recipe will surely help you eat more vegetables. The calcium in this dish helps to boost bone density.*

2 medium Zucchini, 12 inches long
1 medium Onion
1 Tbsp. Olive oil
1/2 lb. Ground beef, 10 percent fat*
1 cup Tomato sauce
8 oz. Mozzarella cheese, part skim,
  shredded

## MENU

*Tuscan White Bean Salad*
**Stuffed Zucchini**
*Crusty Garlic Bread*

**Carnivore or Vegetarian: Lacto-ovo**

Total time: 30 minutes
Serves: 4
Serving size: 1/2 zucchini
Exchange: With meat, 1 reduced fat dairy, 2 high fat meat; vegetarian style, 1 reduced fat dairy, 1 lean fat meat, 1 vegetable

1. Preheat oven to 350°F.
2. Slice zucchini in half lengthwise and hollow out the inside.
3. Dice the removed inside flesh and sauté with onion in olive oil over medium heat until translucent.
4. Add ground beef and sauté until brown.
5. Drain excess fat, then add tomato sauce. Stir 1 more minute.
6. In a baking dish, fill zucchini cavities with meat and vegetable mixture. Top with cheese. Bake at 350°F for 20 minutes or until zucchini is tender.
7. While zucchini is heating, prepare a salad and pasta or bread. *Manga!*

## Serving Suggestion

Serve with crusty garlic bread or pasta and a salad on the side. Each serving of zucchini should be 1/2 cup to 1cup.

**Nutrition Information:**

**With Meat**

CAL 348  CHO 11G  PRO 28G  FAT 13G  CHOL 63MG  CALCIUM 447MG  POTASSIUM 710MG  SODIUM 699MG  FIBER 3G

**Vegetarian**

CAL 264  CHO 16G  PRO 17G  FAT 10G  CHOL 31MG  CALCIUM 438MG  POTASSIUM 350MG  SODIUM 304MG  FIBER 5G

*Vegetarians can substitute 3/4 cup rice and 3/4 cup beans for the meat. This version is half the sodium.

# VEGETABLE STEW WITH BEEF OR TEMPEH

*Great to prepare in advance and serve one or two days later.*

1 lb. Beef chuck stew meat, cut into
  chunks or for vegetarians
1 cup Tempeh, firm (optional)
2 tsp. Olive oil
1 cup Onion, fine dice
1 Tbsp. Garlic, fresh, minced
2 Bay leaves, broken up
1 lb. Russet potatoes, unpeeled, cut
  into chunks
7 cups Water
4 tsp. Beef bouillon concentrate,
  granulated
  Or for vegetarians
4 tsp. Vegetable bouillon concentrate,
  granulated
2 cups Carrots, raw, sliced
8 oz. Mushrooms (packaged), quartered
1 tsp. Marjoram, dried
4 tsp. Cornstarch
16 oz. Tomatoes, crushed (canned)
1 tsp. Thyme, dried
1 tsp. Italian herb seasoning
To taste Pepper, black, freshly ground

> ## MENU
>
> *Mesclun Greens with Apples and
>   Walnuts*
>
> *Vegetable Stew with Beef or
>   Tempeh*
>
> *Herbed Biscuits*

**Carnivore or Vegetarian (optional)**

Total time: 70 minutes
Serves: 4
Serving size: 1-1/2 cups
Exchange: 3 medium fat meat, 3 starch

## Beef Version

1. Using the directions on the package or jar of bouillon concentrate, make 5 cups of beef broth.
2. Heat oil in a large nonstick stockpot over medium heat.
3. Add onion and garlic and sauté until translucent.
4. Add meat and brown.

*(continues)*

# VEGETABLE STEW WITH
# BEEF OR TEMPEH (Continued)

5. Add thyme, marjoram, bay leaves, and beef broth. Cover and simmer 1-1/2 hours or until meat is tender.
6. Stir in potatoes, carrots, and mushrooms. Cover and simmer for 30 minutes.
7. In a bowl, combine 1 cup water and the cornstarch, then add tomatoes, Italian herb seasoning, and black pepper. Stir to mix well and pour into stew.
8. Increase heat to high and bring stew to a boil, then reduce to a simmer.
9. Before serving, remove bay leaves.

## Tempeh Version

1. Using the directions on the package or jar of bouillon concentrate, make 5 cups of vegetable broth.
2. Heat oil in a large nonstick stockpot over medium heat.
3. Add onion and garlic and sauté until translucent.
4. Add thyme, marjoram, bay leaves, and vegetable broth. Cover and simmer 1-1/2 hours.
5. Stir in potatoes, carrots, mushrooms, and tempeh. Cover and simmer for 30 minutes.
6. In a bowl, combine 1 cup water and the cornstarch, then add tomatoes, Italian herb seasoning, and black pepper. Stir to mix well and pour into stew.
7. Increase heat to high and bring stew to a boil, then reduce to a simmer.
8. Before serving, remove bay leaves.

**Nutrition Information:**

**With Beef**

CAL 448  CHO 48G  PRO 30G  FAT 16G  CHOL 70MG  CALCIUM 89MG  POTASSIUM 1,431MG  SODIUM 283MG  FIBER 7G

**With Tempeh**

CAL 186  CHO 30G  PRO 9G  FAT 5G  CHOL 0MG  CALCIUM 104MG  POTASSIUM 1027MG  SODIUM 524MG  FIBER 6G

# Chapter 14

# VEGETABLES

## ALE'S VEGGIE GRATINATI

*This is a super source of potassium*

*Alexandra Gaudio*

**Vegetarian: Vegan**

Total time: 30 minutes
Serves: 4
Serving size: 5 oz.
Exchange: 2 starch, 1 fat

3 Fennel bulbs, fresh, cut 1″ × 1/2″ strips
2 Carrots, fresh, peeled, sliced
1 Onion, fresh, sliced
2 Red potatoes, large dice
3 tsp. Olive oil
4 Tbsp. Parsley, fresh, flat, chopped
1 tsp. Sage, dried
1 tsp. Rosemary, dried
1 Tbsp. Parmesan cheese
To taste Salt (optional)
To taste Pepper, black, ground

1. In a nonstick pot over medium heat, in olive oil, sauté the fennel, carrots, onions, and potatoes, then let simmer over low heat for 5 minutes.
2. Add parsley, sage, and rosemary and cook 15 more minutes.
3. Transfer vegetables to an oven-safe serving dish, top with cheese, and heat under the broiler for 1 minute until the cheese forms a crust. Serve hot.

**Nutrition Information:**
CAL 171  CHO 31G  PRO 5G  FAT 4G  CHOL 1MG  CALCIUM 129MG  POTASSIUM 1,123MG  SODIUM 187MG  FIBER 8G

# ASPARAGUS WITH MINT

1 lb. Asparagus, fresh, cut
  3 inches in length
1/2 cup Water
1/4 cup Parsley, fresh, minced
1–2 Tbsp. Mint, fresh, minced
2 Tbsp. Chives, fresh, minced (or
  1 Tbsp. dried)
To taste Lemon juice, freshly
  squeezed

1. Steam asparagus in a saucepan with water until tender but still firm, either on the stove or in a microwave.
2. Drain water and add remaining ingredients.
3. Serve immediately hot or chill and serve cold.

## About Asparagus

The following key nutrients in asparagus make this vegetable a powerhouse of nutrition, especially when consumed fresh and at least one-half cup per serving:

- *Folate,* which helps to prevent birth defects and decreases levels of homocysteine, a substance associated with heart disease;
- *Beta-carotene,* an anticancer antioxidant; and
- *Potassium* which is important in regulating fluid balance.

Vitamin C levels decrease by 50 percent the longer vegetables sit, so eat them soon after they are purchased or picked. Frozen asparagus retains more nutrients than most fresh vegetables.

**Vegetarian: Vegan**

Total time: Microwave, 3 minutes; stovetop, 10 minutes
Servings: 4
Serving size: 1/2 cup
Exchange: 1 vegetable

**Nutrition Information:**

CAL 18  CHO 3G  PRO 2G  FAT 0G  CHOL 0MG  CALCIUM 20MG  POTASSIUM 151MG  SODIUM 5MG  FIBER 1G

# ASPARAGUS SALAD WITH DIJON VINAIGRETTE

1 lb. Asparagus, steamed

1 Tbsp. Dijon mustard

1 Tbsp. White wine vinegar

2 tsp. Olive oil

1 tsp. Garlic, fresh, minced

1 tsp. Pepper, white, ground

**Vegetarian: Vegan**

Total time: 6 minutes
Servings: 4
Serving size: 4 oz. or 1/2 cup
Exchange: 1 vegetable, 1/2 fat

Whisk together mustard, vinegar, oil, garlic, and pepper. Pour over asparagus, then chill for 3 hours.

## Serving Suggestion

Serve this salad over sliced tomato to make a colorful dish.

**Nutrition Information:**

CAL 59 CHO 7G PRO 4G FAT 3G CHOL 0MG CALCIUM 31MG POTASSIUM 258MG SODIUM 98MG FIBER 2G

# ASPARAGUS, TOMATO, AND CHEESE MELT

*This dish is a great source of calcium.*

**Vegetarian: Lacto-ovo**

1 lb. Asparagus, whole, steamed

2 large Tomatoes, fresh, sliced

8 oz. Jarlsberg cheese, light (or mozzarella, part skim)

To taste Garlic powder

Total time: Microwave, 2 minutes; oven, 15 minutes
Servings: 4
Serving size: 4 oz.
Exchange: 1 fat-free milk, 2 lean meat

1. In a shallow microwavable dish place a layer of 4 cooked asparagus spears, then 2 ounces of cheese, 2 slices of tomato, 2 ounces of cheese, and garlic powder. Repeat layering until all ingredients are used.
2. In microwave: Heat for 1 minute or until cheese is melted.
3. In oven: Bake at 350°F for 10 to 15 minutes or until cheese melts and tomato is tender.

**Nutrition Information:**

CAL 186  CHO 12G  PRO 21G  FAT 7G  CHOL 20MG  CALCIUM 449MG  POTASSIUM 698MG  SODIUM 273MG  FIBER 3G

# BOK CHOY WITH GINGER VINAIGRETTE

*Chef Brian MacMenamin*

**Vegetarian: Vegan**

Total time: 20 minutes
Serves: 4
Serving size: 1/4 (1/2 cup)
Exchange: Without oil, 1 vegetable;
with oil, 1 vegetable

1 lb. Bok choy, cut into 2-inch pieces
1 Tbsp. Champagne wine vinegar
2 tsp. Whole grain mustard
2 tsp. Soy sauce
1 tsp. Sugar
1/2 tsp. Olive oil (optional)
1 small clove Garlic, fresh, minced
1 Tbsp. Ginger, fresh, minced or grated

1. Place bok choy in a steamer basket over boiling water. Cover pan and steam 10 minutes or until stalks begin to turn translucent and are soft when pierced.
2. In a mixing bowl, combine bok choy, vinegar, mustard, soy sauce, sugar, olive oil, garlic, and ginger and whisk to emulsify.
3. Transfer bok choy to a bowl, add dressing, and toss. Serve hot.

**Nutrition Information:**

**Without Oil**

CAL 30  CHO 5G  PRO 2G  FAT 1G  CHOL 0MG  CALCIUM 123MG  POTASSIUM 306MG  SODIUM 288MG  FIBER 1G

**With Oil**

CAL 25  CHO 5G  PRO 2G  FAT 0G  CHOL 0MG  CALCIUM 123MG  POTASSIUM 306MG  SODIUM 288MG  FIBER 1G

# BRAISED FENNEL WITH CARROTS AND ANISE SEEDS

*Chef Brian MacMenamin*

2 Fennel bulbs, cut into strips
2 Carrots, peel on, sliced
3 Tbsp. Parsley, fresh, minced
1 Tbsp. Butter
1/4 tsp. Anise seeds

Total time: 8 minutes
Serves: 6
Serving size: 1/6
Exchange: 1 vegetable

In a skillet over high heat, melt butter, and add fennel and carrots. Sauté until fennel is tender.

## Serving Suggestion

To lower fat, cut the butter and add 1 Tablespoon of apricot liqueur.

**Nutrition Information:**

CAL 50　CHO 8G　PRO 1G　FAT 2G　CHOL 5MG　CALCIUM 49MG　POTASSIUM 400MG　SODIUM 69MG　FIBER 3G

# BROCCOLI WITH GARLIC

1 cup Water
1 lb. Broccoli crowns
5 cloves Garlic, sliced
1 Tbsp. Olive oil
To taste Salt
To taste Pepper, black, ground

1. Bring water to a boil and add broccoli. Simmer for 3 to 5 minutes.
2. Meanwhile, in a small pan, sauté the garlic in oil until tender.
3. Drain the broccoli and add to the garlic.
4. Sauté 1 more minute and transfer to a serving dish.
5. Serve hot.

## About Broccoli

The follow key nutrients in broccoli are powerful nutrients for optimal health, especially when consumed in 1-cup measures.

- *Phytochemicals* such as sulforaphane and dithiolthiones, which deactivate the substances that can cause cancer;
- vitamin C, which boosts the immune system;
- beta-carotene, which inhibits mutations in cells and boosts the immune system;
- vitamin A, which deactivates cancer cells; and
- chromium, which helps to regulate insulin.

Broccoli is also fiber rich, meaning that it helps to regulate blood sugar, gives a feeling of fullness, and aids in bowel movements.

**Vegetarian: Vegan**

Total time: 7 minutes
Serves: 4
Serving size: 1/2 cup
Exchange: 1 vegetable, 1 fat

**Nutrition Information:**

CAL 63  CHO 6G  PRO 3G  FAT 4G  CHOL 0MG  CALCIUM 57MG  POTASSIUM 372MG  SODIUM 68MG  FIBER 3G

# BROCCOLI RABE

2 cups Water

2 lbs. Broccoli rabe

5 cloves Garlic, cut in halves

To taste Pepper, black, ground

10 Black olives

1 Tbsp. Olive oil

**Vegetarian: Vegan**

Total time: 15 minutes
Serves: 4
Serving size: 1/4
Exchange: 1 starch, 1 fat

1. Bring water to a boil in a large pot.
2. Place broccoli rabe, garlic, pepper, and olives in pot and simmer over medium heat, covered, for 15 minutes or until tender. Drain.
3. Serve, drizzled with olive oil.

## Serving Suggestion

Serve over pasta.

**Nutrition Information:**

CAL 124   CHO 17G   PRO 7G   FAT 5G   CHOL 0MG   CALCIUM 126MG   POTASSIUM 733MG   SODIUM 166MG   FIBER 6G

# BRUSSEL SPROUTS

1 lb. Brussel sprouts

1/2 cup Water

To taste Pepper, black, ground

**Vegetarian: Vegan**

Total time: 3–5 minutes
Serves: 4
Serving size: 1/2 cup
Exchange: 1 vegetable

## Microwave

1. Wash sprouts and place in a microwave dish.
2. Add water and cover with microwavable clear wrap or cover.
3. Heat in microwave for 2 to 5 minutes or until tender.
4. Add pepper and serve.

## Stove Top

1. Steam sprouts in water in a covered conventional 1-quart pot until tender.
2. Drain water and add pepper and serve.

## Serving Suggestion

Top with any of the following and toss lightly: 1/4 teaspoon red pepper flakes; or 1/4 teaspoon dried mustard seed; or 1/2 cup yellow raisins; or 1/2 teaspoon minced garlic.

**Nutrition Information:**

CAL 89  CHO 15G  PRO 5G  FAT 1G  CHOL 0MG  CALCIUM 37MG  POTASSIUM 502MG  SODIUM 28MG  FIBER 5G

# CARROTS WITH GINGER AND SESAME SEEDS

*Microwave cooking retains more nutrients than traditional boiling, and ginger aids indigestion.*

6 medium Carrots, cut into 2-inch diagonal
  strips
1 cup Water
1/2 tsp. Ginger, fresh minced
1 Tbsp. Sesame seeds
Pinch Turmeric powder
1 tsp. Sesame seed oil

**Vegetarian: Vegan**

Total time: 4 minutes
Serves: 4
Serving size: 1/2 cup
Exchange: 1 vegetable, 1/2 fat

Place carrots and water in a microwavable bowl with water and cover. Cook 1 to 2 minutes in the microwave until tender but firm. Drain. Add ginger, sesame seeds, turmeric, and oil.

Alternatively, you can steam the carrots in a 1-quart saucepan then add remaining ingredients and serve hot or cold.

**Nutrition Information:**

CAL 44   CHO 5G   PRO 1G   FAT 3G   CHOL 0MG   CALCIUM 17MG   POTASSIUM 160MG   SODIUM 17MG   FIBER 2G

# CAULIFLOWER PURÉE

*This purée looks like mashed potatoes, but this cruciferous vegetable helps reduce the risk of certain types of cancers.*

**Vegetarian: Vegan**

Total time: 30 minutes
Serves: 4
Serving size: 1/4
Exchange: 1 vegetable

1 small Cauliflower, cut in 2-inch pieces
1 quart Water
1/2 cup Parsley, fresh, minced
1/2 tsp. Thyme, dried

1. In a large saucepan, bring water to boil, then add cauliflower. Return to a boil and then lower to medium heat. Cook 30 to 40 minutes or until cauliflower is soft to touch and mushy.
2. Place cauliflower in blender with parsley and thyme and purée 1 to 2 minutes. Serve hot or cold.

**Nutrition Information:**

CAL 20  CHO 4G  PRO 2G  FAT 0G  CHOL 0MG  CALCIUM 33MG  POTASSIUM 244MG  SODIUM 29MG  FIBER 2G

# CLASSIC CUT GREEN BEANS ALMANDINE

1 lb. French cut green beans, frozen, no
  added salt
1/2 cup Chicken or vegetable broth, fat-free,
  low-sodium
2 tsp. Butter (margarine or olive oil optional)
1/4 cup Slivered almonds

**Vegetarian: Vegan**

Total time: 10 minutes
Serves: 4
Serving size: 1/2 cup
Exchange: 1 starch, 1 fat

1. Place green beans in pot with broth on high heat. Bring to boil, then lower and simmer with cover on pot for 8 minutes or until beans are tender. Drain.
2. Alternatively, steam green beans in broth until done, then remove from heat.
3. Sauté almonds in butter, then put on green beans. Toss and serve.

**Nutrition Information:**

CAL 87  CHO 8G  PRO 4G  FAT 5G  CHOL 3MG  CALCIUM 71MG  POTASSIUM 211MG  SODIUM 76MG  FIBER 4G

# COLD LEMON
# BROCCOLI SALAD

1 lb. Broccoli spears, fresh, rinsed
3 cloves Garlic, fresh, minced
1/2 Lemon, fresh
2 Tbsp. Olive oil
To taste Pepper, black, ground
To taste Salt (optional)

**Vegetarian: Vegan**

Total time: 4 minutes
Serves: 6
Serving size: 1/2 cup
Exchange: 1 vegetable, 1/2 fat

1. Place rinsed broccoli in a steam basket and steam in pot with 1 inch of water for 3 minutes.
2. Remove immediately from heat and set in serving bowl.
3. In a separate bowl, mix garlic, lemon, olive oil, salt, and pepper, then pour on broccoli.
4. Toss lightly and serve chilled or at room temperature.

## Suggestion:

Whenever possible support local farmers and avoid transporting costs to our economy as it preserves the environment.

**Nutrition Information:**

CAL 45  CHO 5G  PRO 3G  FAT 2G  CHOL 0MG  CALCIUM 43MG  POTASSIUM 152MG  SODIUM 43MG  FIBER 3G

# GREEN BEANS WITH MUSHROOM BUTTER

*Chef Brian MacMenamin*

| |
|---|
| Total time: 15 minutes |
| Serves: 2 |
| Serving size: 1/2 |
| Exchange: 1 vegetable |

1-1/2 tsp. Butter, unsalted, softened
1/2 cup Portabello mushrooms, minced, sautéed
 until soft and golden
1 tsp. Parsley, minced
1 clove Garlic, minced
1/2 lb. Green beans, trimmed
To taste Salt
To taste Pepper, black, ground

1. Combine butter, mushrooms, parsley, garlic, salt, and pepper in a bowl and mix well.
2. Place beans in a steamer basket over boiling water. Cover pan and steam 10 to 12 minutes or until beans are tender.
3. Transfer beans to a serving bowl and toss with mushroom butter.

**Nutrition Information:**

CAL 63  CHO 7G  PRO 4G  FAT 3G  CHOL 8MG  CALCIUM 34MG  POTASSIUM 367MG  SODIUM 10MG  FIBER 3G

# GRILLED VEGETABLES WITH HERB PESTO

*This dish is low-calorie, color-packed, and bursting with phytonutrients that will boost your skin quality and revitalize your cells.*

*Chef Brian MacMenamin*

**Vegetarian: Lacto-ovo**

Total time: 15–22 minutes
Serves: 10–12
Serving size: 1 cup
Exchange: 1 vegetable, 1 fat

## Pesto

1/2 cup Italian parsley, fresh, packed leaves

1 cup Basil leaves, fresh, packed

4 cloves Garlic, peeled

1-1/2 cups Olive oil, extra virgin

1/4 cup Parmesan cheese, freshly grated

2 Tbsp. Pine nuts

To taste Salt

To taste Pepper, black, freshly ground

1. Rinse the parsley and basil leaves in cool water, then dry thoroughly.
2. Combine the parsley, basil, garlic, and pine nuts in a blender. Slowly add the oil with the machine running, until the pesto is smooth and all the oil is incorporated.
3. Finish by adding the Parmesan and salt and pepper.

## Grilled Vegetables

1 Eggplant, cut into 1/4-inch strips lengthwise

1 small Zucchini, cut into 1/4-inch slices lengthwise

1 Red bell pepper, seeded and cut into quarters

1 small Red onion, sliced into thick rings

1 small Yellow squash, cut into 1/4-inch strips lengthwise

1 bunch Asparagus, woody ends trimmed

4 Portabello mushrooms, stems removed, quartered

*(continues)*

# GRILLED VEGETABLES WITH HERB PESTO (Continued)

1. Preheat oven to 400°F or set a pan on a grill over moderate to high heat.
2. Toss cut vegetables—eggplant, zucchini, bell pepper, onion, squash, asparagus, and mushroom—with three-quarters of the pesto.
3. In the oven or on the grill, cook the vegetables until they are just tender (3 to 5 minutes on each side on the grill, 6 to 8 minutes on each side in the oven).
4. Arrange grilled vegetables on a platter and garnish with pesto.

**Nutrition Information:**

CAL 38  CHO 6G  PRO 2G  FAT 4G  CHOL 2MG  CALCIUM 18MG  POTASSIUM 304MG  SODIUM 6MG  FIBER 2G

*These vegetables can be served warm but are also excellent at room temperature. This recipe makes a large batch of vegetables, so you can have them throughout the week. Keep cold in the refrigerator between uses.

# ITALIAN RATATOUILLE

*The vegetables in this dish are rich sources of fiber, phytonutrients, and vitamins.*

*Rosanne Bordes*

1 Tbsp. Olive oil, extra virgin
1 medium Eggplant, quartered, then sliced into
  1/2-inch wide slivers
1 Red bell pepper, cut into slivers
1 medium Sweet onion, thinly sliced
5 Plum tomatoes, ripe, diced
1 tsp. Basil, fresh, minced
To taste Pepper, black, ground

**Vegetarian: Vegan**

Total time: 26 minutes
Serves: 8
Serving size: 1/2 cup
Exchange: 2 starch, 1 fat

1. In a large skillet over medium heat, sauté the onion in olive oil until softened.
2. Add the sliced pepper and sauté for 3 minutes.
3. Add the eggplant and tomatoes and season with salt and pepper. Cook over medium heat, covered, until the eggplant is soft and translucent, approximately 20 minutes.
4. Add the chopped basil and cook, uncovered, for 3 minutes more. Serve hot or cold.

**Nutrition Information:**

**Four Portions**

CAL 168  CHO 19G  PRO 2G  FAT 11G  CHOL 0MG  CALCIUM 24MG  POTASSIUM 430MG  SODIUM 228MG  FIBER 6G

**Six Portions**

CAL 112  CHO 13G  PRO 2G  FAT 5G  CHOL 0MG  CALCIUM 12MG  POTASSIUM 287MG  SODIUM 152MG  FIBER 4G

**Eight Portions**

CAL 84  CHO 10G  PRO 1G  FAT 3G  CHOL 0MG  CALCIUM 12MG  POTASSIUM 114MG  SODIUM 114MG  FIBER 3G

# ITALIAN-STYLE ZUCCHINI WITH TOMATOES

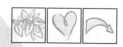

*Together, zucchini and tomatoes boost fiber and lycopene, which reduces the risk of cancer and helps your heart.*

*Chef Brian MacMenamin*

Vegetarian: Vegan

2 tsp. Olive oil

1 clove Garlic, minced

1 medium Red onion, diced

1 cup Italian-style peeled tomatoes, coarsely chopped

1/4 tsp. Oregano, dried

1 medium Zucchini, diced

To taste Salt

To taste Pepper, black, ground

Total time: 20 minutes
Serves: 4
Serving size:
Exchange: 1 vegetable, 1/2 fat

1. Heat olive oil in a heavy saucepan over medium high heat. Add garlic, onions, tomatoes, and oregano and simmer uncovered 2 to 3 minutes.
2. Add zucchini, salt, and pepper. Reduce heat to medium. Cover and simmer 7 to 8 minutes or until zucchini is tender.

**Nutrition Information:**

CAL 46   CHO 7G   PRO 1G   FAT 2G   CHOL 5MG   CALCIUM 22MG   POTASSIUM 280MG   SODIUM 8MG   FIBER 2G

# MUSHROOM MEDLEY

*The anticancer benefits of mushrooms are well known, so enjoy this delicious dish.*

**Vegetarian: Vegan**

15 Baby pearl onions, white
15 Baby red onions
1 Tbsp. Olive oil
10 Wild mushrooms, sliced
10 Mushrooms, white, sliced
1 Tbsp. Sage, fresh (or 1/2 tsp. dried)
To taste Pepper, white, ground

Total time:
Serves: 6
Serving size: 1/2 cup
Exchange: 1 vegetable, 1/2 fat

1. Cut tops and ends off onions; skin can be left on or peeled.
2. Place onions in skillet with oil and sauté over medium heat until translucent.
3. Add mushrooms, sage, and pepper and cook until mushrooms are tender but not mushy.

## Serving Suggestion

Serve over steamed freshly cut green beans or rice.

**Nutrition Information:**

CAL 43   CHO 4G   PRO 2G   FAT 3G   CHOL 0MG   CALCIUM 10MG   POTASSIUM 254MG   SODIUM 3MG   FIBER 1G

# OVEN-ROASTED PEPPERS

*Peppers are a great source of beta-carotene for your eyes and skin.*

4 Red bell peppers

4 Yellow bell peppers

1 Tbsp. Olive oil

1 Tbsp. Balsamic vinegar

2 Tbsp. Capers, drained, rinsed

1 tsp. Oregano, dried

1/2 tsp. Pepper, black, ground

**Vegetarian: Vegan**

Total time: 50 minutes

Serves: 8

Serving size: 1 pepper or 1/2 cup

Exchange: 1 vegetable, 1/2 fat

1. Bake whole peppers on a sheet pan in the oven at 400°F for 30 to 40 minutes or until outside of peppers is slightly brown.
2. Place peppers in a large bowl with a lid or a bowl that can be covered with plastic wrap and cool. Once peppers have cooked, remove skins, and reserve liquid. Tear peppers into strips and place in bowl.
3. Add liquid and remaining ingredients. Cover and chill overnight.

### Serving Suggestion

Serve with crusty garlic bread. Delicious!

**Nutrition Information:**

CAL 49  CHO 8G  PRO 1G  FAT 2G  CHOL 0MG  CALCIUM 15MG  POTASSIUM 241MG  SODIUM 59MG  FIBER 2G

# PARSLEY-STEAMED ARTICHOKES

4 medium Artichokes, fresh

2 cups Water

1/2 cup Italian flat leaf parsley, fresh

6 cloves Garlic, sliced

4 tsp. Olive oil

1/16 tsp. Pepper, black, ground

1/16 tsp. Salt, sea, ground

**Vegetarian: Vegan**

Total time: 32 minutes
Serves: 4
Serving size: 1 artichoke
Exchange: 1 starch, 1 fat

1. Wash artichokes and stuff equal amounts of garlic and parsley between the leaves. Season with salt and pepper. Place in a pot with water and cover. Bring to a beat over high heat, then lower. Simmer with cover on for 30 minutes or until leaves can be removed easily.
2. Remove from pot and drizzle with olive oil before serving.

**Nutrition Information:**

CAL 109  CHO 15G  PRO 5G  FAT 5G  CHOL 0MG  CALCIUM 75MG  POTASSIUM 485MG  SODIUM 157MG  FIBER 7G

# PORTABELLO STUFFED WITH BROCCOLI RABE AND MOZZARELLA

*The anticancer properties in mushrooms make this a winner.*

1 small Onion, yellow, finely diced

1/4 tsp. Garlic, fresh chopped

1 Tbsp. Olive oil

2 cups Water

1 lb. Broccoli rabe

6 medium Portabello mushroom caps

6 oz. Mozzarella cheese, part skim milk, shredded

**Vegetarian: Vegan**

Total time: Conventional oven, 50 minutes; microwave, 15 minutes
Serves: 6
Serving size: 1 mushroom cap
Exchange: 1 reduced fat milk

1. Preheat oven to 350°F.
2. Brush mushroom cap to remove dirt. Remove the stem and chop into fine pieces.
3. Place mushroom stem pieces, garlic, and onion in a saucepan with oil and sauté over medium heat until onion is translucent. Remove from pan and set aside.
4. Place the water in a pot and bring to a boil. Add broccoli rabe and simmer until tender, approximately 10 minutes. Remove from heat and drain well.
5. Put broccoli rabe in saucepan, add the onion mushroom mixture, and sauté for 2 to 3 minutes until blended.
6. Put mushrooms caps on a cookie sheet, stem side up, and place equal amounts of broccoli rabe mixture in the caps of all six mushrooms. Sprinkle with cheese and place in the oven for 5 minutes or until the cheese melts and the mushroom cap is tender.

**Nutrition Information:**

CAL 138  CHO 10g  PRO 12g  FAT 4g  CHOL 15mg  CALCIUM 249mg  POTASSIUM 500mg  SODIUM 179mg  FIBER 3g

# QUICK AND EASY PORTABELLO MUSHROOMS

4 small Portabello mushroom caps

1/4 cup Bread crumbs

4 tsp. Olive oil

Pinch Thyme, dried

**Vegetarian: Vegan**

Serves: 4 time
Serving size: 1 cap
Exchange: 1 vegetable, 1 fat

1. Preheat oven to 425°F.
2. Using a baker's brush, clean dirt from mushroom caps.
3. Place caps in shallow baking pan and top with bread crumbs. Drizzle 1 teaspoon of oil over each mushroom. Place in oven and bake for 10 minutes or until mushrooms are tender. Serve immediately.

## Serving Suggestion

These mushrooms are great with steak or, for vegetarians, with rice and beans.

**Nutrition Information:**

CAL 70  CHO 5G  PRO 1G  FAT 5G  CHOL 0MG  CALCIUM 16MG  POTASSIUM 67MG  SODIUM 59MG  FIBER 0G

# QUICK AND TASTY GLAZED BEETS

*Chef Brian MacMenamin*

1 lb. Golden beets, scrubbed with root and
  1 inch of stem intact
1-1/2 tsp. Cornstarch
1/4 cup Orange juice
3 Tbsp. Apricot jam
4 tsp. Olive oil
1/2 cup Chives, fresh, minced
1/4 cup Parsley, fresh, minced

**Vegetarian: Vegan**

Total time: 55 minutes;
shortcut version, 10 minutes
Serves: 4
Serving size: 1/2 cup
Exchange: 1 starch, 1 fat

1. Place beets in a 350°F oven for 45 minutes to 60 minutes or until tender.
2. Rinse beets under cold water, then allow them to cool to room temperature.
3. Peel and cut beets into quarters and set aside.
4. In a small saucepan, combine cornstarch with juice and apricot jam, stirring over medium low heat until thickened. Add beets and toss. Cook another 5 minutes or until hot.
5. Remove beets from pan and toss with chives and parsley and olive oil as garnish. Serve warm or at room temperature.

## Shortcut Version

No time to cook? Try this quick method: Omit the first step of cooking fresh beets and open a can of beets, then follow the directions for the remaining ingredients. This will cut your time to 10 minutes, although, of course, it will not taste the same as fresh beets.

**Nutrition Information:**

CAL 200  CHO 19G  PRO 1G  FAT 5G  CHOL 0MG  CALCIUM 24MG  POTASSIUM 246MG  SODIUM 123MG  FIBER 2G

# QUICK SWEET CARROTS

*Dorothy Court*

1-1/2 cups Frozen carrots (1 small package)
  or
Precut, shoestring style, fresh carrots
3 Tbsp. Maple syrup
To taste Pepper, black, ground

**Vegetarian: Vegan**

Total time: 5 minutes
Serves: 4
Serving size: 1/3 cup
Exchange: 1 vegetable

In a saucepan, cook carrots in 1 cup of boiling water until tender. Drain water and add syrup and pepper. Serve.

**Nutrition Information:**

CAL 40  CHO 10G  PRO 0G  FAT 0G  CHOL 0MG  CALCIUM 11MG  POTASSIUM 36MG  SODIUM 3MG  FIBER 0G

# RATATOUILLE

*This version of the classic French dish is packed with phytonutrients. August and September is a great time to make this.*

1 Eggplant, unpeeled, cubed

8 medium Tomatoes, quartered

8 oz. White mushrooms, cleaned and sliced

2 Onions, cleaned and sliced

2 Scallions, chopped

1-1/4 cups Water

3 cloves Garlic, minced

1 tsp. Basil, fresh

1/2 tsp. Oregano, dried

To taste Salt

To taste Pepper, black, ground

**Vegetarian: Vegan**

Total time: 35–40 minutes
Serves: 8
Serving size: 1/2 cup
Exchange: 1 starch

---

Place all vegetables in pot and add water and seasonings. Simmer for 20 minutes more until vegetables are soft. Add mushrooms during the last 10 minutes. Serve hot or cold.

**Nutrition Information:**

CAL 65  CHO 14G  PRO 3G  FAT 1G  CHOL 0MG  CALCIUM 24MG  POTASSIUM 604MG  SODIUM 53MG  FIBER 4G

# ROASTED CARROTS AND ONIONS

5 medium Carrots, unpeeled, 4-inch long pieces cut in half

1 medium Onion, yellow, cut into 1/2-inch sliced wedges

1 tsp. Olive oil

1/2 tsp. Balsamic vinegar

1/4 Tbsp. Rosemary, dried, crushed

To taste Garlic powder

To taste Pepper, black, ground

**Vegetarian: Vegan**

Total time: 49 minutes
Serves: 10
Serving size: 4 oz.
Exchange: 1 vegetable

1. Preheat oven to 375°F.
2. Wash carrots and remove blemishes.
3. Coat cookie sheet with oil.
4. In a bowl, add carrots and onion and sprinkle with vinegar, rosemary, garlic powder, and black. Toss lightly and spread evenly over pan.
5. Roast for 45 minutes or until tender. Serve hot or cold.

**Nutrition Information:**

CAL 37   CHO 5G   PRO 2G   FAT 1G   CHOL 0MG   CALCIUM 34MG   POTASSIUM 389MG   SODIUM 45MG   FIBER 2G

# SAUTÉED SUMMER VEGETABLES

*Fresh herbs always boost flavor and are well worth buying. Freeze whatever you have left over.*

**Vegetarian: Vegan**

*Chef Brian MacMenamin*

Total time: 20 minutes
Serves: 6
Serving size: 2/3 cup
Exchange: 1 vegetable, 1/2 fat

1 Tbsp. Olive oil

1 small Zucchini, cut into 1-1/2-inch chunks

1/2 lb. Sugar snap peas, stem and strings
  removed

2 Green onions, cut into 1/2-inch pieces

1 Tbsp. Oregano, fresh, minced (or 1/2 tsp. dried)

1 small Yellow squash, cut into 1-1/2-inch chunks

1 Green bell pepper, diced

1 Red bell pepper, diced

2 Tbsp. Garlic, fresh, minced

Heat oil in a heavy nonstick skillet over medium high heat. Sauté all ingredients 8 to 10 minutes, stirring frequently, until vegetables are golden and tender crisp.

**Nutrition Information:**

CAL 58  CHO 8ɢ  PRO 2ɢ  FAT 3ɢ  CHOL 0ᴍɢ  CALCIUM 38ᴍɢ  POTASSIUM 281ᴍɢ  SODIUM 6ᴍɢ  FIBER 3ɢ

# SESAME BROCCOLI

*Michelle Jackson*

1 head Broccoli
1 Tbsp. Sesame oil
1 Tbsp. Soy sauce
1 Tbsp. Sesame seeds
1 tsp. Red pepper flakes, crushed (optional)

**Vegetarian: Vegan**

Total time: 12 minutes
Serves: 4
Serving size: 1 cup
Exchange: 1-1/4 vegetable, 1 fat

1. Trim the tough stem end from the broccoli, rinse under cool running water, and separate into stalks.
2. Arrange the broccoli in a microwave or conventional steamer.* Cover and cook at high power or over high heat for 4 to 6 minutes or until tender. Drain and transfer to a serving dish.
3. Drizzle the sesame oil and soy sauce over the broccoli. Toss to blend. Sprinkle with sesame seeds and red pepper (optional).

**Nutrition Information:**

CAL 90   CHO 9G   PRO 5G   FAT 5G   CHOL 0MG   CALCIUM 77MG   POTASSIUM 520MG   SODIUM 270MG   FIBER 5G

*Steaming vegetables is better than boiling because it retains the food's color, flavor, texture, and—most important—nutrients.

# SIMPLE SWEET BEETS

*Beets contain powerful phytochemicals that help boost the body's immune response.*

4 medium Beets, fresh, tops cut off,
  quartered with skin on\*
1 quart Water
2 Tbsp. Margarine, 40 percent less fat
To taste Pepper, black, ground

**Vegetarian: Vegan**

Total time: 22 minutes
Serves: 4
Serving size: 1/2 cup
Exchange: 1 vegetable, 1/2 fat

1. Wash beets and cut off tops and bottom halves if too large.
2. Boil beets in water until tender, approximately 20 minutes. Remove from heat and drain.
3. Slice beets, add margarine and pepper, then serve.
4. Optional: Add 1 Tablespoon of cider vinegar and serve beets cold.

**Nutrition Information:**

CAL 38  CHO 5G  PRO 1G  FAT 2G  CHOL 0MG  CALCIUM 12MG  POTASSIUM 150MG  SODIUM 85MG  FIBER 1G

\*Leave the skin on for added vitamins and fiber.

# SPINACH SAUTÉ WITH PINE NUTS

*Boost important nutrients for your eyes and heart with this simple but delicious dish.*

5 cloves Garlic, cut into quarters

1 Tbsp. Olive oil

2 Tbsp. Pine nuts, whole

1 lb. Baby spinach, cleaned, stems removed

1–2 Tbsp. Water

**Vegetarian: Vegan**

Total time: 10–14 minutes
Serves: 4
Serving size: 1/2 cup
Exchange: 1 vegetable, 1 fat,
1/3 very lean protein, 1/4 starch

1. In an 8-inch frying pan, sauté garlic in oil until translucent but not brown.
2. Remove garlic from pan and add pine nuts and brown. Remove nuts and set aside.
3. Return garlic to pan and add spinach and water. Steam sauté over medium high heat, covered, for 5 to 8 minutes or until spinach leaves are wilted and tender. Drain excess water.
4. Place in serving bowl and top with pine nuts. Serve hot or cold.

**Nutrition Information:**

CAL 84  CHO 6G  PRO 5G  FAT 6G  CHOL 0MG  CALCIUM 120MG  POTASSIUM 673MG  SODIUM 90MG  FIBER 3G

# STEAMED SWISS CHARD WITH TOMATOES

*This recipe is packed with folic acid and other phytonutrients that will help protect your eyes.*

**Vegetarian: Vegan**

1 Tbsp. Garlic, minced
1 Tbsp. Olive oil
1 lb. Swiss chard, chopped*
8 oz. Stewed tomatoes, canned

Total time: 20 minutes
Serves: 6
Serving size: 1/2 cup
Exchange: 1 vegetable

1. Sauté garlic in oil in a 3-quart pot.
2. Add Swiss chard and cook until wilted.
3. Add tomatoes, cover, and simmer for 30 minutes.

**Nutrition Information:**

CAL 46  CHO 6G  PRO 2G  FAT 2G  CHOL 0MG  CALCIUM 48MG  POTASSIUM 415MG  SODIUM 215MG  FIBER 2G

*Suggestion: There are different varieties of Swiss chard. Try different types!

# THAI GREEN BEANS

15 oz. French cut green beans, frozen
  (1 package)
2 Tbsp. Hot chili sauce
1 tsp. Garlic, minced
1 tsp. Sesame seed oil

**Vegetarian: Vegan**

Total time: 4 minutes
Serves: 4
Serving size: 1/2 cup
Exchange: 1 vegetable

1. Place green beans in a microwavable bowl and heat in microwave for 2 minutes or until beans are loose and come apart.
2. Add chili sauce, garlic, and sesame seed oil and heat for 1 more minute or until cooked.

**Nutrition Information:**

CAL 47  CHO 8G  PRO 2G  FAT 1G  CHOL 8MG  CALCIUM 50MG  POTASSIUM 155MG  SODIUM 123MG  FIBER 3G

# ZUCCHINI ASPARAGUS STIR-FRY

*New research suggests that pine nuts reduce hunger for hours.*

*Chef Brian MacMenamin*

1 Tbsp. Butter, unsalted, or margarine

1 lb. Asparagus, fresh

1 lb. Zucchini, fresh

1/4 cup Pine nuts

1/3 cup Chives, fresh, chopped

1 Red onion, julienned

**Vegetarian: Vegan
(when made with margarine)**

Total time: 20 minutes
Serves: 4
Serving size: 1 cup
Exchange: 2 vegetable, 2 fat

1. Blanch asparagus and zucchini by emerging in boiling water for 40 seconds, draining, and then shocking in cold water.
2. Cut asparagus into 2-inch pieces.
3. Cut zucchini into thick strips.
4. Melt butter or margarine in a heavy nonstick skillet or wok over medium high heat. Stir-fry asparagus and zucchini and onions approximately 4 minutes, stirring frequently, until asparagus is almost tender.
5. Add pine nuts and stir-fry another 2 minutes or until nuts are golden.
6. Stir in chives and serve.

**Nutrition Information:**

CAL 147  CHO 11g  PRO 6g  FAT 11g  CHOL 8mg  CALCIUM 47mg  POTASSIUM 602mg  SODIUM 24mg  FIBER 5g

# ZUCCHINI CASSEROLE

*There are plenty of phytonutrients and calcium in this one great dish.*

1 medium Zucchini, sliced

1 medium Onion, sliced

2 medium Tomatoes, sliced

8 oz. Mozzarella cheese, part skim milk, shredded

1 Tbsp. Olive oil, seasoned

1/4 tsp. Oregano

To taste Pepper, black, ground

1 sprig Basil, fresh (optional)

**Vegetarian: Lacto-ovo**

Total time: 20 minutes
Serves: 8
Serving size: 1/2 cup
Exchange: 1 vegetable, 1 high fat meat

1. Preheat oven to 350°F.
2. Grease baking pan and place zucchini slices on bottom. Alternate layers of onion, tomato, and shredded mozzarella. Top with remaining zucchini. Drizzle seasoned oil and sprinkle pepper on top.
3. Bake for 20 to 30 minutes or until cheese melts and vegetables are tender.
4. Garnish with basil and serve.

**Nutrition Information:**

CAL 110   CHO 4G   PRO 9G   FAT 7G   CHOL 15MG   CALCIUM 216MG   POTASSIUM 179MG   SODIUM 154MG   FIBER 1G

# Chapter 15

## DIPS, DRESSINGS, SAUCES AND MARINADES

### Dips

---

## ADA'S GUACAMOLE

*Ada Worchowsky*

3 Haas avocados
1-1/2 Scallions, minced
1/4 cup Salsa, mild
1 medium Tomato, chopped
1/2 Lime, juice of, freshly squeezed

**Vegetarian: Vegan**

Total time: 5 minutes
Serves: 10
Serving size: 1/4 cup
Exchange: 1 vegetable, 1 fat

---

Remove pulp from avocado and place in bowl. Add scallions, salsa, tomato, and lime juice and blend, leaving the avocado partly chunky.
Suggestion: For added flavor mix in 2 Tbsp. chopped cilantro.

**Serving Suggestion**
Serve with lightly baked tortilla chips or raw vegetables.

**Nutrition Information:**
CAL 88  CHO 6g  PRO 1g  FAT 8g  CHOL 0mg  CALCIUM 11mg  POTASSIUM 304mg  SODIUM 33mg  FIBER 4g

# THE BEST PARTY SALSA

*Lycopenes in tomatoes help lower the risk of cancer.*

8 large Tomatoes, diced
1 small Onion, diced
1/2 cup Cilantro, fresh, minced
1 Green chili pepper, diced
1 Tbsp. Ketchup

**Vegetarian: Vegan**

Total time: 5 minutes
Serves: 10
Serving size: 1/2 cup
Exchange: 1 vegetable

Mix all ingredients. Serve with raw vegetables.

**Nutrition Information:**
CAL 40  CHO 9G  PRO 1G  FAT 0G  CHOL 0MG  CALCIUM 16MG  POTASSIUM 251MG  SODIUM 16MG  FIBER 1G

# LEMON GARLIC HUMMUS

12 oz. Chickpeas (15-1/2-oz. can), drained
2 Tbsp. Yogurt, plain, fat-free
1 Tbsp. Tahini (sesame seed paste)
1 medium Lemon, freshly squeezed juice
1 Tbsp. Garlic, fresh, minced (or 1/2 tsp. powder)
To taste Pepper, black, ground (optional)

**Vegetarian: Lacto-ovo**

Total time: 6 minutes
Serves: 8
Serving size: 1/4 cup
Exchange: 1 starch, 1/2 lean meat

Blend all ingredients in a blender or food processor to a purée. Serve.

## Serving Suggestion

Use as a dip with fresh, raw vegetables. For a party, hollow out a loaf of pumpernickel bread, fill with dip, and offer the cut up bread for dipping in hummus.

**Nutrition Information:**
CAL 100  CHO 18G  PRO 5G  FAT 2G  CHOL 0MG  CALCIUM 43MG  POTASSIUM 189MG  SODIUM 204MG  FIBER 5G

# LINDA'S QUICK EGGPLANT DIP

1 large Eggplant, unpeeled, diced
1 jar Artichoke hearts, marinated (6.55 oz.),
  drained (reserve 1 Tbsp.)
1 Tbsp. Marinating liquid (from jar)
1-1/2 cups Classico Florentine tomato sauce
1 tsp. Olive oil
1/2 tsp. Garlic powder
20 Olives, black, chopped
To taste Salt
To taste Pepper, black, ground

**Vegetarian: Vegan**

Total time: 6 minutes
Serves: 8
Serving size: 1/2 cup
Exchange: 2 vegetable, 1/2 fat

1. Place all ingredients into a 2-quart glass casserole dish and mix.
2. Cover with a microwavable lid and heat in a microwave for 10 to
   15 minutes. Stir, then microwave again a few minutes until eggplant is
   tender.
3. Remove from microwave and thoroughly mix.

## Serving Suggestion

Serve as an appetizer or snack with toasted pita or 1/2-inch slices of French
bread.

**Nutrition Information:**

CAL 72  CHO 12G  PRO 2G  FAT 3G  CALCIUM 28MG  POTASSIUM 456MG  SODIUM* 450MG  FIBER 4G

*Sodium will be lower if you omit salt.

# VEGETABLE HERB DIP

*This delicious dip has no fat and is high in calcium.*

8 oz. Greek yogurt, fat-free

4 oz. Sour cream, fat-free

1 tsp. Vegetable bouillon base

1 Tbsp. Parsley, dried

1/4 tsp. Thyme, dried

Dash Basil, dried

1/4 tsp. Garlic powder

1 tsp. Teriyaki sauce

**Vegetarian: Lacto-ovo**

Total time: 5 minutes
Serves: 4
Serving size: 2 oz.
Exchange: 1/4 dairy

Mix all ingredients together. Chill and serve with vegetables.

**Nutrition Information:**

CAL 58  CHO 10G  PRO 5G  FAT 0G  CHOL 3MG  CALCIUM 157MG  POTASSIUM 204MG  SODIUM 353MG  FIBER 0G

# *Dressings*

## BALSAMIC VINAIGRETTE

2 Tbsp. White or red balsamic vinegar*
2 Tbsp. Olive oil
1 tsp. Basil, dried (or 2 Tbsp. fresh)
To taste Pepper, black, ground

**Vegetarian: Vegan**

Serves: 4
Serving size: 1 Tbsp.
Exchange: 1-1/2 fat

Whisk all ingredients together well before pouring over salad.

**Nutrition Information:**

CAL 61  CHO 0G  PRO 0G  FAT 7G  CHOL 0MG  CALCIUM 3MG  POTASSIUM 14MG  SODIUM 0MG  FIBER 0G

*White balsamic vinegar has a milder flavor.

## CARLA'S DIJON VINAIGRETTE

*Carla Arpino*

**Vegetarian: Vegan**

Servings: 8
Serving size: 1 Tbsp.
Exchange: 2 fats

1/4 cup Red wine vinegar
2 tsp. Dijon-style mustard
1/2 cup Olive oil
To taste Fresh herbs of choice (e.g., basil, parsley, oregano)

Pour ingredients into a bowl and whisk together or put in a jar and shake well before pouring over salad.

**Nutrition Information:**

CAL 121  CHO 0G  PRO 0G  FAT 10G  CHOL 0MG  CALCIUM 0MG  POTASSIUM 2MG  SODIUM 16MG  FIBER 0G

# LEMON GARLIC DRESSING

2 Tbsp. Olive oil
1 Tbsp. Balsamic vinegar
1 Tbsp. Lemon juice, freshly squeezed
2 cloves Garlic, fresh, minced
1/2 tsp. Salt (optional)
To taste Pepper, black, ground (optional)

**Vegetarian: Vegan**

Servings: 4
Serving size: 1 Tbsp.
Exchange: 1 fat

Whisk all ingredients together before pouring over salad.

**Nutrition Information:**

CAL 63  CHO 1G  PRO 0G  FAT 7G  CHOL 0MG  CALCIUM 4MG  POTASSIUM 14MG  SODIUM 296MG*  FIBER 0G

*Zero milligram if salt is omitted.

# REDUCED FAT THOUSAND ISLAND DRESSING

1/4 cup Mayonnaise (Hellman's or Best Foods
   Light)
1/4 cup Ketchup
3 Tbsp. Pickle relish, sweet

**Vegetarian: Lacto-ovo**

Makes about 4 oz.
Serves: 6
Serving size: 2 Tbsp.
Exchange: 1 fat

In a small bowl, blend all ingredients with a whisk until smooth. Store in a glass container and use within one week.

**Nutrition Information:**

CAL 63  CHO 7G  PRO 0G  FAT 4G  CHOL 4MG  CALCIUM 3MG  POTASSIUM 61MG  SODIUM 309MG  FIBER 0G

# SESAME DRESSING

1/4 cup Rice vinegar

2 Tbsp. Sesame seed oil

1 Tbsp. Teriyaki sauce

1 Scallion, thinly sliced

1 tsp. Hot chili sauce (optional)

**Vegetarian: Vegan**

Servings: 8–10
Serving size: 1 Tbsp.
Exchange: 1/2 fat

Blend all ingredients. Chill and serve with mandarin salad (see index for recipe).

**Nutrition Information:**

CAL 30  CHO 1G  PRO 0G  FAT 3G  CHOL 0MG  CALCIUM 2MG  POTASSIUM 16MG  SODIUM 77MG  FIBER 0G

# TASTY BUTTERMILK RANCH DRESSING

1/4 cup Buttermilk, fat-free

1/4 cup Mayonnaise, Hellman's or Best Foods
  Light

2 tsp. Dijon-style mustard

3 Tbsp. Yogurt, plain, 2 percent fat

1 Tbsp. Cider vinegar

2 tsp. Parsley, dried

1 tsp. Garlic powder

1 tsp. Olive oil

To taste Salt

To taste Pepper, black, ground

**Vegetarian: Lacto-ovo**

Serves: 6
Serving size: 2 Tbsp.
(makes approximately 3/4 cup)
Exchange: 1/2 starch, 1 fat

1. In a small bowl, blend all ingredients with a whisk until smooth.
2. Season with salt and pepper.

### Serving Suggestion

Make ahead and store in a glass container. Can keep up to one week.

**Nutrition Information:**

CAL 52  CHO 2G  PRO 1G  FAT 4G  CHOL 4MG  CALCIUM 30MG  POTASSIUM 49MG  SODIUM 184MG  FIBER 0G

# YOGURT DILL DRESSING

1 cup Yogurt, plain, fat-free
1 Tbsp. Dill, fresh, minced
2 Tbsp. Mint, fresh, minced
1/2 tsp. Dijon-style mustard
1/4 tsp. Garlic powder

**Vegetarian: Lacto-ovo**

Serves: 8 (makes ~1 cup)
Serving size: 1 oz.
Exchange: Free

Blend all ingredients and chill.

## Serving Suggestion

Serve with Mediterranean cucumber salad (see index for recipe).

**Nutrition Information:**

CAL 19  CHO 2G  PRO 2G  FAT 0G  CHOL 2MG  CALCIUM 52MG  POTASSIUM 68MG  SODIUM 28MG  FIBER 0MG

## *Marinades*

# GINGER MARINADE

*Barbara Lewis*

1 cup Sake (Japanese rice wine)
As desired Ginger root, raw, sliced

Serves: 4
Serving size: Not applicable
Exchange: 1 bread

Place ingredients in a covered container with salmon and let sit in the refrigerator for 2 to 6 hours before steaming fish. See index for steamed salmon in ginger marinade.

**Nutrition Information:**
CAL 94  CHO 14G  PRO 1G  FAT 1G  CHOL 0MG  CALCIUM 15MG  POTASSIUM 320MG  SODIUM 12MG  FIBER 1G

# LAMB MARINADE

1/2 cup Canola oil

1/2 cup Sherry, dry

1/4 cup Hoisin sauce

7 cloves Garlic, fresh, sliced

1 small Ginger root, raw, sliced

To taste Pepper, red, ground

Serves: 6
Serving size: Not applicable
Exchange: 1/2 fat when used to
marinate meat

Mix all ingredients to blend.

## Serving Suggestion

Place lamb in a container with a fitted lid, coat the meat with the marinade, and keep in the refrigerator for 6 to 24 hours before roasting.

**Nutrition Information:**

CAL 143  CHO 8G  PRO 1G  FAT 10G  CHOL 0MG  CALCIUM 19MG  POTASSIUM 84MG  SODIUM 232MG  FIBER 1G

## *Sauces*

# BARBECUE SAUCE, HOME-STYLE

8 oz. Tomato sauce, canned or jarred

2 Tbsp. Brown sugar, packed

2 Tbsp. Molasses

1 small Onion, chopped

1 Tbsp. Apple cider vinegar or distilled vinegar

1 Tbsp. Garlic, minced (or 1/2 tsp. powder)

To taste Pepper, black, ground (optional)

**Vegetarian: Vegan**

Total time: 3 minutes
Serves: 10
Serving size: 2 Tbsp.
Exchange: 1 starch, 1 fruit

Blend all ingredients in a blender or food processor to a purée. Serve.

### Serving Suggestion

Use as a coating sauce before grilling chicken.

**Nutrition Information:**

CAL 72  CHO 18G  PRO 0G  FAT 0G  CHOL 0MG  CALCIUM 33MG  POTASSIUM 79MG  SODIUM 204MG  FIBER 0G

# EASY LOW-SUGAR CRANBERRY SAUCE

*This sauce features less sugar and more fiber than the usual variety.*

12 oz. Cranberries, fresh, whole

1/4 cup Water

1/4 cup Pecans, chopped

1/2 medium Orange, fresh, diced

1 tsp. Sugar substitute

or

1 Tbsp. Brown sugar (optional)

**Vegetarian: Vegan**

Total time: 20 minutes
Serves: 8
Serving size: 1/2 cup
Exchange: 1/2 fruit, 1/2 fat

1. Place rinsed cranberries and water in a pot and simmer over medium heat until the cranberries are soft and blended, approximately 10 minutes.
2. Remove from heat and add pecans, orange, and sweetener (sugar or substitute).
3. Mix thoroughly and pour in a serving dish. Chill until ready to serve. Keeps up to 1 week.

**Nutrition Information:**

**Without Splenda or Sugar**

CAL 50  CHO 7G  PRO 1G  FAT 3G  CHOL 0MG  CALCIUM 9MG  POTASSIUM 60MG  SODIUM 0MG  FIBER 2G

# MUSHROOM SAUCE

1 small Onion, diced

1 Tbsp. Butter

1 lb. Mushrooms, white, sliced

1/4 cup Parsley, fresh, minced (or 1 Tbsp. dried)

To taste Pepper, black, freshly ground

1/2 cup Water or low-sodium vegetable broth

2–3 Tbsp. Cornstarch

**Vegetarian: Lacto-ovo**

Total time: 15 minutes
Serves: 6
Serving size: 1/3 cup
Exchange: 1 vegetable

1. In a skillet over medium heat, sauté onions in butter.
2. When onion becomes translucent, add mushrooms and parsley and simmer 3 minutes or until parsley wilts, then remove from heat.
3. In a separate bowl, whisk cornstarch into cold water or cold vegetable broth. Pour into saucepan with mushrooms over medium heat for 5 minutes or until sauce thickens (the more cornstarch, the thicker the sauce).
4. Season with pepper.

## Serving Suggestion

Serve over breaded baked chicken breasts or your favorite rice.

**Nutrition Information:**

CAL 62  CHO 11ɢ  PRO 0ɢ  FAT 2ɢ  CHOL 10ᴍɢ  CALCIUM 4ᴍɢ  POTASSIUM 259ᴍɢ  SODIUM 14ᴍɢ  FIBER 0ɢ

# PEANUT SAUCE

*This recipe was first introduced to me by a nanny I hired from Holland. I have modified it to enhance its nutrient density. My children love to eat it over rice or pasta. It makes for an easy vegetarian meal and adds a balance of calcium, protein, and "good" monounsaturated fats.*

1/2 cup Peanut butter, chunky style,
  reduced fat*
1/2 cup Yogurt, fat-free
1/4 tsp. Teriyaki sauce
1/4 tsp. Soy sauce
To taste Dried chili peppers (optional)

**Vegetarian: Lacto-ovo**

Total time: 10 minutes
Serves: 4
Serving size: 1/4 cup
Exchange: 1 medium fat meat,
1 starch, 1 fat

Place all ingredients in a saucepan over low heat. Stir to blend ingredients. Cook until all sauce is smooth.

**Nutrition Information:**

CAL 203  CHO 15G  PRO 11G  FAT 11G  CHOL 1MG  CALCIUM 74MG  POTASSIUM 322MG  SODIUM 252MG  FIBER 2G

*Use defatted peanut butter and lower the calories and fat. Better 'n Peanut Butter is a brand to look for in stores such as Whole Foods and Trader Joe's.

# QUICK HOMEMADE TOMATO SAUCE

*This sauce is rich in lycopenes, which reduce the risk of prostate cancer. It also contains no sugar unlike many store brands.*

4 large Tomatoes, fresh, washed, diced

1 Tbsp. Olive oil

1 small Onion, diced

10 cloves Garlic, fresh, minced

1 bunch Basil, fresh, minced

1 Tbsp. Oregano, dried

10 oz. Peas (1 package frozen), thawed

**Vegetarian: Vegan**

Total time: 30 minutes
Serves: 4
Serving size: 1/4 cup
Exchange: 1 starch, 1 vegetable, 1 fat

1. In a large pot, bring diced tomatoes to a boil. Reduce heat to low and simmer for 25 minutes or until liquid has reduced, adding water only if needed.
2. In a separate pan, sauté the onion, garlic, basil, and oregano.
3. Add the sauté mix to the tomato reduction along with the peas. Simmer 15 more minutes.
4. Serve over pasta.

## Serving Suggestion

Cook your favorite pasta (penne is great) and pour this tomato sauce over it. Enjoy!

**Nutrition Information:**

CAL 135  CHO 21G  PRO 6G  FAT 4G  CHOL 0MG  CALCIUM 79MG  POTASSIUM 617MG  SODIUM 56MG  FIBER 6G

# SAUCE AU POIVRE

*Chef Brian MacMenamin*

1 tsp. Black peppercorns, whole
1 Tbsp. Vegetable oil
1 medium Shallot, minced
1/2 cup Chicken broth
1 Tbsp. Cognac or balsamic vinegar
1 tsp. Butter, unsalted

Total time: 10 minutes
Serves: 4
Serving size: 3 Tbsp.
Exchange: 1/2 fat

1. Coarsely crush peppercorns with a mortar and pestle or wrap in a kitchen towel and press on peppercorns with the bottom of a heavy skillet.
2. Sauté shallots in skillet in oil over medium heat until tender.
3. Add chicken broth, cognac or vinegar, and butter to skillet and let cook 5 minutes over medium heat.

**Nutrition Information:**

CAL 35  CHO 0G  PRO 0G  FAT 3G  CHOL 4MG  CALCIUM 3MG  POTASSIUM 20MG  SODIUM 74MG  FIBER 0G

# Chapter 16

# DESSERTS

## AMARETTO DIP WITH STRAWBERRIES

*This recipe makes a quick, healthy, and delicious dessert or snack for guests.*

*Dorothy Court*

2 cups Strawberry yogurt, fat-free
1/4 cup Cool Whip
1/3 cup Amaretto liqueur
2 quarts Strawberries, fresh, whole, cleaned

**Vegetarian: Lacto-ovo**

Total time: 5 minutes
Serves: 12
Serving size: 1/2 cup dip, 6 berries
Exchange: 1 starch

Blend yogurt with amaretto. Serve in a bowl with strawberries surrounding the dip.

**Nutrition Information:**

CAL 91   CHO 18G   PRO 3G   FAT 1G   CHOL 1MG   CALCIUM 78MG   POTASSIUM 227MG   SODIUM 25MG   FIBER 2G

# APPLE BETTY

*This simple dessert boosts phytonutrients and fiber for optimal health.*

1/4 tsp. Canola oil
5 medium Apples, cored, thinly sliced
1 Tbsp. Lemon juice
1/2 cup Brown sugar
1/2 cup Flour, unbleached
1/4 cup Flaxseed meal
1 tsp. Cinnamon, ground
1/4 tsp. Nutmeg, ground
1/3 cup Butter, soft (almond butter optional)

**Vegetarian: Lacto-ovo**

Total time: 55 minutes
Serves: 6
Serving size: 1/2 cup
Exchange: 1 fruit, 1 bread, 2 fat

1. Preheat oven to 375°F.
2. Coat the bottom of a 9-inch pie plate with canola oil, then mix apples and lemon juice and place in plate.
3. Combine sugar, flour, flaxseed meal, cinnamon, and nutmeg, then cut in the butter to make a crumbly topping. Sprinkle over apples.
4. Bake for 30 to 40 minutes. Topping should be crisp. Serve warm.

## Serving Suggestion

Try this as an alternative to junk food snacks and get the benefit of phytonutrients that boost the immune system. Almond butter has no saturated fat.

**Nutrition Information:**

CAL 223  CHO 28G  PRO 2G  FAT 13G  CHOL 27MG  CALCIUM 27MG  POTASSIUM 184MG  SODIUM 70MG  FIBER 4G

# AUGUST FRESH FRUIT WITH GINGERSNAP COOKIES

1 cup Peaches, fresh, pitted, sliced

1 cup Nectarines, fresh, pitted, sliced

1 cup Black plums, fresh, pitted, sliced

1 cup Blueberries, fresh

1 cup Light whipped cream (optional)

2 Tbsp. Apricot brandy (optional)

16 Gingersnaps

**Vegetarian: Lacto-ovo**

Total time: 15 minutes
Serves: 8
Serving size: 1/2 cup
Exchange: With cream, 2 fruit,
1 fat; without cream, 2 fruit

1. Mix and portion peaches, nectarines, plums, and blueberries onto dessert dishes.
2. Arrange two gingersnaps on each side of the fruit and top with whipped cream.

## Serving Suggestion

Top with light whipped cream (on page 361 of this chapter). Optional: drizzle with apricot brandy before topping with whipped cream for an adult luncheon.

**Nutrition Information:**

**With Cream**

CAL 142  CHO 25G  PRO 1G  FAT 4G  CHOL 9MG  CALCIUM 20MG  POTASSIUM 170MG  SODIUM 85MG  FIBER 2G

**Without Cream**

CAL 97  CHO 22G  PRO 0G  FAT 0G  CHOL 0MG  CALCIUM 0MG  POTASSIUM 133MG  SODIUM 73MG  FIBER 2G

# BAKED APPLE WITH CINNAMON

2 large Macintosh apples, cored
1/2 cup Ginger ale
1/2 tsp. Cinnamon, ground
1/2 tsp. Cardamom, ground
1/4 tsp. Nutmeg, ground
2 tsp. Brown sugar (or sugar substitute
  equivalent)

**Vegetarian: Vegan**

Total time: Conventional oven,
50 minutes; microwave, 7 minutes
Serves: 2
Serving size: 1 apple
Exchange: 3 fruit

## Oven Method

1. Preheat oven to 350°F.
2. Core apples and place in 2-inch-deep baking dish.
3. Pour ginger ale over apples and add cinnamon, cardamom, nutmeg, and sugar or Splenda.
4. Bake 45 minutes or until apples are soft. Serve hot or cold.

## Microwave Method

Follow the cooking preparation above but heat 4–5 minutes on high heat until apples are soft. Serve hot or cold.

**Nutrition Information:**

**With Sugar**

CAL 169  CHO 43G  PRO 0G  FAT 1G  CHOL 0MG  CALCIUM 24MG  POTASSIUM 248MG  SODIUM 7MG  FIBER 5G

# BANANA CREAM

*This recipe makes a great after-school snack.*

1 large Banana
4 Tbsp. Cool Whip Lite
1 cup Greek yogurt, fat-free
1 tsp. Rum extract or vanilla extract
4 Graham cracker rectangles, crushed
3 Strawberries, fresh, sliced

**Vegetarian: Lacto-ovo**

Total time: 7 minutes
Serves: 3
Serving size: 2/3 cup
Exchange: 1 fruit, 1 starch,
1/2 fat-free milk

1. Place banana, 2 Tablespoons of Cool Whip, yogurt, and rum extract or vanilla extract in a blender and purée.
2. Place 2/3-cup portions of purée in individual dessert bowls. Top with crackers, remaining Cool Whip, and berries. Serve immediately.

**Nutrition Information:**
CAL 182  CHO 34G  PRO 6G  FAT 3G  CHOL 2G  CALCIUM 177MG  POTASSIUM 436MG  SODIUM 172MG  FIBER 2G

# CHERRY YOGURT PARFAIT

*This dessert naturally boosts calcium absorption.*

2 cups Yogurt, vanilla, fat-free
2 cups Cherries, jarred in light syrup,
    drained
4 Tbsp. Flaxseed meal
4 Mint leaves, fresh

**Vegetarian: Lacto-ovo**

Total time: 6 minutes
Serves: 4
Serving size: 1 cup
Exchange: 1 fat dairy, 1 fruit, 1/2 fat

Place 1/2 cup of yogurt in each of four serving bowls. Top with 1/2 cup of cherries, then add flaxseed meal. Serve garnished with fresh mint leaves.

**Nutrition Information:**
CAL 201  CHO 40G  PRO 8G  FAT 3G  CHOL 3MG  CALCIUM 219MG  POTASSIUM 448MG  SODIUM 69MG  FIBER 6G

# FAT-FREE LEMON MOUSSE

*Chef Brian MacMenamin*

**Vegetarian: Lacto-ovo**

2 Tbsp. Water
2 tsp. Gelatin, unflavored
1 cup Half-and-half, fat-free
4 Tbsp. Sugar
1 Tbsp. Lemon peel, finely grated
2 large Egg whites
1/8 tsp. Cream of tartar

Total time: 30 minutes
Serves: 4
Serving size: 1/2 cup
Exchange: 1 starch

1. Pour 2 Tablespoons water into a small saucepan and sprinkle the gelatin over the water. Let stand until gelatin softens, approximately 10 minutes. Over very low heat, stir just until the gelatin dissolves, approximately 1 minute.
2. Stir in fat-free half-and-half, 2 Tablespoons sugar, and grated lemon peel. Stir over very low heat until sugar dissolves, approximately 2 minutes (do not boil).
3. Transfer gelatin mixture to a large bowl then set bowl in another large bowl filled halfway with ice water; stir until mixture is cool, approximately 5 minutes.
4. Using electric mixer, beat egg whites with cream of tartar in medium bowl until soft peaks form. Gradually add 2 Tablespoons of sugar and beat until stiff but not dry.
5. Carefully fold egg whites into gelatin mixture just until blended.
6. Divide mousse among four wine glasses and chill in refrigerator until mousse is softly set.
7. Serve mousse cold.

## Serving Suggestion

Garnish with fresh mint.

**Nutrition Information:**

CAL 98  CHO 18G  PRO 4G  FAT 1G  CHOL 3MG  CALCIUM 62MG  POTASSIUM 170MG  SODIUM 117MG  FIBER 0G

# FRESH APPLE SAUCE WITH NUTMEG

*The fiber and cinnamon in this dish help insulin regulate blood sugar.*

**Vegetarian: Vegan**

10 medium Granny Smith apples, cored, sliced

4 medium Macintosh apples, cored, sliced

4 medium Delicious apples, cored, sliced

1/2 cup Apple cider, pasteurized

1 Tbsp. Cinnamon, ground

1 tsp. Nutmeg, ground

1/4 cup Brown sugar (sugar substitute equivalent optional)

Total time: 55 minutes
Serves: 12
Serving size: 1/2 cup
Exchange: With sugar, 2-1/2 fruit; with sugar substitute, 2 fruit

1. Place apples (with skin for more fiber) in saucepan with cider and simmer over medium high heat, uncovered, for 40 minutes. Stir to prevent sticking as needed, every 4 to 6 minutes.
2. Add cinnamon, nutmeg, and brown sugar until you have a chunky sauce.

## Serving Suggestion

Top with a sprinkling of ground flaxseed meal for more flavor and nutrients.

**Nutrition Information:**

**With Sugar**

CAL 151  CHO 40G  PRO 0G  FAT 1G  CHOL 0MG  CALCIUM 23MG  POTASSIUM 292MG  SODIUM 3MG  FIBER 5G

**With Splenda**

CAL 135  CHO 36G  PRO 0G  FAT 1G  CHOL 9MG  CALCIUM 23MG  POTASSIUM 292MG  SODIUM 3MG  FIBER 5G

# FRESH FRUIT SUPREME

*This dessert is power-packed with antioxidants and phytonutrients that help your immune system.*

2 Kiwi fruit, peeled, sliced
2 medium Oranges, peeled, sliced
1 medium Pear, sliced
1 medium Apple, sliced
1 medium Cantaloupe, peeled, large dice
1/4 cup Mint leaves, fresh
1/2 cup Almond slivers

**Vegetarian: Vegan**

Total time: 10 minutes
Serves: 8–10
Serving size: 1 cup
Exchange: 1 fruit, 1 fat

Toss all ingredients except almonds to mix. Chill and serve, sprinkled with almonds.

## Serving Suggestion

To add even more flavor, sprinkle with cinnamon and cardamom.

**Nutrition Information:**

CAL 109  CHO 17G  PRO 3G  FAT 45G  CHOL 0MG  CALCIUM 51MG  POTASSIUM 347MG  SODIUM 5MG  FIBER 4G

# GRAPE-NUTS® CUSTARD

*This is a yummy calcium-rich dessert.*

*Dr. Gary Federici*

**Vegetarian: Lacto-ovo**

1 quart Milk, 2 percent fat
3/4 cup Post Grape-Nuts
4 Eggs (or equivalent amount of egg
  substitute such as Egg Beaters)
8 Tbsp. Sugar (or equivalent amount of sugar substitute)
Pinch salt
To taste Nutmeg, ground
1 tsp. Vanilla extract (or more to taste)

Total time: 50 minutes
Serves: 8
Serving size: 1/2 cup
Exchange: 1 starch, 1 reduced fat dairy

1. Preheat oven to 350°F.
2. Scald milk (do not boil) with Grape-Nuts in it. Remove from heat and let stand.
3. In another bowl, beat eggs, sugar, salt, nutmeg, and vanilla to blend.
4. Add milk and Grape-Nuts to mixture (add a few white raisins if you like), mix, and then pour into an ovenproof dish.
5. Place ovenproof dish in another baking pan filled with a little water. Bake for 40 minutes, then remove from heat.
6. Serve warm or chilled.

## Serving Suggestion

Sprinkle top with cinnamon.

**Nutrition Information:**

CAL 157  CHO 28G  PRO 7G  FAT 3G  CHOL 10MG  CALCIUM 151MG  POTASSIUM 242MG  SODIUM 162MG  FIBER 1G

# LIGHT COUNTRY APPLE PIE

*The cinnamon in this pie helps insulin work better.*

## Pastry

**Vegetarian: Lacto-ovo**

1-1/4 cup Flour, unbleached
1/4 cup Whole wheat flour
2 Tbsp. Brown sugar, unbleached (optional)
  or Splenda
Pinch Salt
10 Tbsp. Light butter, unbeaten, softened
3–4 Tbsp. Ice water

> Total time: 2 hours with dough
> Serves: 12
> Serving size: 1/12
> Exchange: 1 starch, 1 fruit, 1 fat

1. Place the flour, sugar, and salt in a food processor with a steel blade or mix with a pastry cutter. Add butter and mix until crumbly.
2. Add water and blend to form into a ball.
3. Wrap ball with plastic and chill 1 hour in refrigerator.
4. Flute edges to seal pie crust and place on oven to bake, reduce heat to 350°F, and bake for 45 minutes or until golden brown.

## Filling

2 lbs. Granny Smith apples, peeled, cored, cut into 1/4-inch wide slices
1 lb. Macintosh apples, peeled, cored, cut into 1/2-inch slices
1 Tbsp. Lemon juice, fresh
1 Tbsp. Cinnamon, ground
1/2 tsp. Nutmeg, ground
1/4 tsp. Allspice, ground

## Making the Filling

1. Place apples, lemon juice, cinnamon, nutmeg, and allspice in a bowl and thoroughly mix together.

## Making the Pie

1. Preheat oven to 450°F.
2. Remove dough from refrigerator and divide in half and place on floured surface. Roll out two 9-inch crusts and put one in a pie plate or tin.
3. Add apple filling and top with remaining crust.

*(continues)*

# LIGHT COUNTRY
# APPLE PIE (Continued)

4. Trim edges of both crusts and seal their edges together by using a fork. Cut a cross in the top crust to vent steam during baking.
5. Bake 15 minutes at 450°F, then reduce heat to 350°F and bake for 35 to 40 minutes.
6. Serve pie warm or at room temperature.

**Nutrition Information:**

**With Sugar**

| | | | | | | | | |
|---|---|---|---|---|---|---|---|---|
| CAL 171 | CHO 31G | PRO 2G | FAT 5G | CHOL 12MG | CALCIUM 18MG | POTASSIUM 165MG | SODIUM 48MG | FIBER 3G |

# LIGHT WHIPPED CREAM

1 cup Light whipping cream

1 Tbsp. Sugar

Pour cream into a chilled bowl and whip with a hand mixer on high until firm but not stiff (do not overmix). Add sugar and blend. Serve.

**Vegetarian: Lacto-ovo**

Total time: 10 minutes
Serves: 8
Serving size: 1 oz.
Exchange: 1-1/4 fat

**Nutrition Information:**

| | | | | | | | | |
|---|---|---|---|---|---|---|---|---|
| CAL 65 | CHO 3G | PRO 1G | FAT 6G | CHOL 20MG | CALCIUM 29MG | POTASSIUM 37MG | SODIUM 12MG | FIBER 0G |

# LOWER-IN-FAT TIRAMISU

*Michelle Jackson*

**Vegetarian: Lacto-ovo**

1 loaf Pound cake*
2 cups Vanilla yogurt, fat-free
8 oz. Cool Whip Lite (or equivalent reduced fat whipped topping)
1 cup Coffee, brewed or instant
2 Tbsp. Cocoa powder

Total time: 3 hours, 10 minutes
(10 minutes preparation, 3 hours chilling)
Serves: 16
Serving size: 1 slice
Exchange:1-1/2 starch, 1-1/2 fats

1. Cut pound cake into 16 slices approximately 1/2-inch thick.
2. In a large bowl, stir Cool Whip topping into yogurt.
3. Spread 3/4 cup of the yogurt mixture thinly on the bottom and up the sides of a 13 × 9 × 2–inch regular baking dish.
4. Brush both sides of cake slices with coffee.
5. Layer half of the cake slices and half of the remaining yogurt mixture in the dish and then repeat.
6. Sprinkle cocoa powder over the top, then cover and refrigerate for at least 3 hours.
7. Store in refrigerator.

## Serving Suggestion
Serve with fresh fruit.

**Nutrition Information:**

CAL 167  CHO 22G  PRO 4G  FAT 7G  CHOL 35MG  CALCIUM 78MG  POTASSIUM 117MG  SODIUM 56MG  FIBER 1G

*For vegetarians, make sure the pound cake is made with only vegetable sources and dairy products. Lard is animal fat.

# NEW PUMPKIN PIE WITH AN OLD-FASHIONED FLAVOR

*This recipe not only tastes great but also boosts isoflavones and beta-carotene and is lower in fat than the traditional pie.*

16 oz. Pumpkin purée, canned or fresh

10 oz. Tofu (soft or silken), low fat

1/4 cup Brown sugar

1/4 cup Sugar, granulated (optional)

1/4 cup Equivalent sugar substitute

1 tsp. Cinnamon, ground

1/4 tsp. Ginger, ground

1/4 tsp. Cloves, ground

1/8 tsp. Nutmeg, ground

1/8 tsp. Allspice, ground

1/8 tsp. Salt

1 Pie shell, 9 inches, unbaked*

**Vegetarian: Lacto-ovo**

Total time: 70 minutes
Serves: 10
Serving size: 1/10
Exchange: 2 starch, 2 fat, 1/2 fruit

1. Preheat oven to 425°F.
2. Cream together the pumpkin and sugar.
3. In a blender, add tofu and thoroughly blend with cinnamon, ginger, cloves, nutmeg, allspice, and salt.
4. Pour the tofu mixture into the pie shell.
5. Bake at 425°F for 15 minutes, then lower the heat to 350°F and bake for an additional 40 minutes.

**Nutrition Information:**

CAL 240  CHO 38G  PRO 5G  FAT 8G  CHOL 44MG  CALCIUM 37MG  POTASSIUM 437MG  SODIUM 349MG  FIBER 3G

*Vegetarians: Check to make sure the premade pie crust does not contain animal sources such as lard.

# PINEAPPLE AND FRUIT TRIFLE

*This is a great low-fat summertime dessert!*

1 small Pineapple, fresh

12 oz. Peaches in natural syrup (1 can), drained

12 oz. Fruit cocktail in natural syrup (1 can), drained

1 cup Strawberries (frozen), thawed and sliced

1 Angel food cake, prepared*

2 packages Vanilla pudding, sugar-free, prepared with fat-free milk

2/3 cup Sherry

1 cup Cool Whip Lite

**Vegetarian: Lacto-ovo**

Total time: 1 hour, 20 minutes
Serves: 12–15
Serving size: 1/15
Exchange: 2 starch, I fruit

1. Tear angel food cake into chunks.
2. Cut up pineapple and in a bowl mix with peaches, fruit cocktail, and strawberries.
3. Place half of the cake chunks in a trifle dish and pour one-half of the sherry on top. Add one-half of the mixed fruit on top of the angel food cake and sherry, then add one-half of the vanilla pudding. Repeat with the rest of ingredients.
4. Top the trifle with Cool Whip Lite.
5. Chill for at least 1 hour.

**Nutrition Information:**

**CAL 196  CHO 44G  PRO 5G  FAT 0G  CHOL 1MG  CALCIUM 104MG  POTASSIUM 376MG  SODIUM 527MG  FIBER 2G**

*Vegetarians: Check the labels of convenience products to be sure they meet your requirements.

# WHOLE GRAIN BREAD PUDDING

2 large Eggs, slightly beaten

2 cups Milk, fat-free

1/2 tsp. Vanilla extract

1 tsp. Cinnamon, ground

1/16 tsp. Salt

2 cups Whole wheat or multigrain bread, 2 to 3
  days old

1/4 cup Brown sugar

1/4 cup Raisins

**Vegetarian: Lacto-ovo**

Total time: 50 minutes
Serves: 6
Serving size: 1/2 cup
Exchange: 1-1/2 starch

1. Preheat oven to 350°F.
2. Mix together eggs, milk, vanilla extract, cinnamon, and salt and lightly stir.
3. Pour mixture into a 9-inch square pan and bake for about 45 minutes or until knife inserted into middle comes out clean.

**Nutrition Information:**

CAL 126  CHO 20G  PRO 6G  FAT 2G  CHOL 72MG  CALCIUM 131MG  POTASSIUM 225MG  SODIUM 161MG  FIBER 1G

# ZUCCHINI CAKE

*Zucchini is loaded with nutrients for your heart and immune system. Eating a vegetable never got better.*

3 medium Eggs, well beaten
1/2 cup Sugar
1/2 cup Canola oil
3 Tbsp. Butter
2 tsp. Vanilla extract
2 cups Zucchini, coarsely grated
1 Tbsp. Lemon rind, grated
1-1/2 cups All-purpose flour
1/2 cup Flaxseed meal
2 tsp. Cinnamon, ground
1 tsp. Cardamom, ground
2 tsp. Baking soda
1/4 tsp. Baking powder
1/8 tsp. Salt
1/4 cup Walnuts, chopped

**Vegetarian: Lacto-ovo**

Total time: 55 minutes
Serves: 12
Serving size: 1/12
Exchange: 2 starch, 1 fat

1. Preheat oven to 350°F.
2. Grease a 8-1/2 × 4-1/2 × 2-1/2–inch baking pan.
3. In a bowl, mix sugar and butter, then add beaten eggs and vanilla and blend well. The mixture should be lemon colored and thick.
4. Thoroughly blend in the grated zucchini and lemon rind, then the flour, flaxseed meal, cinnamon, cardamom, baking soda, baking powder, salt, and walnuts.
5. Spoon batter into pan.
6. Bake for 1 hour or until inserted knife or toothpick comes out clean from center.
7. Cool in pan for 15 minutes, then turn out onto serving dish. Let cool before slicing.

**Nutrition Information:**

CAL 158  CHO 28G  PRO 4G  FAT 9G  CHOL 48MG  CALCIUM 98MG  POTASSIUM 149MG  SODIUM 179MG  FIBER 3G

# References

Ainsworth, B. E., Haskell, W. L., Leon, A.S., et al. "Compendium of Physical Activities: Classification of Energy Costs of Human Physical Activities." *Medicine and Science in Sports and Exercise* 25, no. 1 (1993): 71–80.

American Diabetes Association. "Evidence-Based Nutrition Principles and Recommendations for the Treatment and Prevention of Diabetes and Related Complications." *Diabetes Care* 25 (2002): 202–212.

American Diabetes Association. "Standards of Medical Care in Diabetes, 2005." *Diabetes Care* 28, supp. 1 (2005): s11–s13.

American Heart Association. *The American Dietetic Association's Complete Food and Nutrition Guide.* Minnetonka, MN: Chronimed Publishing, 1998.

Anderson, J. W., Randles, K. M., Kendall, C. W., et al. "Carbohydrate and Fiber Recommendations for Individuals with Diabetes: A Quantitative Assessment and Meta-Analysis of the Evidence." *Journal of the American College of Nutrition* 23 (2004): 5–17.

Anderson, R. A., and Polansky, M. M. "Tea Enhances Insulin Activity." *Journal of Agricultural and Food Chemistry* 50 (2002): 7182–7186.

Arad, Y., Spadro, L. A., Roth, M., Newstein, D., and Guerci, A. D. "Treatment of Asymptomatic Adults with Elevated Coronary Calcium Scores with Atorvastatin, Vitamin C, and Vitamin E: The St. Francis Hearts Study Randomized Clinical Trial." *Journal of the American College of Cardiology* 5, no. 46 (2005): 173–175.

Arts, I. C., Jacobs, D. R. Jr., Gross, M., Harnack, L. J., and Folsom, A. R. "Dietary Catechins and Cancer Incidence among Postmenopausal Women: The Iowa Women's Health Study (United States)." *Cancer Causes and Control* 13, no. 4 (2002): 373–382.

Balk, E. et al. "Effects of Omega-3 Fatty Acids on Cardiovascular Risk Factors and Intermediate Markers of Cardiovascular Disease." *Evidence Report/Technology Assessment no. 93.* Prepared by Tufts-New England Medical Center Evidence-Based Practice Center. Rockville, MD: Agency for Healthcare Research and Quality, March 2004 (Publication no. 04-E010-2).

Barlow, S. E., and Dietz, W. H. "Obesity Evaluation and Treatment: Expert Committee Recommendations. *Journal of Pediatrics* 102, no. 3 (1998): e29.

Bellisle, F. "Effects of Diet on Behaviour and Cognition in Children." *British Journal of Nutrition* 92, supp. 2 (2004).

Bellizzi, M. C., and Dietz, W. H. "Workshop on Childhood Obesity: Summary of the Discussion." *American Journal of Clinical Nutrition* 70 (1999): 173S–175S.

Bourre, J. M. "Roles of Unsaturated Fatty Acids (especially Omega-3 Fatty Acids) in the Brain at Various Ages and during Aging." *Journal of Nutrition, Health, and Aging* 8, no. 3 (2004).

Brand-Miller, J., Haynes, S., Petocez, P., et al. "Low Glycemic Index Diets in the Management of Diabetes." *Diabetes Care* 26 (2003): 2261–2267.

# REFERENCES

Bray, G. A., Nielsen, S. J., and Popkin, B. M. "Consumption of High-Fructose Corn Syrup in Beverages May Play a Role in the Epidemic of Obesity." *American Journal of Clinical Nutrition* 79, no. 4 (2004): 1090.

Burani, J. *Good Carbs, Bad Carbs,* 2d ed. New York: Marlowe & Co., 2005.

Burani, J., and Palma, J. L. "Low-Glycemic Index Carbohydrates: An Effective Behavioral Change for Glycemic Control and Weight Management in Patients with Type 1 and Type 2 Diabetes." *The Diabetes Educator* 32, no. 1 (2006): 78–88.

Campbell, T. C., and Campbell, T. M. "The China study: starting Implications for Diet, Weight Loss, and Long Term Health." Dallas, Texas, Benbella Books, 2005.

Centers for Disease Control and Prevention. "What Is Epi Info?" Online at http://www.cdc.gov/epiinfo/.

_____. *Table for Calculated Body Mass Index Values for Selected Heights and Weights for Ages 2 to 20.* Online at http://www.cdc.gov/nccdphp/dnpa/bmi/00binaries/bmi-tables.pdf.

_____. National Center for Chronic Disease Prevention and Health Promotion, Division of Nutrition and Physical Activity. *Promoting Physical Activity: A Guide for Community Action.* Champaign, IL: Human Kinetics, 1999.

Chantre, P., and Lairon, D. "Recent Findings of Green Tea Extract AR25 (Exolise) and Its Activity for the Treatment of Obesity." *Phytomedicine* 9, no. 1 (2002): 3–8.

Committee on Nutrition of the American Academy of Pediatrics. "Policy Statement: Prevention of Pediatrics Overweight and Obesity." *Pediatrics* 112, no. 2 (2003): 424–430.

Cordain, L., et al. "Fatty Acid Analysis of Wild Ruminant Tissues: Evolutionary Implications for Reducing Diet-Related Chronic Disease." *European Journal of Clinical Nutrition* 56, no. 3 (2002): 181–191.

Daniels, S. R., Khoury, P. R., and Morrison, J. A. "The Utility of Body Mass Index as a Measure of Body Fatness in Children and Adolescents: Differences by Race and Gender." *Pediatrics* 99, no. 6 (1997): 804–807.

Dennison, B. A., Rockwell, H. L., and Baker, S. L. "Excess Fruit Juice Consumption by Preschool Children Is Associated with Short Stature and Obesity." *Pediatrics* 99 (1997): 15–22.

Diabetes and Nutrition Study Group (DNSG) of the European Association for the Study of Diabetes. "Recommendations for the Nutritional Management of Patients with Diabetes Mellitus." *European Journal of Clinical Nutrition* 54 (2000): 353–355.

Dietz, W. H., and Bellizzi, M. C. "Introduction: The Use of BMI to Assess Obesity in Children." *American Journal of Clinical Nutrition* 70, supp. (1999): 123s–125s.

Dwivedi, C., Natarajan, K., and Matthees, D. P. "Chemopreventive Effects of Dietary Flaxseed Oil on Colon Tumor Development." *Nutrition and Cancer Journal* 51, no. 1 (2005): 52–58.

Ebell, Mark H. "The Vitamin E Saga: Lessons in Patient-Oriented Evidence." *American Family Physician* (June 1, 2005): 71 (11): 2052, 2054.

Elliot, S. S., Keim, N. L., Stern, J. S., Teff, K., and Havel, P. J. "Fructose, Weight Gain, and the Insulin Resistance Syndrome." *American Journal of Clinical Nutrition* 76, no. 5 (2002): 911–922

Etter, J.-F., Perneger, T. V., and Ronchi, A. "Distributions of Smokers by Stage: International Comparison and Association with Smoking Prevalence." *Preventive Medicine* 26 (1997): 580–585

Farooki, A., Schnelder, S. H. "Increased Cancer-related Mortality for Patients with Type of Diabetes Who Use Sulfonylureas or Insulin: Response to Bowker et al." *Diabetes Care* 29 (8)(2006): 1989–1990.

Fava, J. L., Norman, G. J., Levesque, D. A., Redding, C. A., Johnson, S., Evers, K., and Reich, T. *Measuring Decisional Balance for Stress Management.* Paper presented at the Nineteenth Annual Scientific Sessions of the Society of Behavioral Medicine, New Orleans, March 1998.

Fava, J. L., Norman, G. J., Redding, C. A., Keller, S., Robbins, M. L., Maddock, J. E., Evers, K., and Dewart, S. *The Multidimensional Stress Management Behaviors Inventory.* Kingston, RI: Stress Management Working Group, Cancer Prevention Research Center, University of Rhode Island, 1997.

Fava, J. L., Norman, G. J., Redding, C. A., Levesque, D. A., Evers, K., and Johnson, S. *A Process of Change Measure for Stress Management.* Paper presented at the Nineteenth Annual Scientific Sessions of the Society of Behavioral Medicine, New Orleans, March 1998.

Fiorito, L., et al. "Girls Calcium Intake is Associated with Bone Mineral Content during Middle Childhood." *Journal of Nutrition* 136 (2006): 1281–1286.

Foster-Powell, K., Holt, S., and Brand-Miller, J. C. "International Table of Glycemic Index and Glycemic Load Values: 2002." *American Journal of Clinical Nutrition* 76, no. 1 (2002): 5–56.

Freedman, D. S., Dietz, W. H., Srinivasan, S. R., and Berenson, G. S. "The Relation of Overweight to Cardiovascular Risk Factors among Children and Adolescents: The Bogalusa Heart Study." *Pediatrics* 103 (1999): 1175–1182.

Gao, X. et al. The 2005 USDA Food Guide Pyramid 15 Associated with more Adequate Nutrient Intakes within Energy Constraints than the 1992 Pyramid Journal of Nutrition. 136 (2006): 1341–1346 Source: The KeyStone Center. The KeyStone Forum on Away-from-Here Foods. Opportunities for Preventing Weight Gain and Obesity. www.keystone.org.

Garn, S. M., and LaVelle, M. "Two-Decade Follow-Up of Fatness in Early Childhood." *American Journal of Diseases of Children* 139 (1985): 181–185.

Garrison, Robert, and Somer, Elizabeth. *The Nutrition Desk Reference*. New Canaan, CT: Keats Publishing, 1995 (pp. 65–222).

Gershoff, Stanley. *The Tufts University Guide to Total Nutrition*. New York: Harper Perennial, 1996 (pp. 27–54).

Gochfeld, M., Burger, J. "Good fish/bad fish: A composite benefit-risk by dose curve." *Neurotoxicology* 24, no. 4 (2005): 511–20.

Grizis, F. C. "Nutrition in Women Across the Life Span" *Nursing Clinics in North America* 27, no. 4 (1999): 971–982.

Guo, S. S., and Chumlea, W. C. "Tracking of BMI in Children in Relation to Overweight in Adulthood." *American Journal of Clinical Nutrition* 70, supp. (1999): 145s–148s.

Guo, S. S., Roche, A. F., Chumlea, W. C., Gardner, J. D., and Siervogel, R. M. "The Predictive Value of Childhood Body Mass Index Values for Overweight at Age 35 Years." *American Journal of Clinical Nutrition* 59 (1994): 810–819.

Haag, M. "Essential Fatty Acids and the Brain." *Canadian Journal of Psychiatry* 48, no. 3 (2003).

Hakim, I. A., et al. "Effect of Increased Tea Consumption on Oxidative DNA Damage among Smokers: A Randomized Controlled Study." *Journal of Nutrition* 133, no. 10 (2003): 3303S–3309S.

Harris, K. M., Gordon-Larsen, P., Chantala, K., et al. "Longitudinal Trends in Race/Ethnic Disparities in Leading Health Indicators from Adolescence to Young Adulthood. *Archives of Pediatrics and Adolescent Medicine.* 160, no. 1 (2006): 74–81.

Hegarty, V. M., May, H. M., and Khaw, K. T. "Tea Drinking and Bone Mineral Density in Older Women." *American Journal of Clinical Nutrition* 71 (2000): 1003–1007.

Hoolihan, L. "Beyond Calcium: The Protective Attributes of Dairy Products and Their Constituents." *Nutrition Today* 38, no. 2 (2004): 70–76.

Isemura, M., et al. "Tea Catechins and Related Polyphenols as Anti-Cancer Agents." *Biofactors* 13, nos. 1–4 (2000): 81–85.

Jenkins, D. J., Kendall, C. W., Augustin, L. S., et al. "Glycemic Index: Overview of Implications and Disease." *American Journal of Clinical Nutrition* 76 (2002): 266S–273S.

Katz, Nikita B. "Omega-3 Fatty Acids: A Clinical Update." March 2004, Institute For Natural Resources, BioMed.

Katz, O., and Katz, N. B. "Non-Traditional Approaches: Anxiety, Insomnia, and Depression." Sept. 2003. Institute for Natural Resources, BioMed.

KidsHealth. "Vitamins and Minerals." Online at: http://www.kidshealth.org/teen/food_fitness/nutrition/vitamins_minerals.html.

_____. "Vitamin Chart." Online at: http://www.kidshealth.org/teen/misc/vitamin_chart.html.

Leibman, B. "Antioxidants . . . Still Hazy After All These Years." *Nutrition Action Newsletter* (Center for Science in the Public Interest) 32, no. 9 (2005): H2.

Li, N., Zheng, S., Han, C., and Chen, J. "The Chemoprotective Effects of Tea on Human Oral Precancerous Mucosa Lesions." *Proceedings of the Society for Experimental Biology and Medicine* 220 (1999): 218–224.

Ludwig, D. "Dietary Glycemic Index and Obesity." *Journal of Nutrition* 130 (2000): 280S–283S.

MacLean, C. H., et al. "Effects of Omega-3 Fatty Acids on Cancer Risk: A Systematic Review." *Journal of the American Medical Association* 295, no. 4 (2006): 403–415.

# REFERENCES

MacLean, C. H., et al. *Effects of Omega-3 Fatty Acids on Cognitive Function with Aging, Dementia, and Neurological Diseases.* Evidence Report/Technology Assessment no. 114. AHRQ Publication No. 05-E011-2. Rockville, MD: Agency for Healthcare Research and Quality, February 2005.

MacLean, C. H., et al. *Effects of Omega-3 Fatty Acids on Lipids and Glycemic Control in Type II Diabetes and the Metabolic Syndrome and on Inflammatory Bowel Disease, Rheumatoid Arthritis, Renal Disease, Systemic Lupus Erythematosus, and Osteoporosis.* Evidence Report/Technology Assessment no. 89. AHRQ Publication No. 04-E012-2. Rockville, MD: Agency for Healthcare Research and Quality, March 2004.

Mahady, G. B. "Do Soy Isoflavones Cause Endometrial Hyperplasia?" *Nutrion Review* 63, no. 11 (2005): 392–397.

McCaffree, J. "Childhood Eating Patterns: The Roles Parents Play." *Journal of the American Diet Association* 103 (2003): 1587.

McConahy, K. L., Smiciklas-Wright, H., Mitchell, D. C., and Picciano, M. F. "Portion Size of Common Foods Predicts Energy Intake among Pre-School Aged Children." *Journal of the American Diet Association* 104 (2004): 975–979.

Mendoza, J., Drewnowski, A., Christakis, D. A., "Dietory Energy Density Is Associated with Selected Predictors of Obesity in U.S. Children." *Journal of Nutrition* 136 (2006): 1318–1322.

Miller, E. R., III, et al. "Meta-Analysis: High-Dosage Vitamin E Supplementation May Increase All-Cause Mortality." *Annals of Internal Medicine* 142 (2005): 37–46.

Mochi, H. "Women and Diabetes: Preventing Coronary Heart Disease." *Diabetes Self-Management* (Jan.–Feb. 2006): 85–89.

Moore, V. M., et al. "Dietary Composition of Pregnant Women Is Related to Size of Baby at Birth." *Journal of Nutrition* 134, no. 7 (2004): 1820–6.

Napier, Kristine M. *Eat to Heal: The Phytochemcial Diet and Nutrition Plan.* New York: Warner Books, 1998.

National Institutes of Health Office of Dietary Supplements. *Dietary Supplement Fact Sheet: Calcium.* Online at: http://www.ods.od.nih.gov/factsheets/calcium.asp.

———. *Dietary Supplement Fact Sheet: Folate.* Online at: http://www.ods.od.nih.gov/factsheets/folate.asp.

———. *Dietary Supplement Fact Sheet: Iron.* Online at: http://www.ods.od.nih.gov/factsheets/iron.asp.

———. *Dietary Supplement Fact Sheet: Vitamin A.* Online at: http://www.ods.od.nih.gov/factsheets/vitamina.asp.

———. *Dietary Supplement Fact Sheet: Vitamin B6.* Online at: http://www.ods.od.nih.gov/factsheets/vitaminb6.asp.

———. *Dietary Supplement Fact Sheet: Vitamin B12.* Online at: http://www.ods.od.nih.gov/factsheets/vitaminb12.asp.

———. *Dietary Supplement Fact Sheet: Vitamin D.* Online at: http://www.ods.od.nih.gov/factsheets/vitamind.asp.

———. *Dietary Supplement Fact Sheet: Vitamin E.* Online at: http://www.ods.od.nih.gov/factsheets/vitamine.asp.

———. *Dietary Supplement Fact Sheet: Zinc.* Online at: http://www.ods.od.nih.gov/factsheets/cc/zinc.asp.

Palmer, S. *Today's Dietitian* 7, no. 7 (Vol. ): 41–44.

Pediatric Committee on Nutrition. "The Use and Misuse of Fruit Juice in Pediatrics." *Pediatrics* 107 (2001): 1210–1213.

Pittas, A. G., Das, K. S., Hajduk, C. L., et al. "A Low Glycemic Load Diet Facilitates Greater Weight Loss in Overweight Adults with High Insulin Secretion but Not Adults with Low Insulin Secretion in the CALERIE trial." *Diabetes Care* 28, no. 12 (2005): 2939–2941.

Sacco, M., et al. "Primary Prevention of Cardiovascular Events with Low-Dose Aspirin and Vitamin E in Type 2 Diabetic Patients: Results of the Primary Prevention Project (PPP) Trial." *Diabetes Care* 26 (2003): 3264–3272.

Sacks, F. M., et al. *Soy Protein, Isoflavones, and Cardiovascular Health. An American Heart Association Science Advisory for Professionals from the Nutrition Committee.* Circulation, Dallas, TX: American Heart Association, Jan. 17, 2006.

Schachter, H., et al. *Health Effects of Omega-3 Fatty Acids on Asthma.* Evidence Report/Technology Assessment no. 94. Prepared by University of Ottawa Evidence-Based Practice Center. AHRQ Publication No. 04-E013-2. Rockville, MD: Agency for Healthcare Research and Quality, March 2004.

Sharma, A., Belna, J., Logan, J., Espat, J., and Hurteau, J. A. "The Effects of Omega-3 Fatty Acids on Growth Regulation of Epithelial Ovarian Cancer Cell Lines." *Gynecological Oncology* 99, no. 1 (2005): 58–64.

Shattuck, Deborah. "Eat Your Vegetables: Make Them Delicious." *Journal of the American Diet Association* (Oct. 2001), 10, 1130–1132.

Silverman, Harold. *The Vitamin Book*. New York: Bantam Books, 1985.

Simopoulos, A. P. "Essential Fatty Acids in Health and Chronic Disease." *American Journal of Clinical Nutrition* 79, no. 3 (2004): 523–524.

Skinner, J. D., Carruth, B. R., Moran, J., Houck, K., and Coletta, F. "Fruit Juice is Not Related to Children's Growth." *Pediatrics* 103 (1999): 58–64.

Stanner, S. A., Hughs, J., Kelly, C. N., and Buttriss, J. "A Review of the Epidemiological Evidence for the 'Antioxidant Hypothesis.'" *Public Health Nutrition* 7 (2004): 407–422.

Steinbeck, K. S. "The Importance of Physical Activity in the Prevention of Overweight and Obesity in Childhood: A Review and Opinion." *Obesity Reviews* 2 (2001): 117–130.

Strawbridge, W. J., Wallhagen, M. I., and Sherma, S. J. "New NHLBI Clinical Guidelines for Obesity and Overweight: Will They Promote Health?" *American Journal of Public Health* 90 (2000): 340–343.

Sun, C. L., et al. "Urinary Tea Polyphenols in Relation to Gastric and Esophageal Cancers: A Prospective Study of Men in Shanghai, China." *Carcinogenesis* 23, no. 9 (2002): 1497–1503.

Tea Council of the USA. *Tea and Health: An Overview of Research on Potential Health Benefits of Tea.* New York: Author, 2004.

Turner-McGrievy, B. "Vegetarian Meal Plan, Beneficial for Type 2 Diabetes?" *Diabetes Self-Management* (Jan.–Feb. 2006): 12–19.

U.S. Department of Agriculture. *Nutrition and Your Health: Dietary Guidelines for Americans* (2005 Dietary Guidelines Advisory Committee Report; online at: www.health.gov/dietaryguidelines/dga2005/report/PDF/D4_Fats.pdf).

Velicer, W. F, Prochaska, J. O., Fava, J. L., Norman, G. J., and Redding, C. A. "Detailed Overview of the Transtheoretical Model." Material adapted from "Smoking Cessation and Stress Management: Applications of the Transtheoretical Model of Behavior Change." *Homeostasis* 38 (1998): 216–233. Online at: www.uri.edu/research/cprc/TTM/detailedoverview.

Wang, C., et al. "Effects of Omega-3 Fatty Acids on Cardiovascular Disease." Evidence Report/Technology Assessment no. 94. Prepared by Tufts-New England Medical Center Evidence-Based Practice Center. AHRQ Publication No. 04-E009-2. Rockville, MD: Agency for Healthcare Research and Quality, March 2004.

Wesnes, K. A., et al. "Breakfast Reduces Declines in Attention and Memory over the Morning in School Children." *Appetite* 41, no. 3 (2003): 329–331.

Winstone, D., Kuhn, M. A., and Der Marderosian, A. H. *Herbal Therapy and Supplements*. Philadelphia: Lippincott Williams & Wilkins, 2001.

Wood, C. E., Register, T. C., Franke, A. A., Anthony, M. S., and Cline, J. M. "Dietary Soy Isoflavones Inhibit Estrogen Effects in the Postmenopausal Breast." *Cancer Research* 66, no. 2 (2006): 1241–1249.

Wu, C. H., et al. "Epidemiological Evidence of Increased Bone Mineral Density in Habitual Tea Drinkers." *Archives of Internal Medicine* 162, no. 9 (2002): 1001–1006.

Yu, H., Oho, T., Xu, L. X. "Effects of Several Tea Components on Acid Resistances of Human Tooth Enamel." *Journal of Dentistry* 13 (1995): 101–105.

Zablocki, Elaine. "High Insulin Levels Linked to Breast Cancer Death." Online at Web MD.com: http://healthboards.webmd.com/content/article/25/1728_57897.htm (May 25, 2000).

Zheng, W., Doyle, T. J., Kushi, L. H., et al. "Tea Consumption and Cancer Incidence among Postmenopausal Women." *American Journal of Epidemiology* 144 (1996): 175–81.

## IMPORTANT WEB SITES

American College of Sports Medicine: www.acsm.org
American Diabetic Association: www.eatright.org
American Diabetes Association: www.diabetes.org

# REFERENCES

American Heart Association: www.americanheart.org

Centers for Disease Control Division of Nutrition and Physical Activity, National Center for Chronic Disease Prevention and Health Promotion: www.cdc.gov/nccdphp/dnpa

Environmental Protection Agency: www.epa.gov/

Food and Drug Administration: www.fda.gov

Glycemic Index: www.glycemicindex.com

New York State Health Department: http://www.health.state.ny.us/

Office of Dietary Supplements, National Institutes of Health, Bethesda, Maryland: http://ods.od.nih.gov

United States Department of Agribusiness (USDA): www.mypyramid.org

# Index